IMAGES
of America

MIDLAND

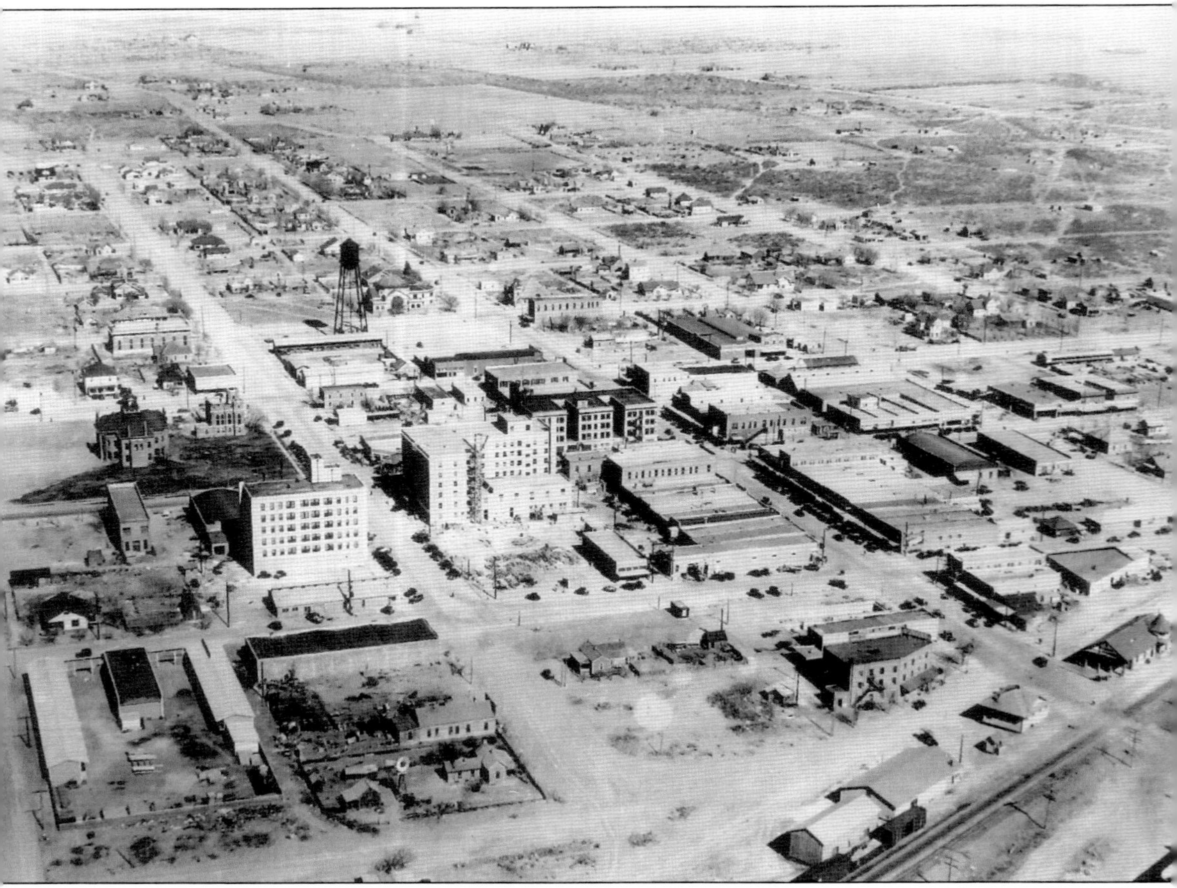

In 1928, Midland was poised at the transition point between ranching center and financial capital of the Permian Basin. Elements of both cities appear in this photograph from February 8. The Scharbauer Hotel (center) nears completion with scaffolding forming a spinal column up the building. The stone courthouse and jail remain (far left). The Texas and Pacific Depot (lower right) symbolically marks the city's beginning, while a windmill and barn (lower left) preserve a trace of earlier days. (Courtesy of the Midland Historical Museum.)

On the Cover: An assembly of plows pulled by Henry M. Halff's Oil Pull tractor sits in front of the Llano Hotel, which housed the Midland National Bank, sometime around 1920. Henry Halff was an ardent advocate of Midland development, supporting everything from irrigation projects to polo teams. This photograph of businessmen, farmers, and townsfolk in front of one of Midland's major financial institutions captures the enterprising spirit of Midland before the petroleum era. (Courtesy of the Midland Historical Museum.)

IMAGES
of America

MIDLAND

James Collett

ARCADIA
PUBLISHING

ISBN 978-0-7385-7896-5

Published by Arcadia Publishing
Charleston, South Carolina

Printed in the United States of America

Library of Congress Control Number: 2009941022

For all general information contact Arcadia Publishing at:
Telephone 843-853-2070
Fax 843-853-0044
E-mail sales@arcadiapublishing.com
For customer service and orders:
Toll-Free 1-888-313-2665

Visit us on the Internet at www.arcadiapublishing.com

To all my pioneer ancestors who saw the beauty in this land and stayed so that I could call it home

Contents

Acknowledgments 6

Introduction 7

1. From Midway to Midland 9
2. Windmill City in the Land of the High Sky 31
3. Big Dreams in the Permian Basin 69
4. Tough Times in Depression and War 85
5. Boom and Bust and Boom in the Tall City 101
6. On the World Stage in the 21st Century 123

ACKNOWLEDGMENTS

I would like to thank those who built all the great archives collections that have preserved the many images of Midland's colorful history and for their generous sharing of images. The Midland Historical Museum and its staff, especially Nancy McKinley, have done a masterful job of collecting many irreplaceable images and files on the history of this city. Unless otherwise noted, photographs are from the Midland Historical Museum collection. The Permian Historical Society should also be commended for the archival collection they have accumulated at the University of Texas of the Permian Basin in Odessa, Texas, which includes materials far beyond Midland. The Nita Stewart Haley Memorial Library in Midland has one of the finest collections of western images and history around, and their photograph archives are superbly organized. I thank Burr Williams, Shirley Ireland, Ron Hodges, and Jeff George for sharing their photographs. Thanks also to all those individuals who have helped me learn more about Midland's fascinating history. Finally, I thank my mother, Snooks, for giving me my great love of history and the past and my wife, Jo Ann, for being my unfailing friend, supporter, and partner.

Introduction

On June 23, 1881, the Texas and Pacific Railroad construction crew reached the halfway point between Fort Worth and El Paso, Texas. At that time, they were crossing the southern edge of the Llano Estacado—a huge mesaland sprawling across the lower Great Plains. The site—flat, arid, treeless terrain miles from any surface water—held no particular promise. The only current "resident" was Lem Medlin, an itinerant hunter who sold the workers buffalo and antelope meat. The Texas and Pacific crew placed a car beside the rails and named it Midway Station. From that less than auspicious beginning, Midland, Texas, grew into the "Tall City," becoming an important player in the world petroleum industry and gaining recognition in both state and national arenas for its hometown citizens who rose to positions of political power.

Following the completion of the Texas and Pacific Railroad line in December 1881, the first settlers arrived. Sheep raising quickly gave way to cattle ranches, and founders like the Scharbauer family and the Cowden brothers established vast spreads stretching westward into New Mexico.

The Midland Town Company of Zanesville, Ohio, promoted the area's potential across the Midwest, exaggerating amenities and glossing over the disadvantages. In 1884, the company drilled a water well and auctioned land for a town. They were so successful that the community petitioned for a post office and became Midland, as the name Midway was already a bit overused in Texas. The following year, Midland County was formed from Tom Green County and a wood-frame courthouse was quickly erected.

Over the next two decades, the small community grew into a farm and ranch center. Banks, churches, schools, and the *Staked Plains*, Midland's first newspaper, all began in what many called "Windmill Town" because of the prevalence of the mills in both the town and countryside. The Scharbauer family developed a line of Hereford cattle nationally recognized for their quality. Henry Halff touted the bounty produced on the surrounding farms.

Midland continued to grow through the opening decades of the 20th century. The city survived a series of disastrous fires, the worst of which destroyed most of downtown. The first Midland college—Midland Christian—was founded in 1910. A new three-story stone courthouse and jail were erected, and prominent buildings began to line Main and Wall Streets.

By 1920, the region's growth had stabilized; the usable land was all pretty much occupied. Though Midland continued to thrive, many believed the city might have reached its full maturity. They could not have been more wrong.

In 1923, the Santa Rita No. 1 oil well inaugurated the Permian Basin oil boom. Throughout the 1920s, a series of discovery wells opened new oil fields across the region. Communities arose overnight, boomed during the drilling phase, and then rapidly declined into smaller, more stable oil towns. Midland, with no local production of its own, set out to avoid this fate by becoming a regional nexus of petroleum production, once again taking advantage of its location at the center of the Permian Basin fields.

Several enterprising businessmen risked their money and reputations to construct buildings designed to attract the larger oil companies. John Thomas, a local doctor, built the first multistory office building. Rancher Clarence Scharbauer erected a 250-room hotel. Thomas Hogan outdid them all, raising the ornately decorated 12-story Petroleum Building. His detractors labeled it "Hogan's Folly," but oil had redefined West Texas and Midland began its move from Windmill Town to Tall City.

The young metropolis endured tough times in the Depression as prices fell and production slowed. Office buildings sat empty until renewed oil exploration in the mid-1930s helped the local economy improve faster than much of the nation.

Midland again redefined itself following the United States' entry into World War II when Sloan Field, the local airport, played an important role in the war effort. Clarence Scharbauer donated an additional 450 acres to what was already the largest airfield in the area, and local leaders convinced the air force to establish a bombardier training field. The school opened in February 1942 and quickly became one of the largest in the world. Class after class graduated to join the massive bombing operations in the Atlantic and Pacific theaters. The school operated until January 1945, when the airport resumed its role as a regional center for air travel.

Following the end of the war, Midland grew exponentially as the nation entered a long period of prosperity, which included an almost insatiable demand for petroleum products. By 1960, the city had over 60,000 residents. The downtown area contained a number of structures that dwarfed Hogan's Petroleum Building and were visible for miles on the surrounding plains. Housing major oil companies, financiers, and a myriad of oil-related industries, they gave the city the look it still bears today.

Throughout the final three decades of the century, Midland experienced the booms and busts of the petroleum industry: at times so flush that workers slept in their cars because no housing remained available, at times with a downtown of buildings more empty than occupied. Fortunes were made and lost as the roller-coaster ride of petroleum prices ran its course and families like that of George W. Bush came to Midland to take their chances. The ups and downs continue in the new century, and oil remains a critical piece of Midland's current economy. However, the city continues to work to diversify its economic base, and wind and water have grown in importance as regional resources.

As the new century began, two prominent Midland citizens assumed significant roles in government. George W. Bush, who lived in Midland as a youngster, served as governor of Texas from 1995 to 2001 and won the presidency of the United States in the 2000 election. Bush made his last public speech in Midland before flying to Washington to assume office as the 43rd President of the United States. In 2009, Bush returned to Midland for his first public appearance as a past president. Another Midland citizen, Tom Craddick, played a historic role in the Texas Legislature when, in January 2003, he became the first Republican Speaker of the Texas House in over 130 years.

From its location in the midst of West Texas, upon the southern edge of the Llano Estacado, in the central area of the American nation, Midland has invented and reinvented itself in a location whose importance is defined in terms of its relationship to those things surrounding it. Like the mythical Phoenix, the city has leveraged its self-made reputation to adapt and flourish in unforgiving environments, both natural and economic. Midland has redefined itself from railroad town to ranching center, from oil financial hub to military resource, and back again to oil leader. As the 21st century begins with its new challenges for the petroleum industry, Midland will seek once again to adapt to a new future in West Texas.

One

From Midway to Midland

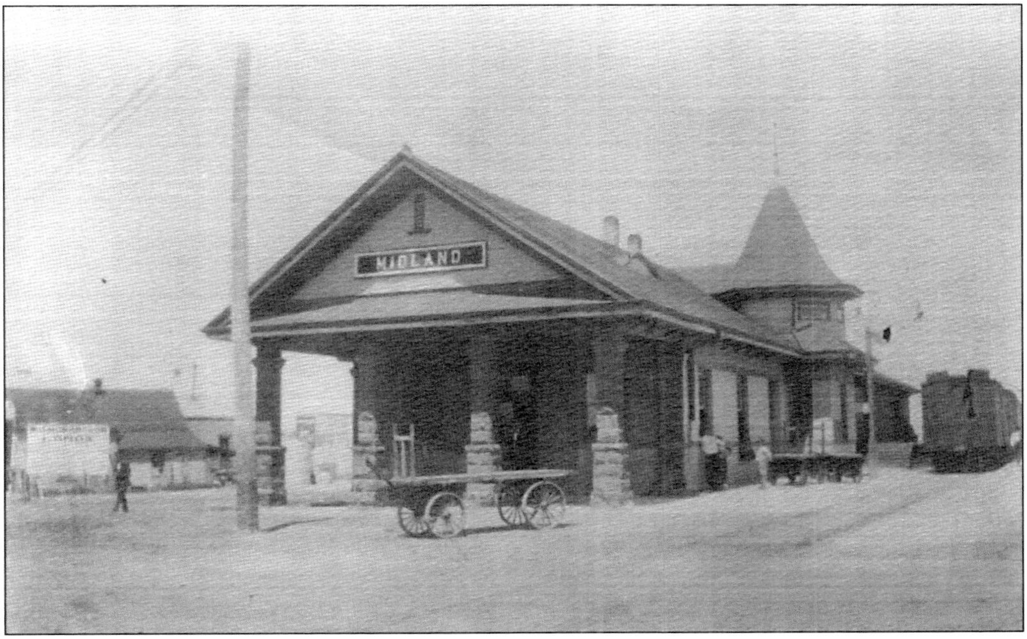

On June 23, 1881, the Texas and Pacific construction crew drove a spike into the line 340 miles from their starting point in Dallas to mark the halfway point between Fort Worth and El Paso. According to the *Dallas Weekly Herald* of June 9, 1881, a "distinguished speaker" praised their "great energy and efficiency." From that humble beginning, Midland grew into a thriving community by the time the first permanent depot was constructed in 1890. The photograph was taken around 1895.

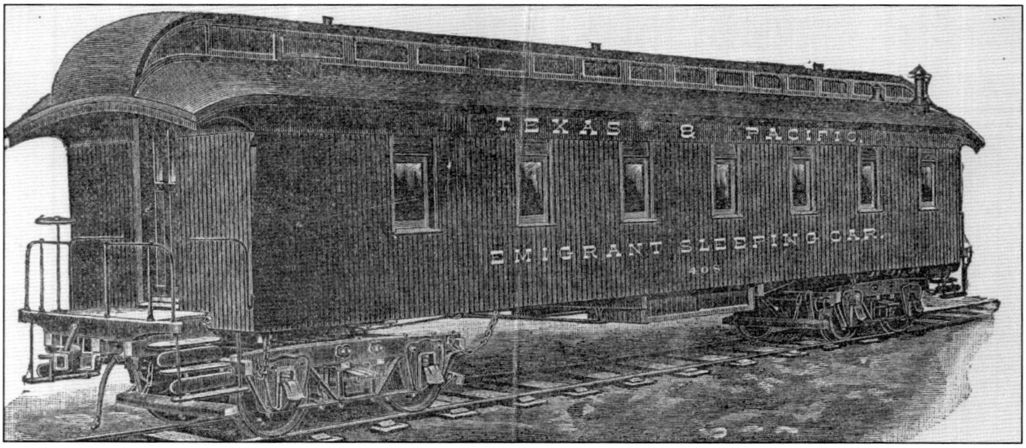

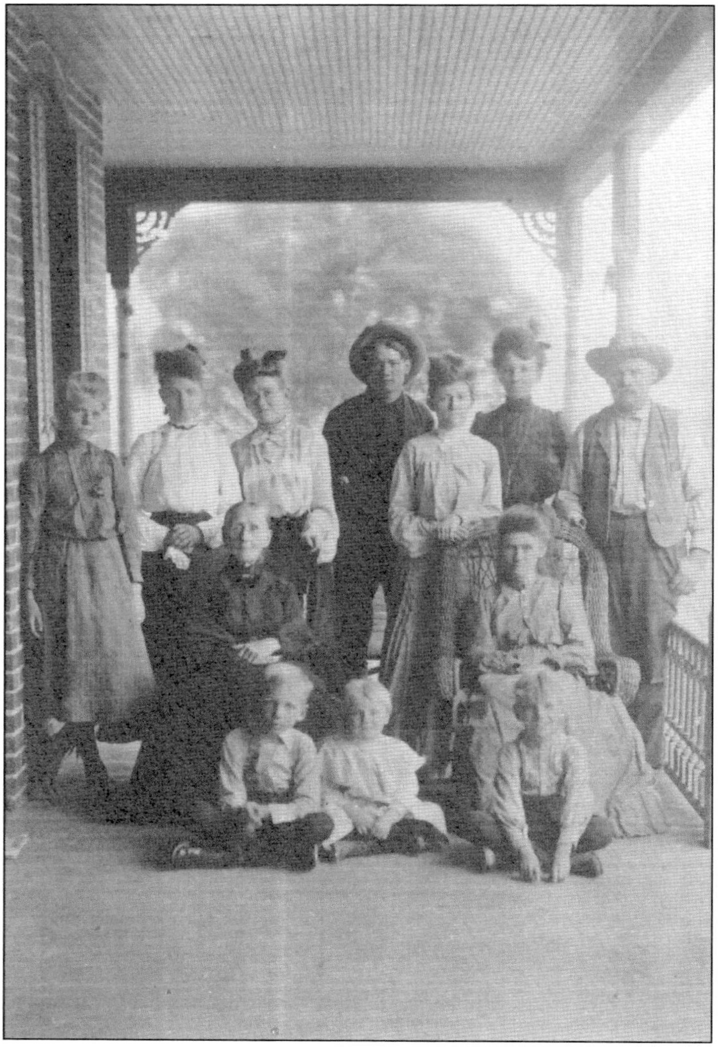

A sleeping car like this served as the first section house for Midway until a more permanent structure was erected. Few people settled the empty plain at first. In 1884, an Ohio real estate company promoted the area throughout the Midwest. By the end of year, 100 families lived in the area. The U.S. Postal Service rejected Midway, as several Texas cities already bore that name. Midland was officially on the map.

Herman Nelson Garrett (on the far right, with his family in 1903) is often claimed as Midland's first settler. In 1882, the one-armed Garrett drove a flock of 300 sheep east from El Paso. He crossed the Pecos River on planks laid along the railroad track. He built his camp at Mustang Springs, 10 miles north of Midland. Several other sheep men soon followed his lead.

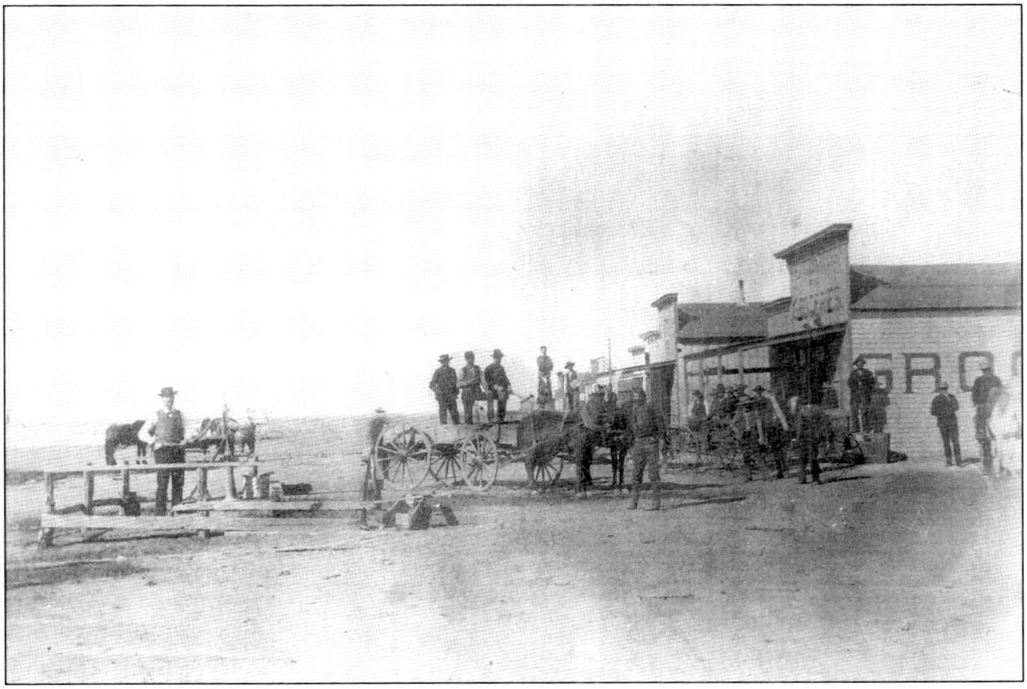

The Midland Town Company of Zanesville, Ohio, dug the first water well for the city by hand in 1884. It measured 6 feet wide and extended 50 feet into the West Texas soil. A hand pump supplied water to wooden buckets. Before the well was dug, water was shipped by rail from Monahans, 50 miles to the west. The well also supplied water for the community cattle trough.

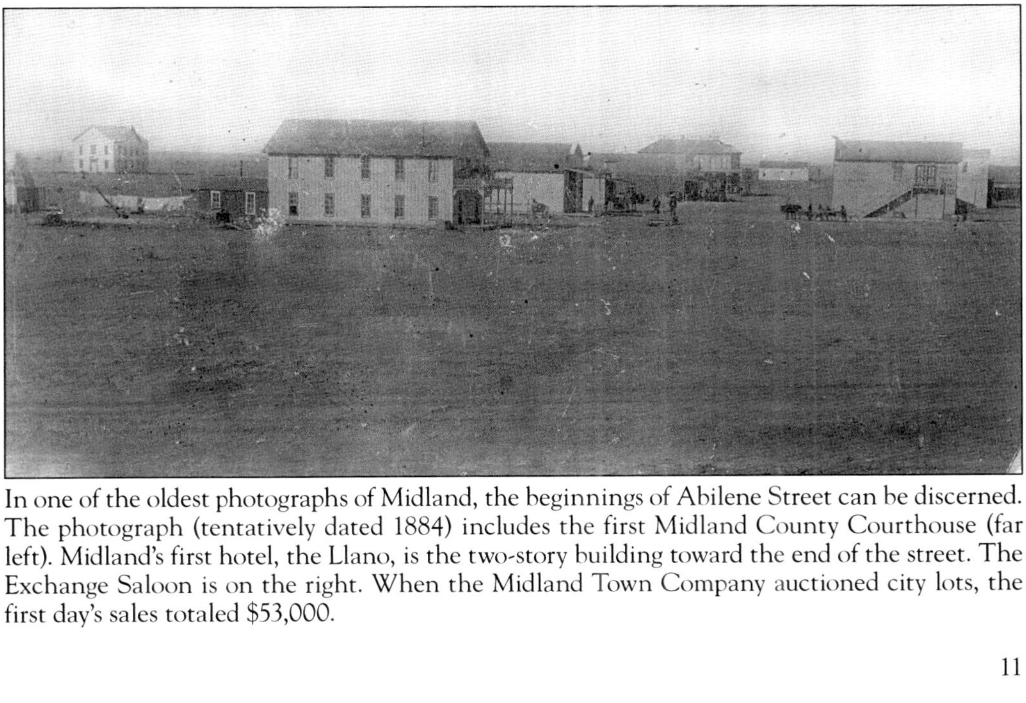

In one of the oldest photographs of Midland, the beginnings of Abilene Street can be discerned. The photograph (tentatively dated 1884) includes the first Midland County Courthouse (far left). Midland's first hotel, the Llano, is the two-story building toward the end of the street. The Exchange Saloon is on the right. When the Midland Town Company auctioned city lots, the first day's sales totaled $53,000.

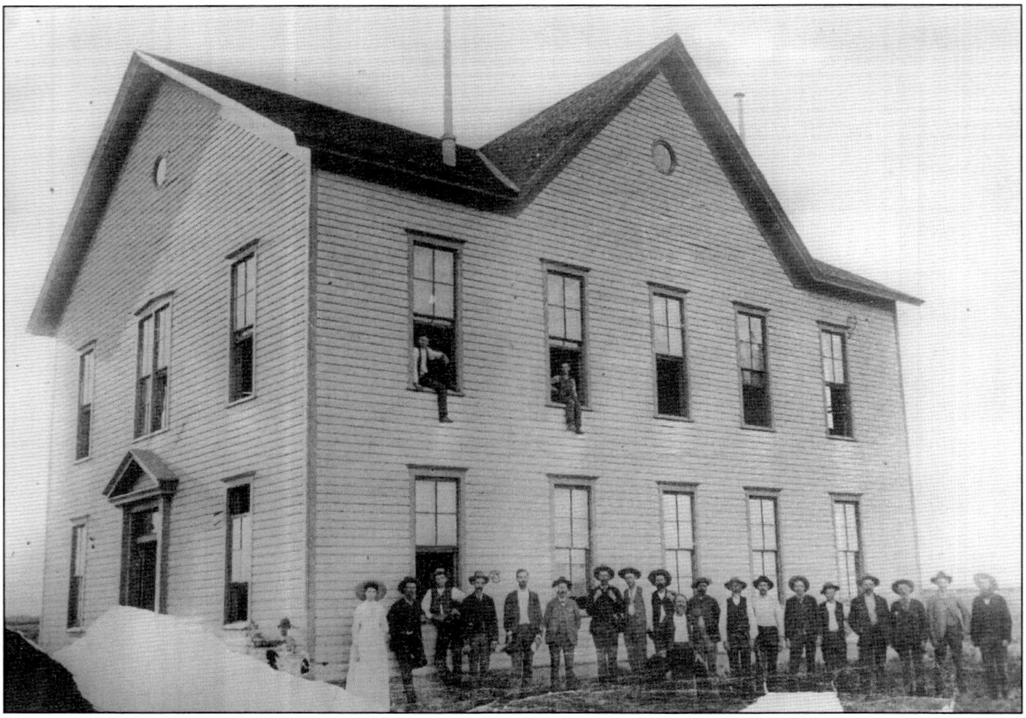

In 1885, Midland County was carved from Tom Green County and organized in June. On August 25, the first county commissioners court met, with Judge E. B. Lancaster presiding. The court accepted the bid of the Midland Town Company to provide $3,000 toward the construction of a courthouse to be erected on land owned by the company. That courthouse, pictured here, was a two-story, wood-frame structure. (Courtesy of the Permian Historical Society Archives.)

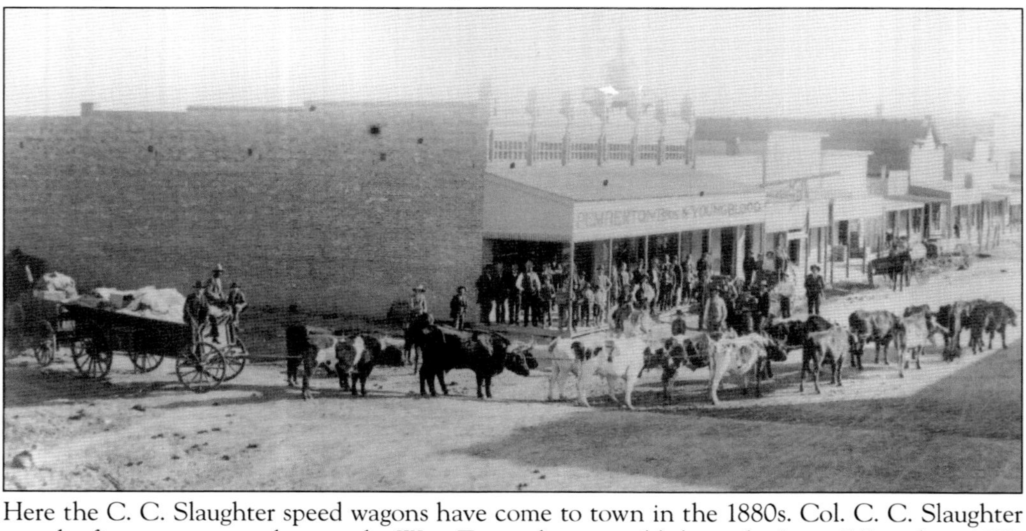

Here the C. C. Slaughter speed wagons have come to town in the 1880s. Col. C. C. Slaughter was the first to move cattle onto the West Texas plains, establishing the Long S Ranch in 1879, 50 miles north of Monahans. Slaughter began his career as a freighter hauling hides and lumber. He continued to use his wagons to carry supplies to his vast ranch, reputed to have been over 24 million acres in size.

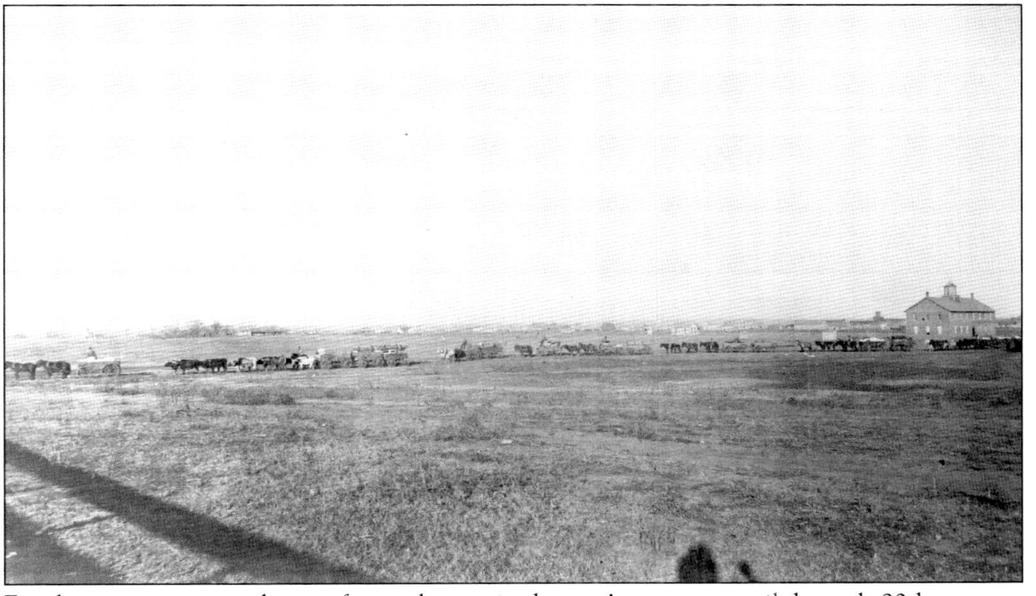

Freight wagons remained a significant element in the area's economy until the early 20th century. Here a freight line departs from Midland on its way to Fort Davis in 1898. (Courtesy of the Permian Historical Society Archives.)

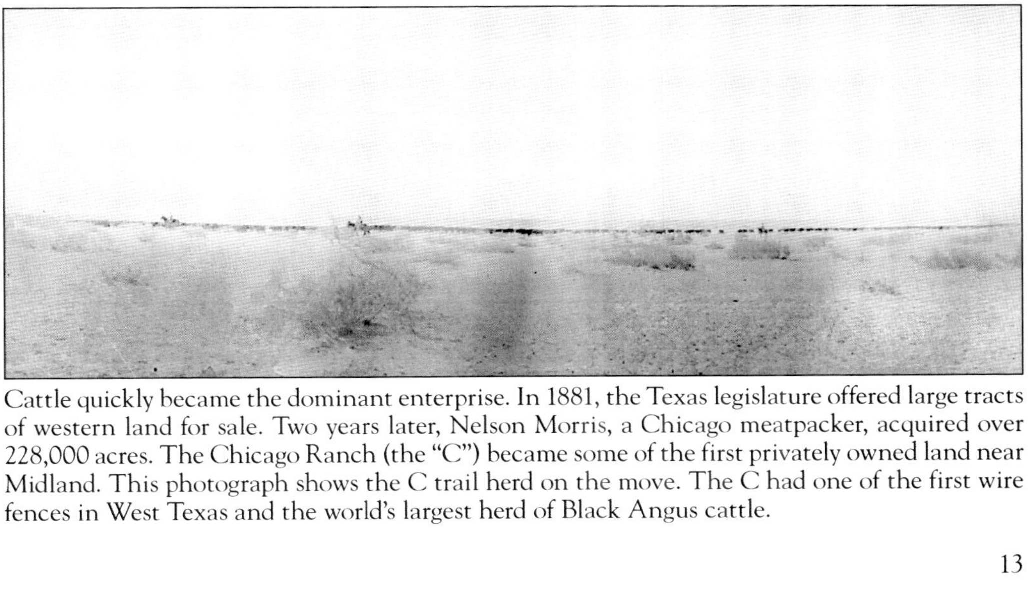

Cattle quickly became the dominant enterprise. In 1881, the Texas legislature offered large tracts of western land for sale. Two years later, Nelson Morris, a Chicago meatpacker, acquired over 228,000 acres. The Chicago Ranch (the "C") became some of the first privately owned land near Midland. This photograph shows the C trail herd on the move. The C had one of the first wire fences in West Texas and the world's largest herd of Black Angus cattle.

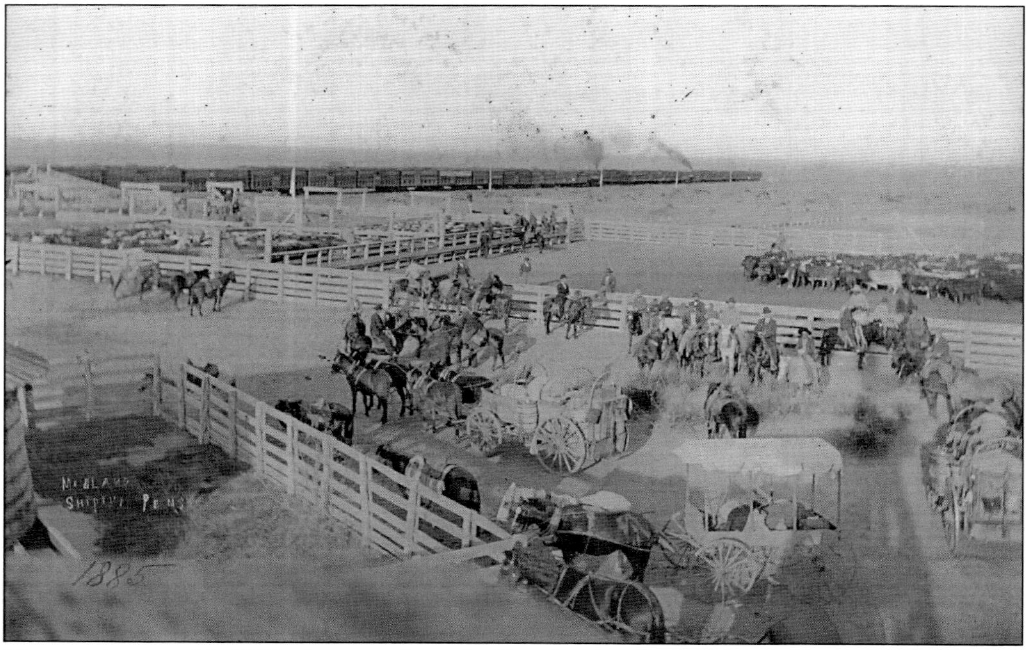

The caption on this 1885 photograph reads, "Loading cattle for Indian Territory at Midland, Texas, Ezra White, agent for T and P." Midland quickly became a major shipping point for the region's cattle. C. C. Slaughter branded 15,000 Angus cows a year in both 1887 and 1888. The Cowden brothers—W. H., George, John, and Buck—established the vast JAL Ranch along the New Mexico–Texas border.

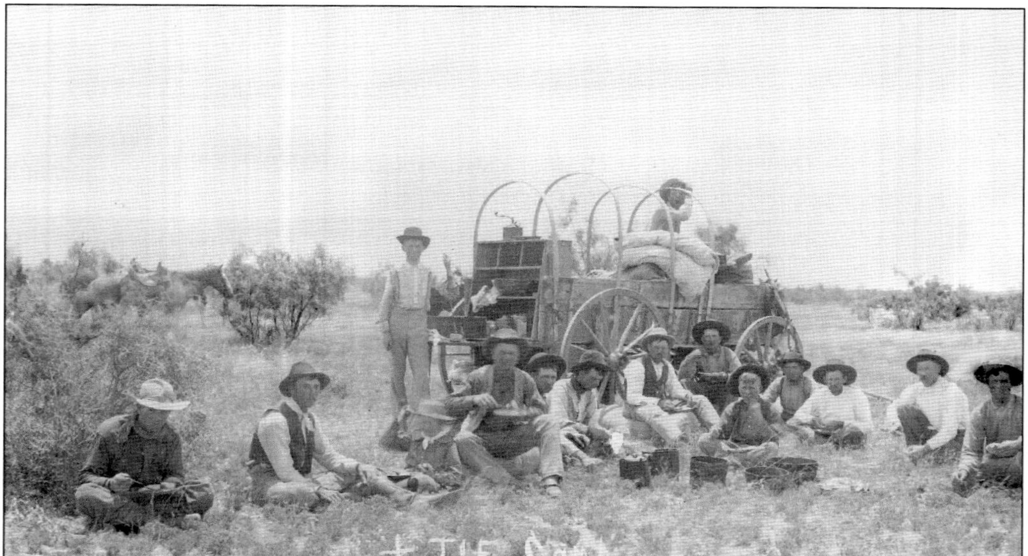

Photographer E. E. Hoyt captured lunch at the Cross Tie Camp. Tom Martin, W. Peppers, and Lump Mooney started the Cross Tie and Railway Ranch south of Midland in 1884. Tom Martin fenced his first pasture with flat wire at a cost of $200 per mile of fence. The Cross Tie brand was registered in 1902.

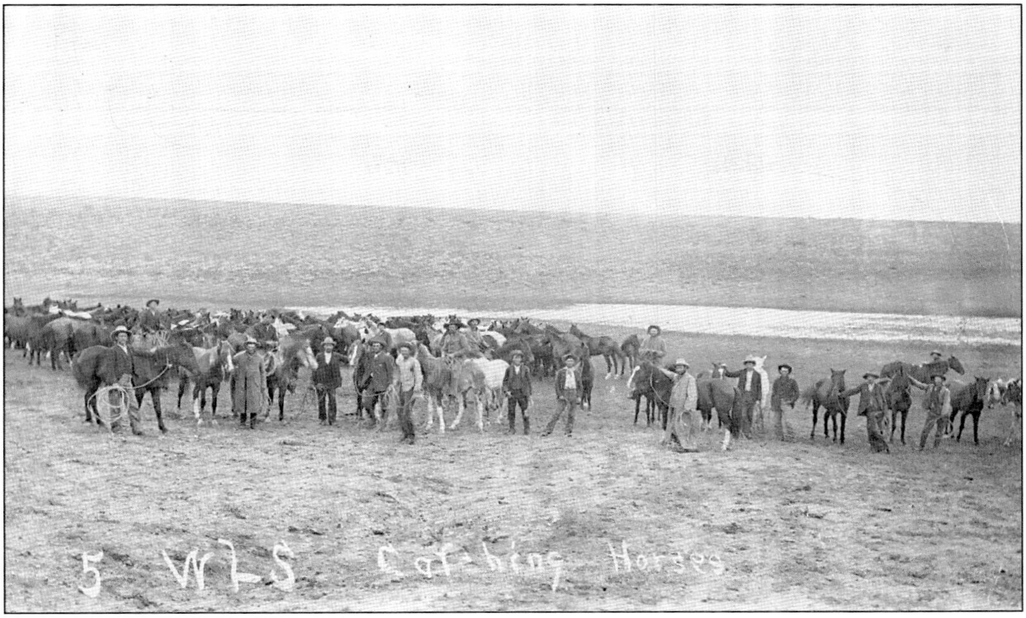

In 1884, Major Wells began the Five Wells Ranch 40 miles north of Midland. The rolling plains proved an excellent environment for cattle and horses. Depressions in the land provided surface pools when rain was plentiful. The Five Wells cowboys catch horses from the remuda in 1890.

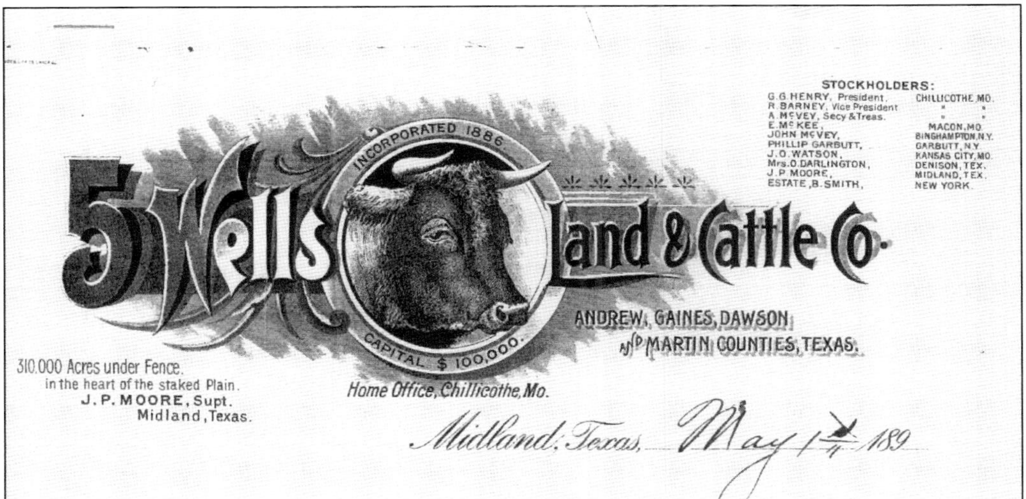

The Five Wells stationery boasted the ranch's prowess. The corporate venture headquartered in Chillicothe, Missouri, drew not only stockholders and corporate heads, but also young men seeking adventure. The files of the Midland Historical Museum include correspondence from the family of George McNair of Rochester, New York, regarding his untimely death on the ranch from tuberculosis in 1896.

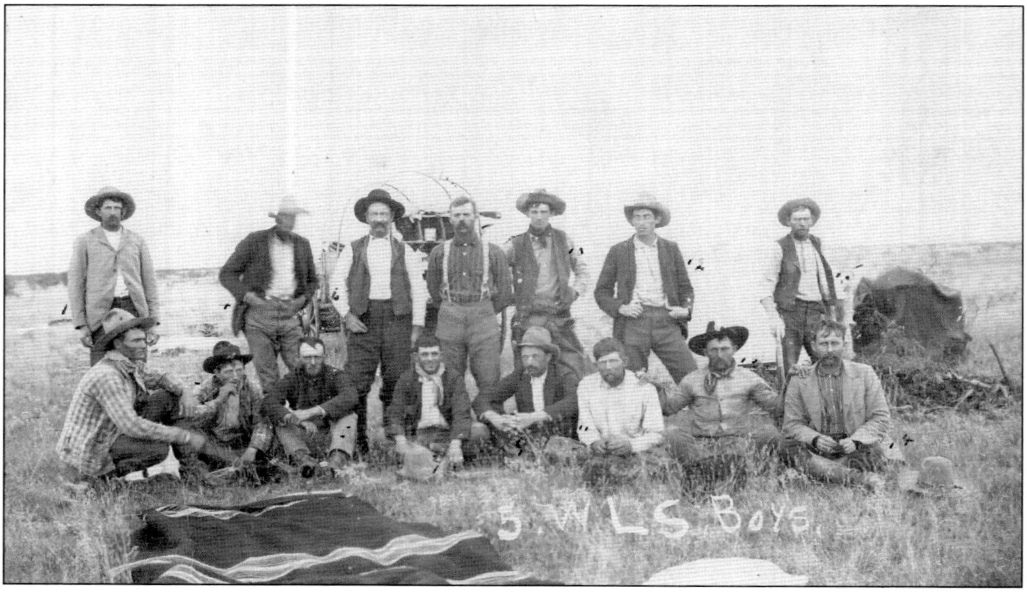

The Five Wells cowboys strike a pose for early-day photographer E. E. Hoyt in 1890. Identified from left to right are (first row) Timberline, Wild Bill, Jim Darling, Tom Hudspeth, Elmer Greenlee, Jim Herrell, Ben Boydston, and John Deering; (second row) Andrew Allen, Doc Sears, Henry Williams, Jim Darling, Top Herd, T. O. Midkiff, and unidentified cook. John Scharbauer, sheep man turned rancher turned banker, acquired the ranch in 1895.

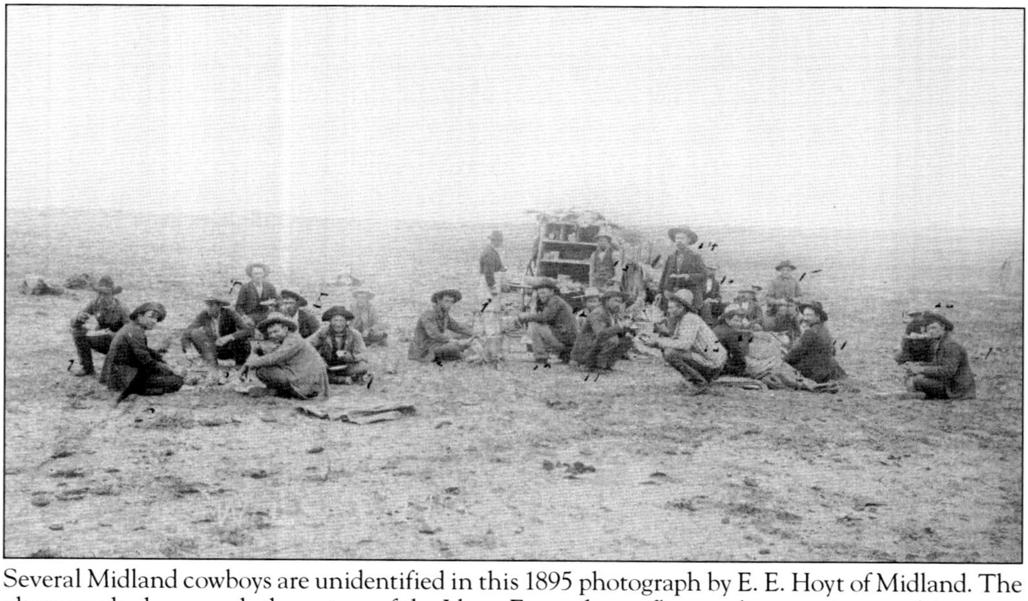

Several Midland cowboys are unidentified in this 1895 photograph by E. E. Hoyt of Midland. The photograph also records the nature of the Llano Estacado—a flat, treeless terrain stretching away to the horizon. Those around the chuck wagon are, from left to right, Ben Boydston, unidentified, T. O. Midkiff, Frank Shelton, unidentified cowboy, Tom Hudspeth, Wild Bill, unidentified cowboy, Bud Roggins, unidentified cook (left of chuck wagon), Jim Doublin, Doc Sears, unidentified cook (right of chuck wagon), Roy Davis, Henry Williams (standing), Timberline, Elmer Greenlee, Kid Gene Barrett, two unidentified cowboys, Jim Smith, Ben Glasscock, and unidentified cowboy.

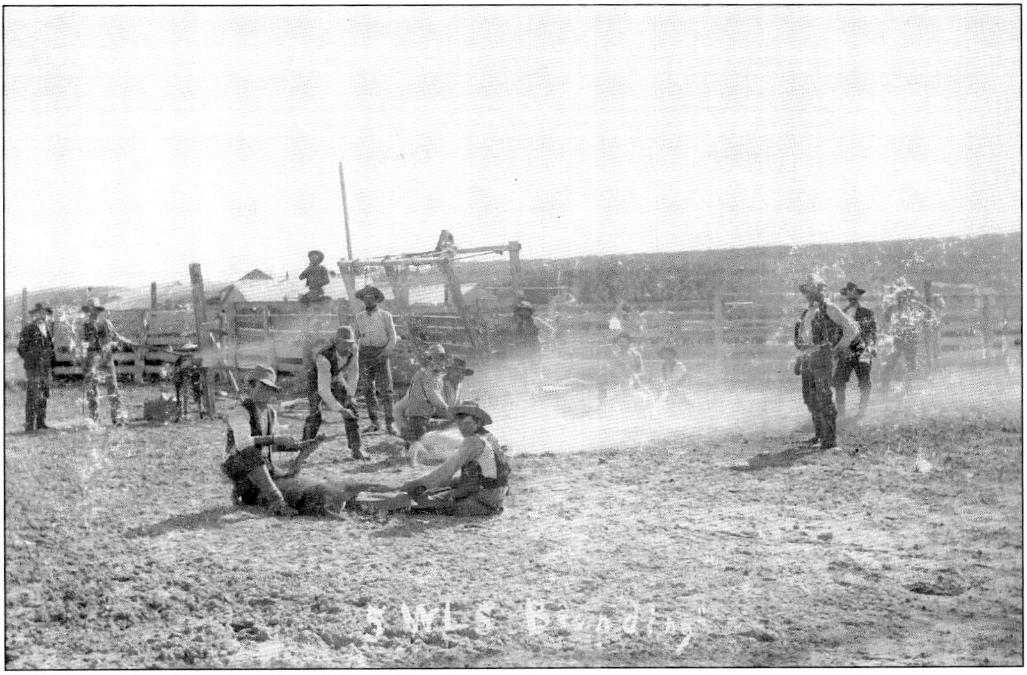

Another early-day Five Wells photograph depicts the reality of ranch work in this branding scene. Years later, a young man named Elmer Kelton, born at the Five Wells Horse Camp in 1926, would write a number of award-winning Western novels that provided highly realistic depictions of life on West Texas ranches. Cowboys in the photograph are Harry Tolbert, Clarence Scharbauer, Eb Dickson, Wilber Wadley, Ed Rountree, and Millard Eidson.

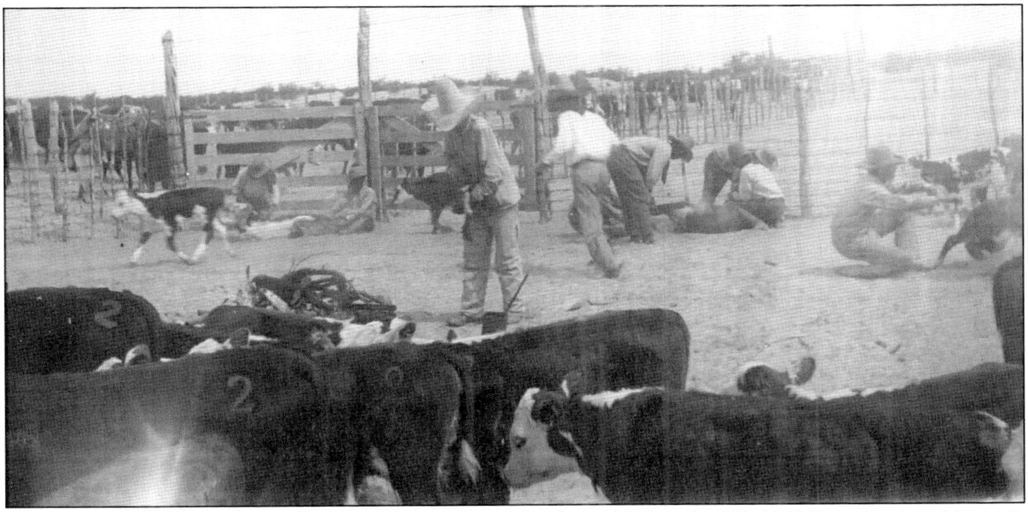

Given the outfits worn by the men in this picture, this branding at the Waddell Ranch probably took place later than the one above, but the work remained the same. Brands provided an identifying mark for the cattle, but also came to symbolize the ranch itself and the men who worked there. The cowboys, ranch foremen, and landowners all took pride in "riding for the brand." Today, even in industries far removed from cattle raising, companies still find identity and pride in what continue to be called their "brand" names.

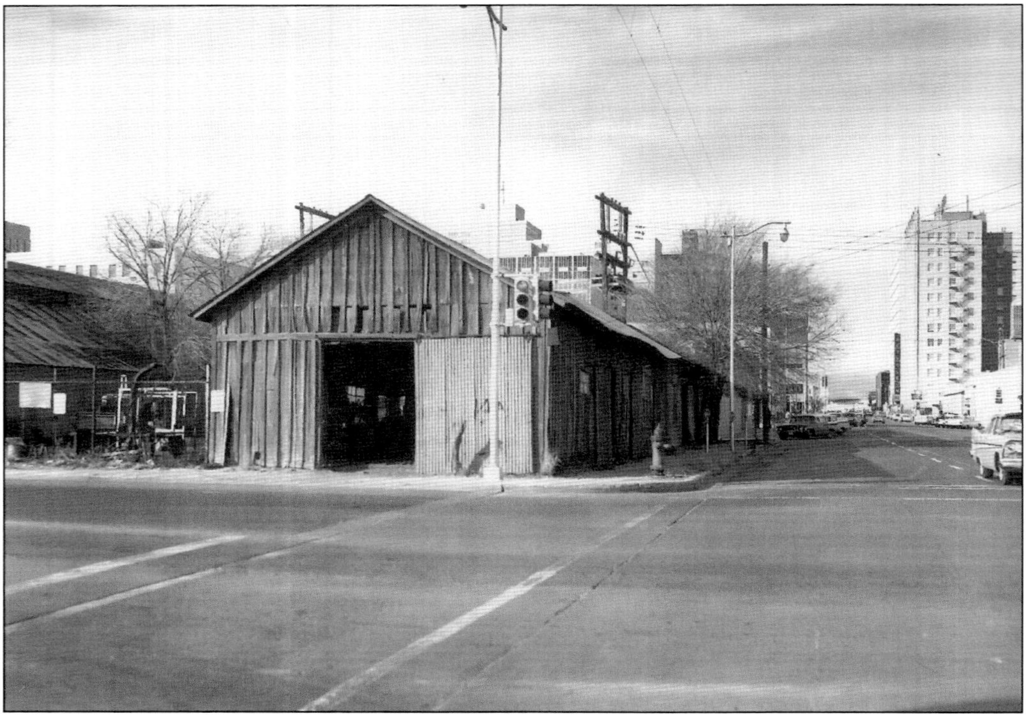

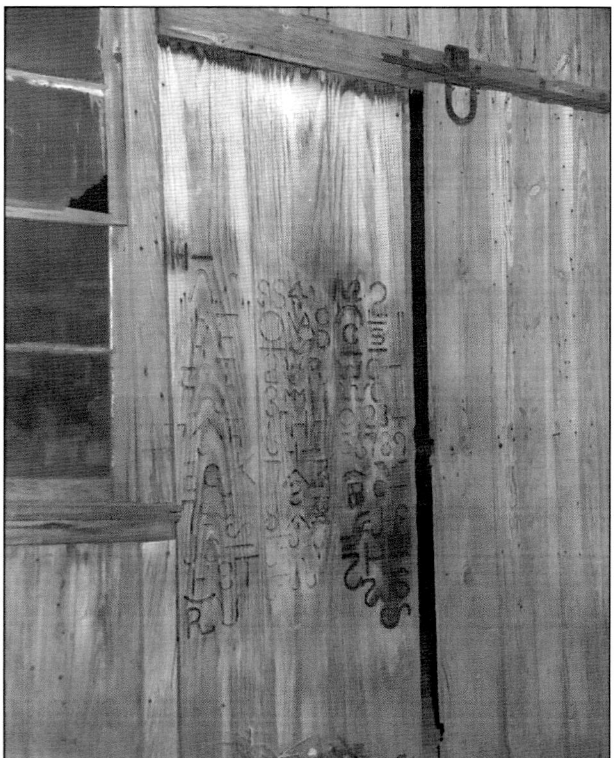

Midland's master blacksmith was John Valentine Pliska. This was his shop, which appears insignificant against a 1960s Midland background. On his way to Mexico in 1903, Pliska stopped in Midland. He walked a couple of blocks to the local blacksmith shop, took a job, and remained the rest of his life. In October 1905, Pliska became the first person to become a naturalized citizen in Midland County.

In addition to making horseshoes and repairing wagons and windmills, Pliska became a master maker of branding irons. To test the irons he would heat them and then burn the brand into the heavy doors of his shop. In 1936, the Texas Centennial exhibited two of his doors, filled with famous brands. The doors became part of the University of Texas Museum collection.

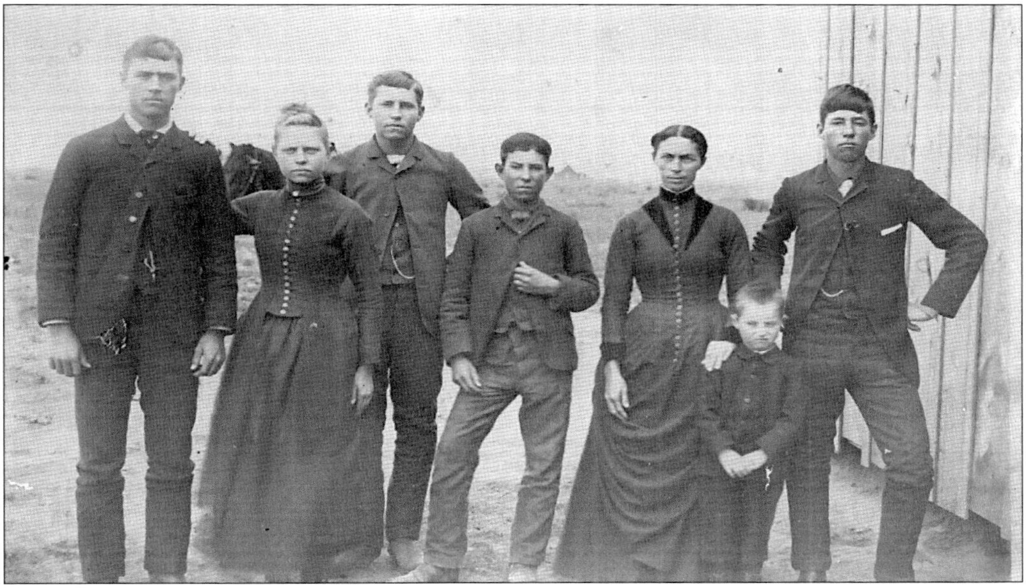

In the early 1880s, widow Nancy Vest brought her family to Midland seeking a new start. They spent the first night in the home of a Texas Ranger, as her husband had also been a ranger. Nancy Vest worked as a practical nurse and boarded ranch children in her home. The Vest boys worked as ranch hands for area outfits. The Vests typified the early settlers drawn to the opportunities offered on the Midland frontier. This 1890 photograph includes, from left to right, Bill, Mollie, Ab, John, Nancy, Doc, and Tom.

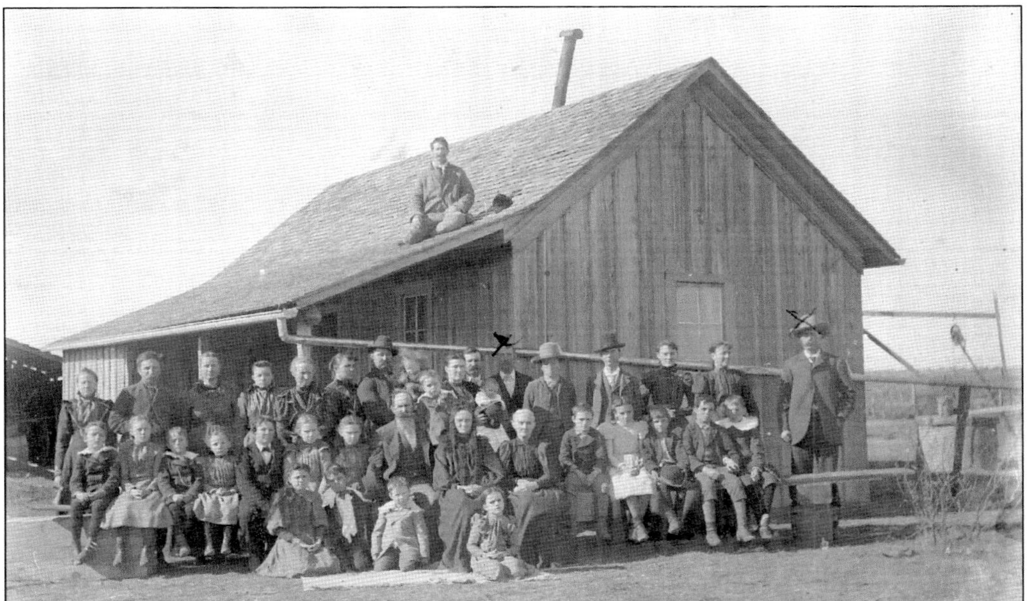

This was Midland's first school (around 1886) on north Big Spring Street, near Illinois Street. Nancy Vest and Mrs. Daugherty donated the land. Among the group of parents and children are Clarence Scharbauer and Mary McIntire (Mollie) Vest. The school was rebuilt the following year.

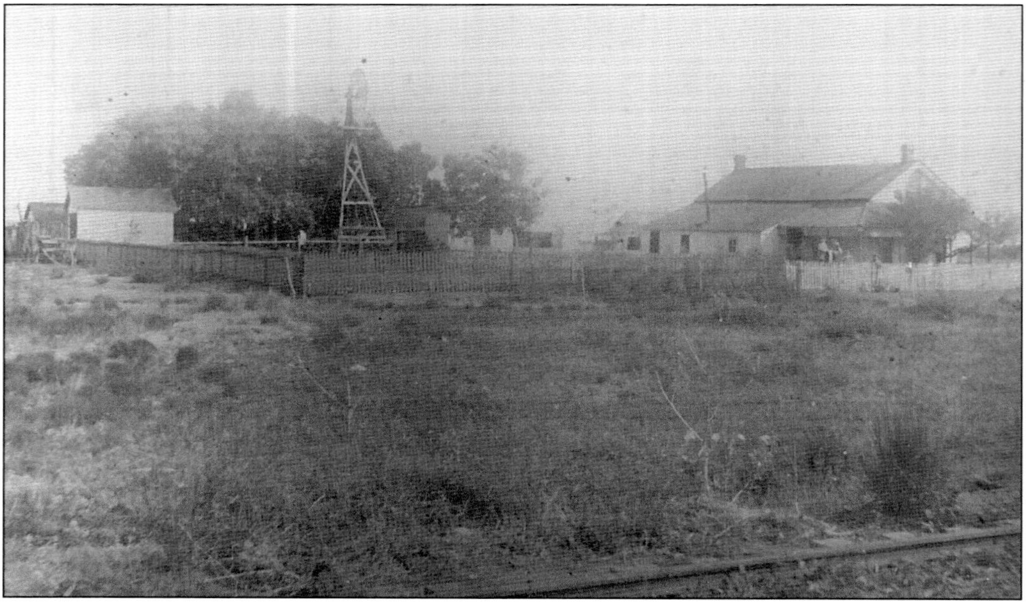

In 1886 and 1887, nature dealt the West two devastating blows. A drought dried up much of the scarce surface water. The following winter was among the worst in recorded history. Yet, while many Westerners fled east, promoters continued to tout Midland's virtues. Germania, a railroad stop a few miles east, targeted European immigrants with photographs such as this of a prosperous-looking home beside the tracks.

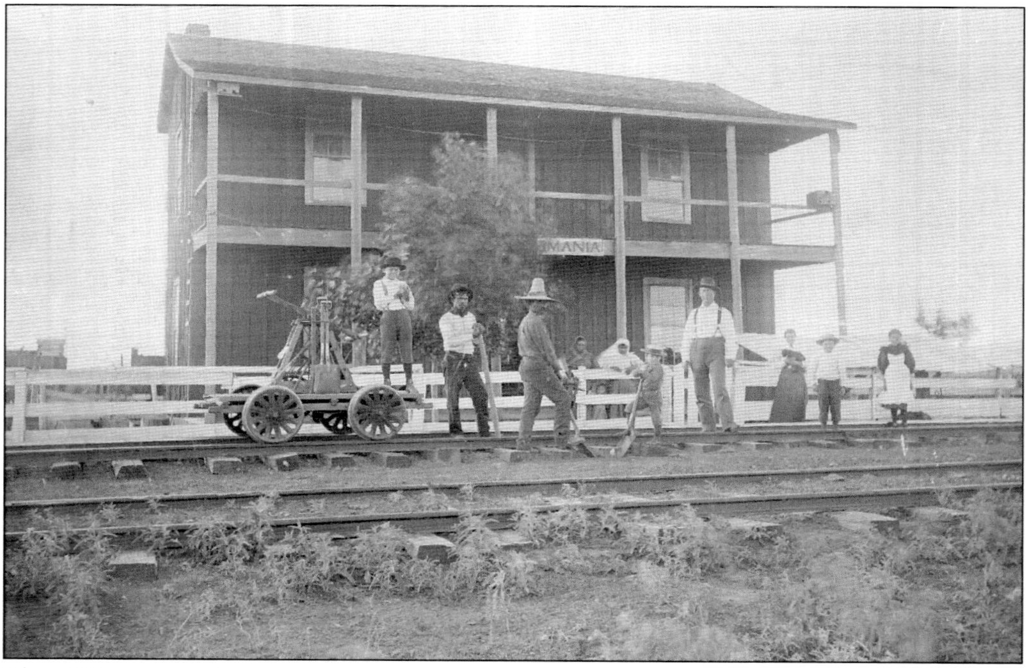

This 1895 picture of the first section house in Germania, with its choreographed pose, clearly sought to appeal to special ethnic groups and immigrants. Despite the promoters' best efforts, Germania did not survive.

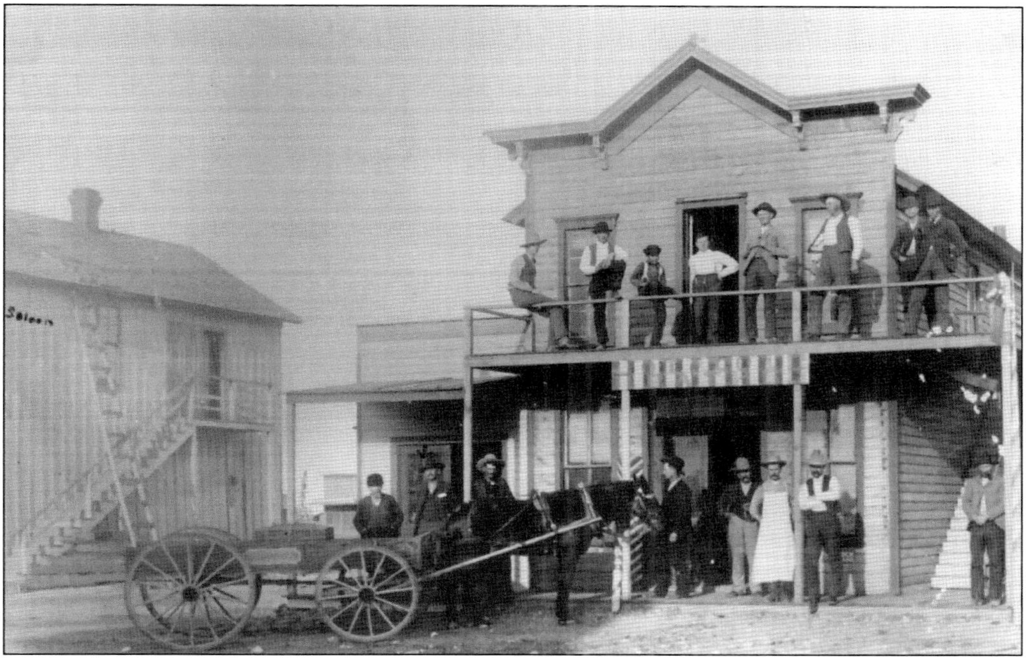

The handwritten caption on this photograph reads, "Looking north on Main Street from railroad tracks, barber shop on first floor, rooming house on second floor." It most likely dates from the late 1880s or early 1890s.

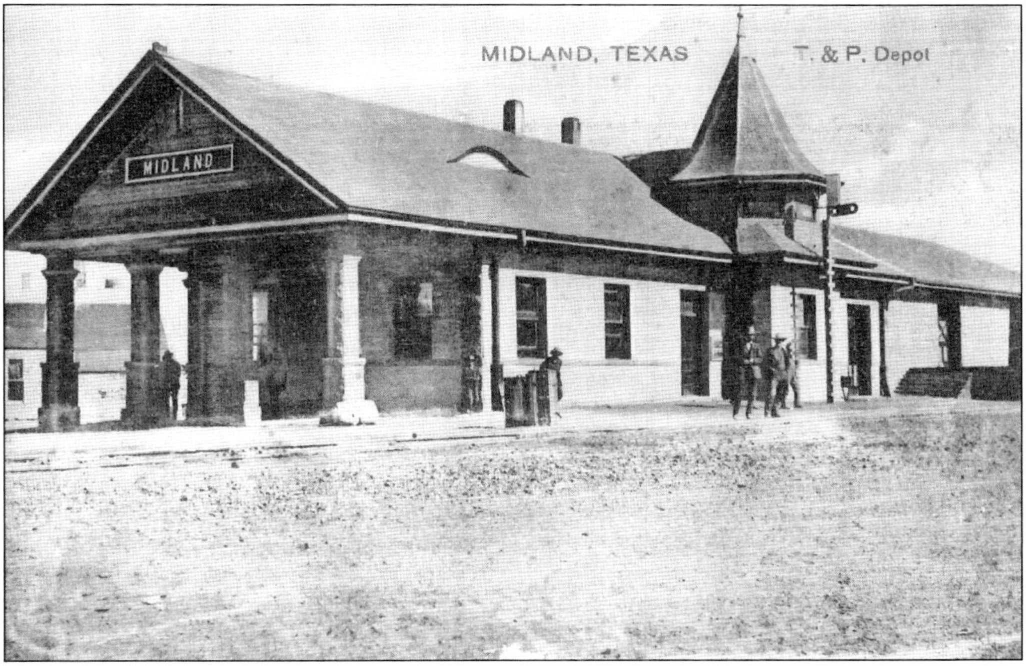

In 1890, the Texas and Pacific Railroad constructed a new depot of red sandstone from the Barstow Quarry in western Ward County. This depot, shown here on an old postcard, remained a focal point of the community for the next several decades.

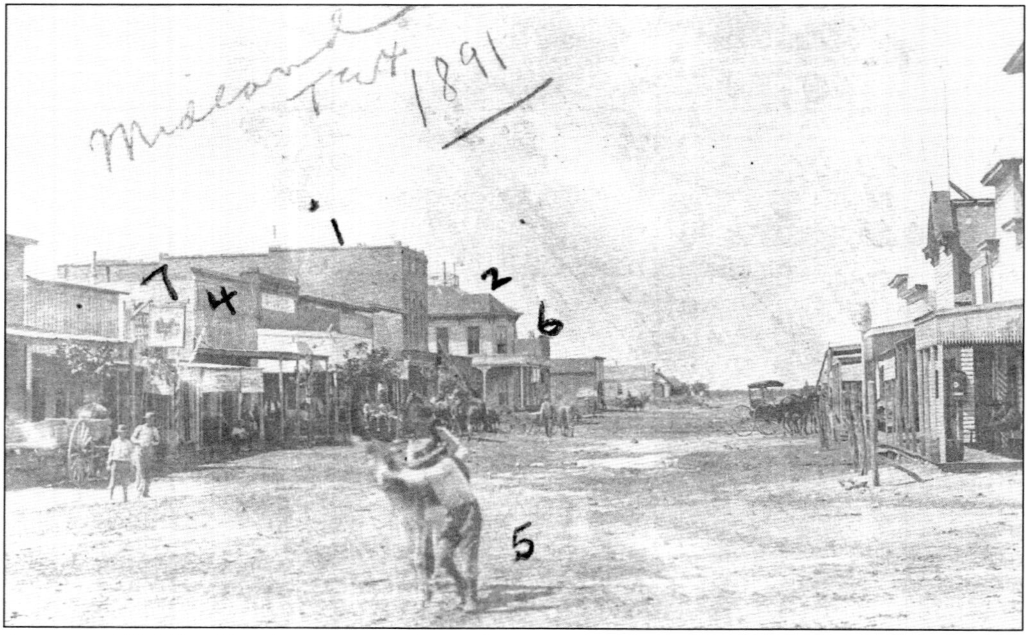

Ten-year-old Midland had become a market and social center for area ranches. This 1891 photograph identifies the following: 1.) First National Bank, 2.) Llano Hotel, 4.) Henry Rohlfing Confectioner, and 7.) Swain Saddle Shop. In the center of the photograph are 5.) Wilbur Wadley, an outstanding cowboy, and his uncooperative donkey. (Courtesy of the Permian Historical Society Archives.)

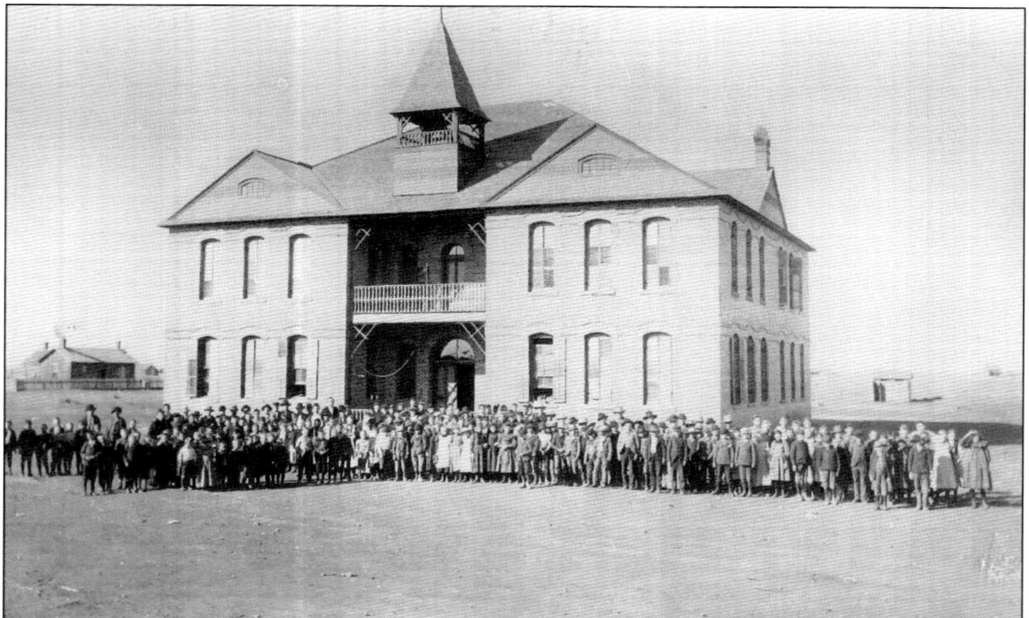

By 1890, Midland County had over 1,000 residents and 722 people lived in the city. Families and proud citizens pose in front of the North School building in 1893, located between Big Spring and Colorado Streets. Built at a cost of $9,000, the school was paid for by public subscription within 24 hours.

On August 23, 1885, six members organized Midland's first church. In 1889, the congregation constructed a small frame church in the 100 block of north Abilene Street. In 1894, Mary McIntire (Mollie) Vest and Frank McCormick became the first couple married in First Methodist. Some 300 guests attended. The wedding supper at their new home was cooked outside in a wash pot.

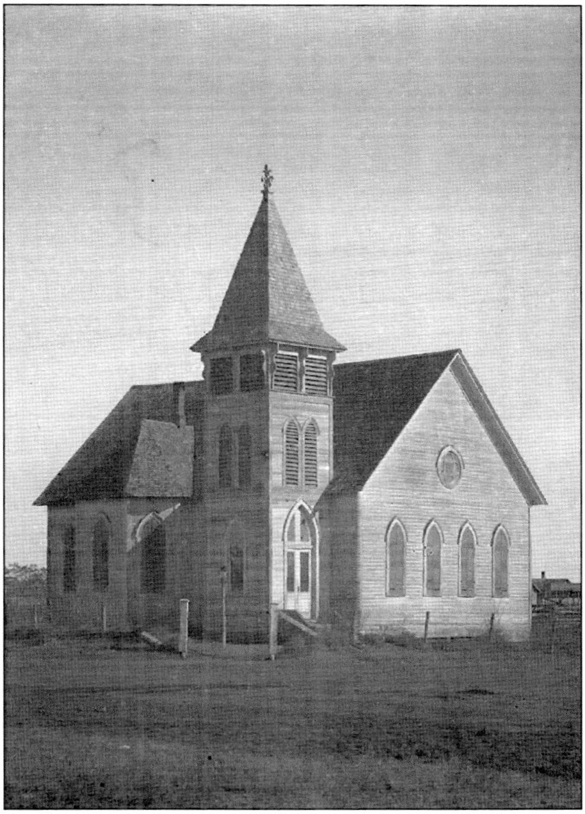

H. G. Symonds took the famous photograph below, which he titled "Sand Storm passed over Midland, Texas, February 20, 1894, 6 p.m." The dark cloud looms over the small houses and windmills. Huge storms develop and sweep across the Llano, pushing dust clouds for miles. These storms became more infamous during the 1930s Dust Bowl years. The almost constant wind that blows across the plains also brought power to turn the windmills as a reliable water source.

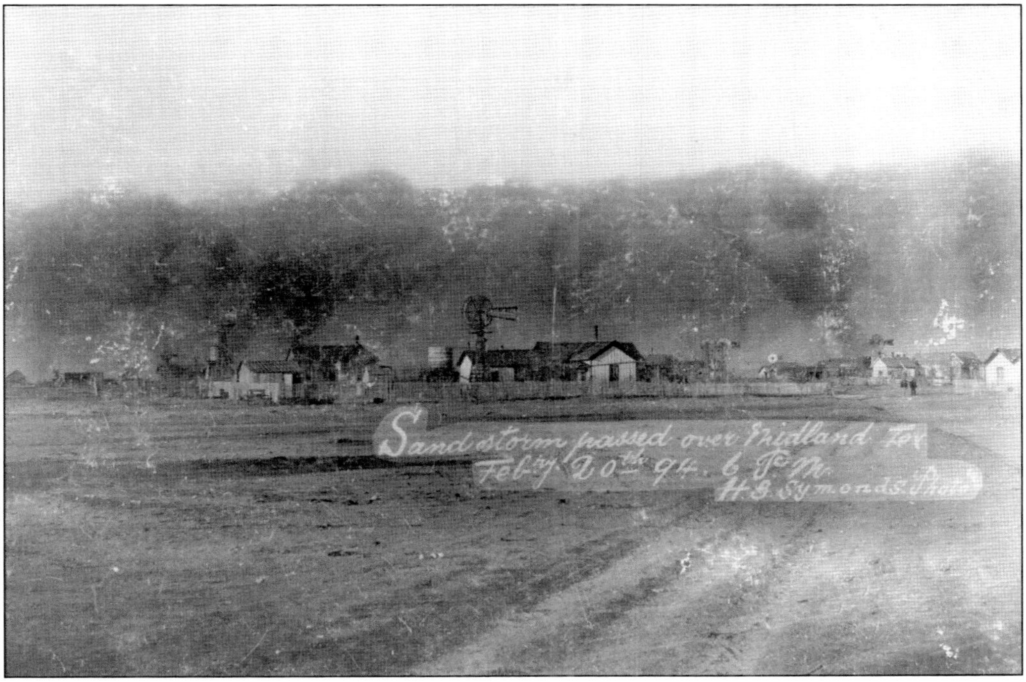

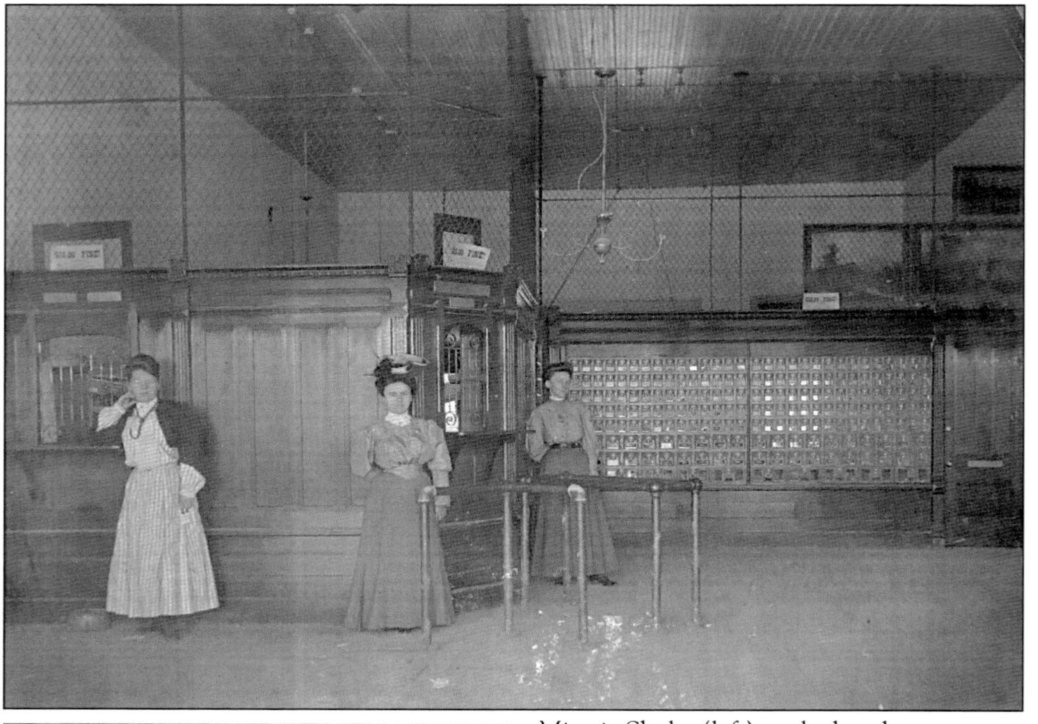

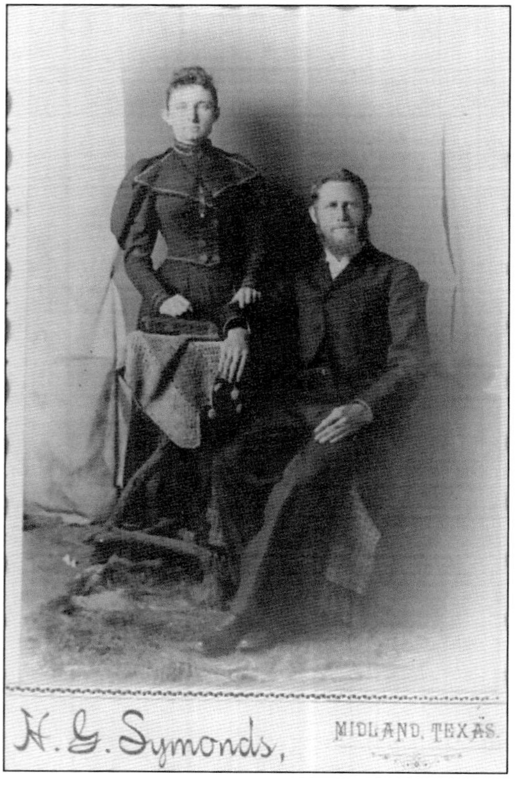

Minnie Sholte (left) worked at the Midland Post Office, shown here in 1895. The other two women are Mrs. Ray (center) and Ethel Richardson.

The Baptists organized in January 1886, led by their first minister, Rev. S. B. Callaway. The initial congregation had 26 members but grew quickly. In 1886, the Baptists erected their first church and offered it to all denominations that wished to hold services. In November 1894, Midland's Baptist pastor, Rev. G. H. M. Wilson, and his wife sat for their photograph in the studio of H. G. Symonds. Wilson was the church's first full-time pastor.

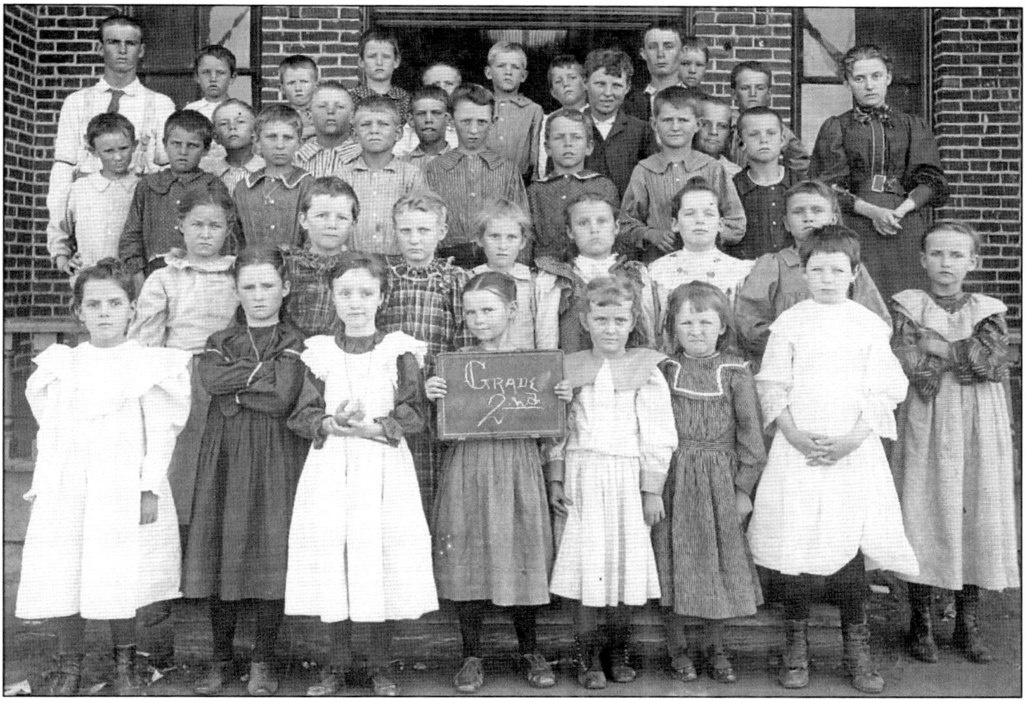

In 1896, the students of Mamie Stokes line up, girls in front, for their picture in front of their redbrick schoolhouse at 301 West Illinois Street. A few children appear a bit old for that grade, but the lines between grades were a bit hazy before the standardization of curriculum.

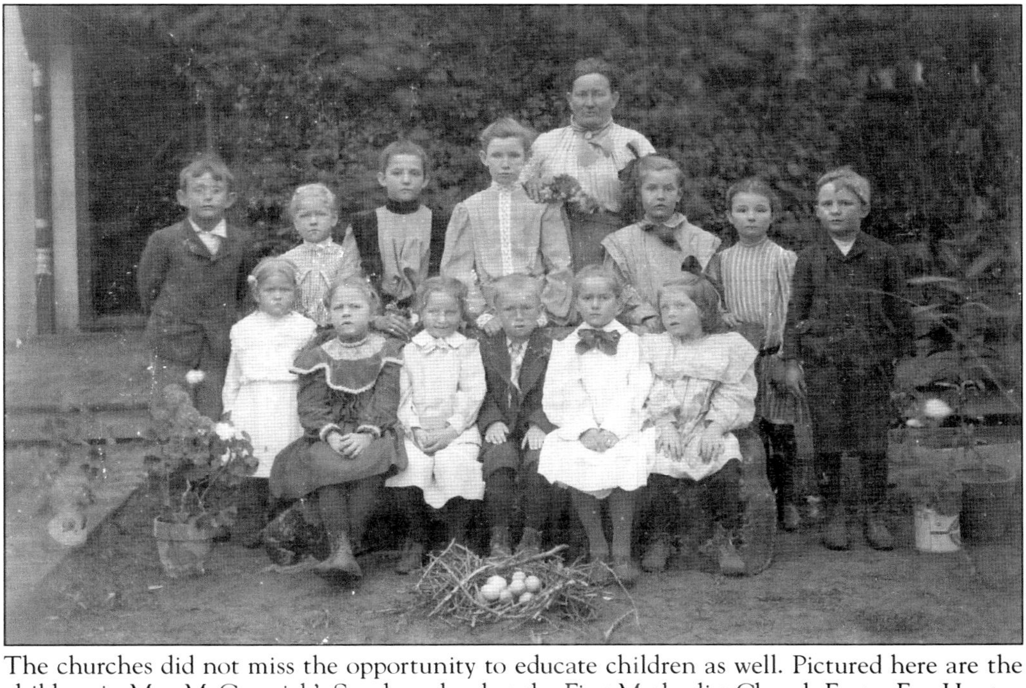

The churches did not miss the opportunity to educate children as well. Pictured here are the children in Mrs. McCormick's Sunday school at the First Methodist Church Easter Egg Hunt.

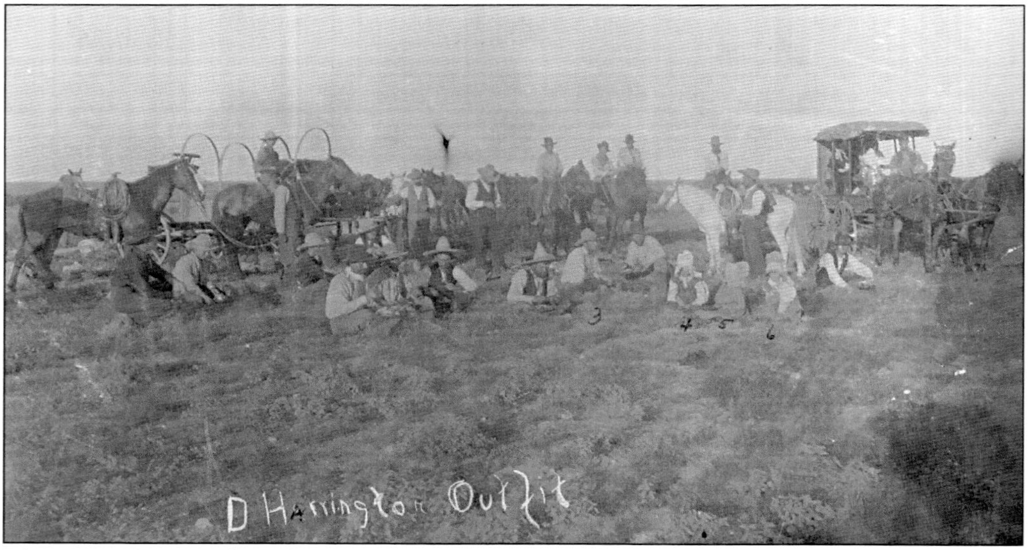

This 1894 photograph of the D. Harrington outfit south of Midland is rare in that it includes women. The women remain in the buggy while the girls sit with the cowboys. Identified here are 1.) Tas. Harrington (by wagon on left), 2.) E. Dive Harrington, 3.) W. W. Harrington, 4.) Irene, 5.) Dot Twinning (a cousin), and 6.) Pearl Harrington.

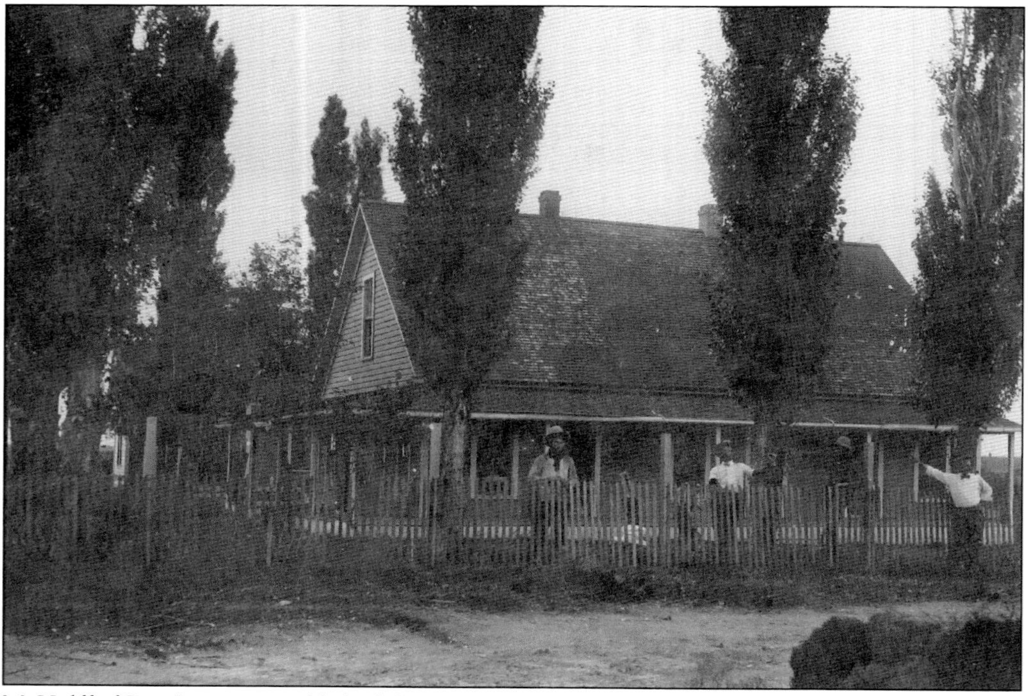

M. Halff of San Antonio established the Quien Sabe Ranch in the early 1890s. The ranch covered over 500 sections stretching southeast from the edge of Midland. The ranch ran some 10,000 head of cattle over its first dozen years. According to the *Handbook of Texas*, "Quién sabe?" (Spanish for "Who knows?") was the answer that local Mexican cowboys gave when asked the origin of the ranch's unusual cattle brand. This is the Quien Sabe headquarters around 1909.

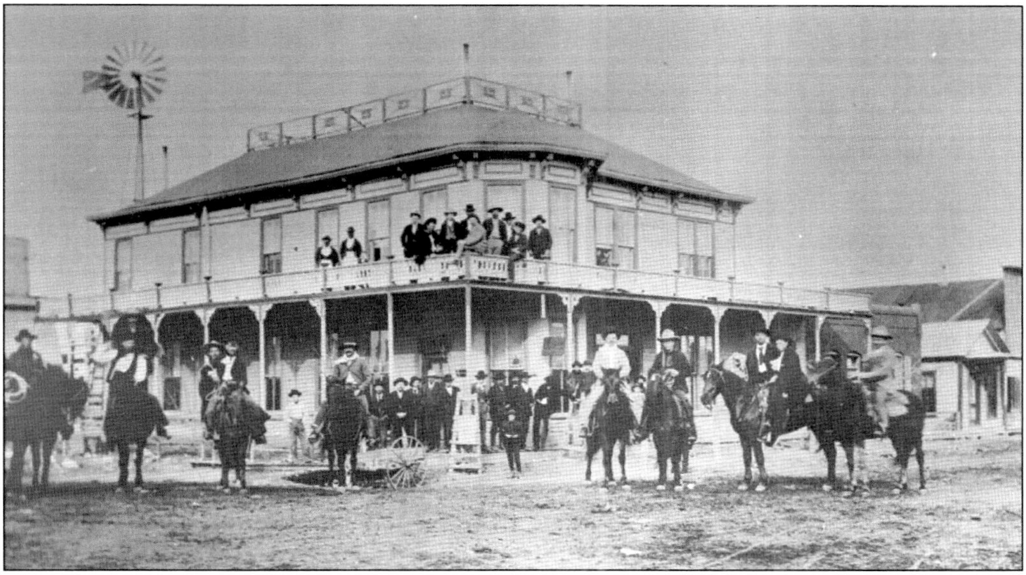

On Christmas Day 1895, a group of cowboys came to Midland to celebrate. They lined up in front of the Llano Hotel to have their picture taken. The Llano, located on a prominent downtown corner, was already a landmark in the area. The group included members from three families that produced well-known cowboys—the Gardners, the Vests, and the McGonagills. (Courtesy of the Permian Historical Society Archives.)

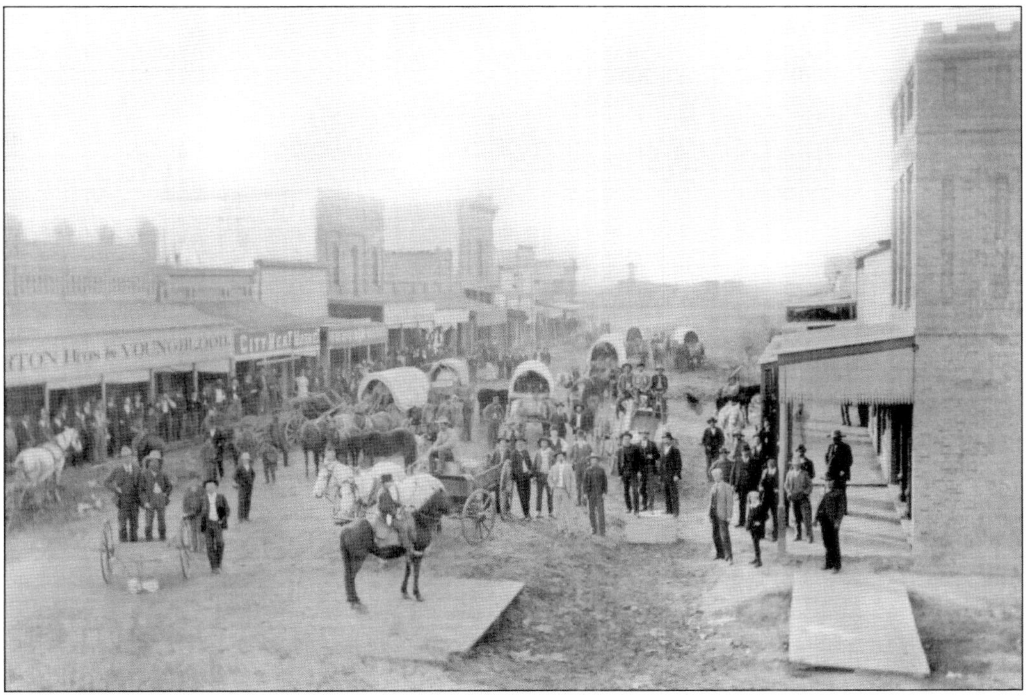

On that same Christmas Day, the busy crowd along Abilene (later renamed Main) Street paused long enough for the photographer on the balcony of the Llano Hotel to capture this scene. (Courtesy of the Nita Stewart Haley Memorial Library, Midland, Texas.)

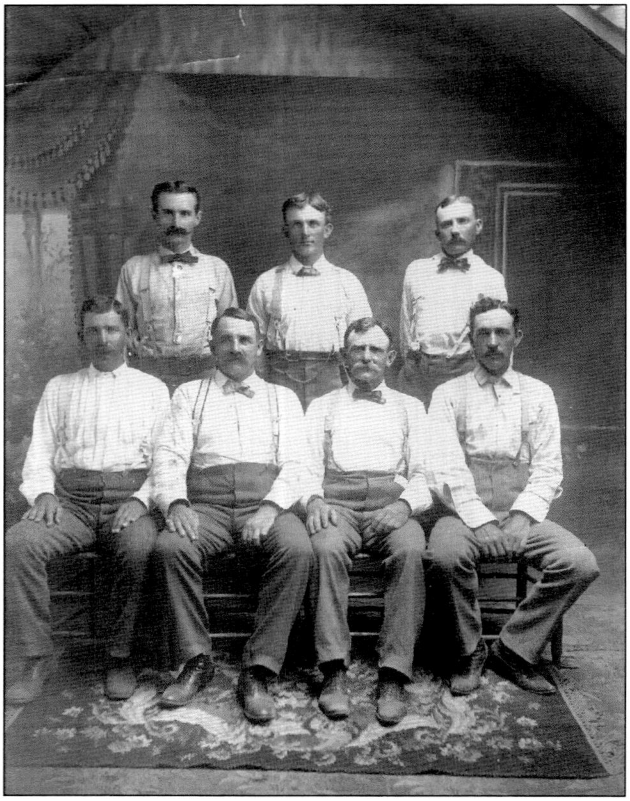

John Scharbauer came to Midland in 1887 and quickly moved into cattle raising near Marienfeld (now Stanton), east of Midland. Scharbauer saw the benefits of scientifically improved livestock. He brought in registered Herefords, once paying $5,000 for a single bull, Sir Jones. His cattle gained national recognition. This 1895 photograph includes, from left to right, (first row) Burl Aycock, John Scharbauer, Chris Scharbauer, and George D. Elliott; (second row) Jim Flanigan, Clarence Scharbauer, and Louie Wall.

The 1900 photograph below provides a look behind the scenes at the Midland Post Office at 108 East Missouri Street. Postal worker Mae Dyer is sorting mail, and Minnie Sholte, another employee, sits by the window. The cowgirl is unidentified.

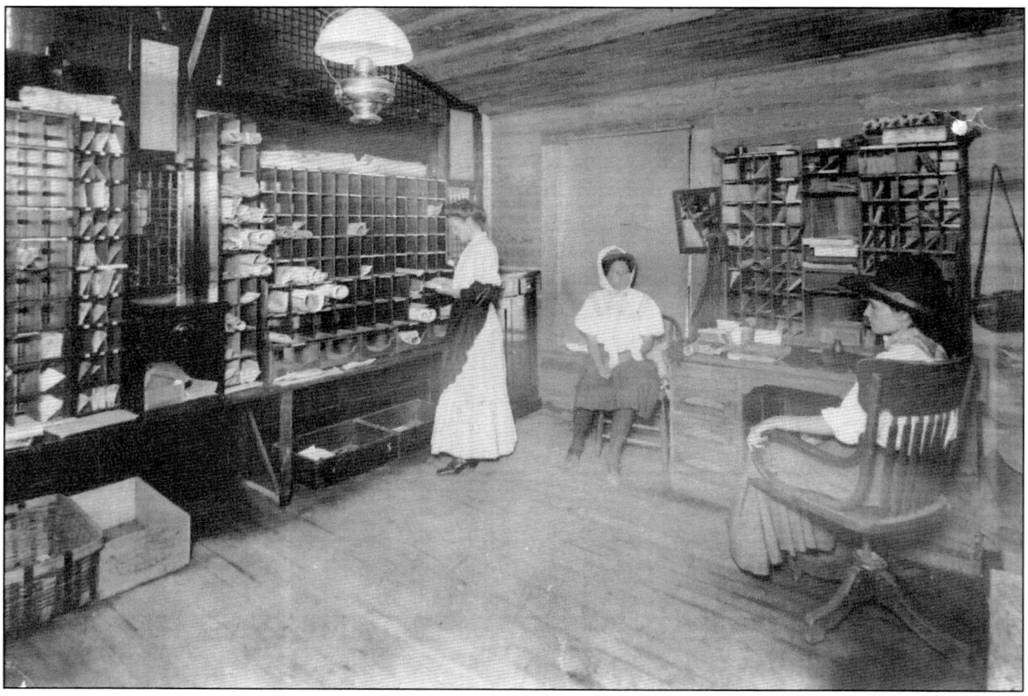

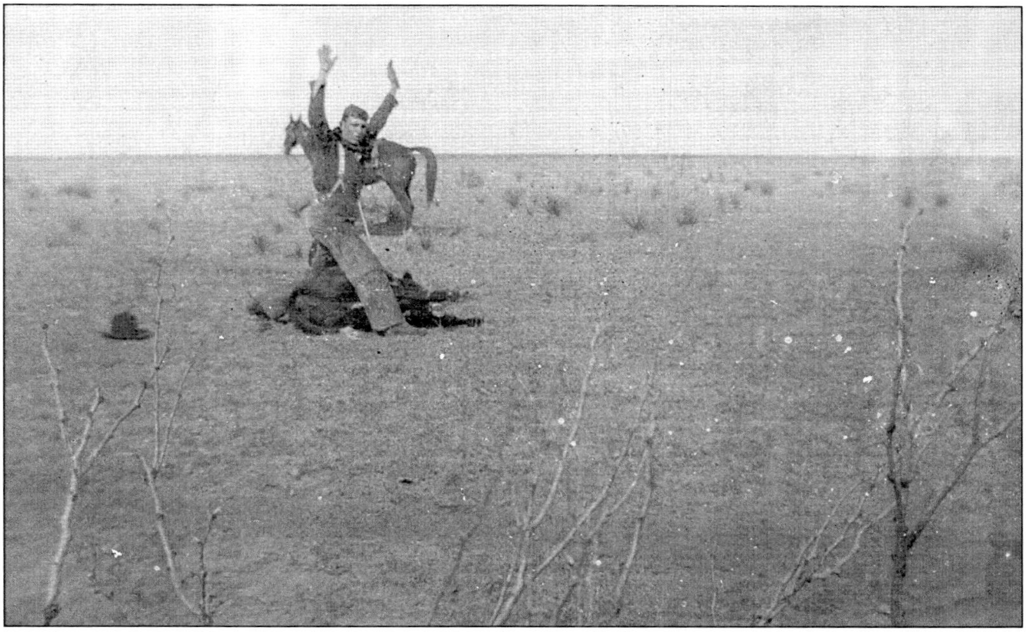

As the number of large cattle ranches grew along with the number of highly skilled cowboys working them, these young men naturally began to match their talents against one another. People enjoyed watching these competitions, and thus, the rodeo was born. Though not the first, Midland's 1898 Cowboy Carnival was among the earliest forerunners of the modern event. Here a cowboy raises his hand to signal the conclusion of his calf roping.

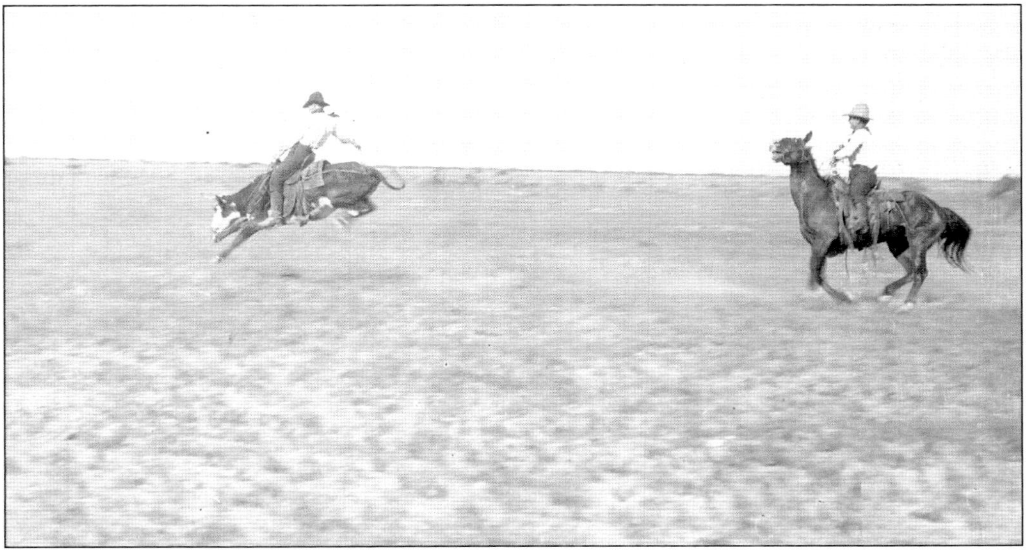

Promoters advertised the 1898 Cowboy Carnival across the state. Some 2,500 people attended—nearly double the city's population. The first day was filled with bronco riding, steer roping, and other events, along with barbecue and beer. That night, a "norther" swept in, dropping 14 inches of snow. The carnival ended as spectators and competitors rushed to catch any train, even a freighter, out of town. Henry Rohlfing, photographer and local confectionery store owner, took this photograph around the time of the carnival. (Courtesy of the Permian Historical Society Archives.)

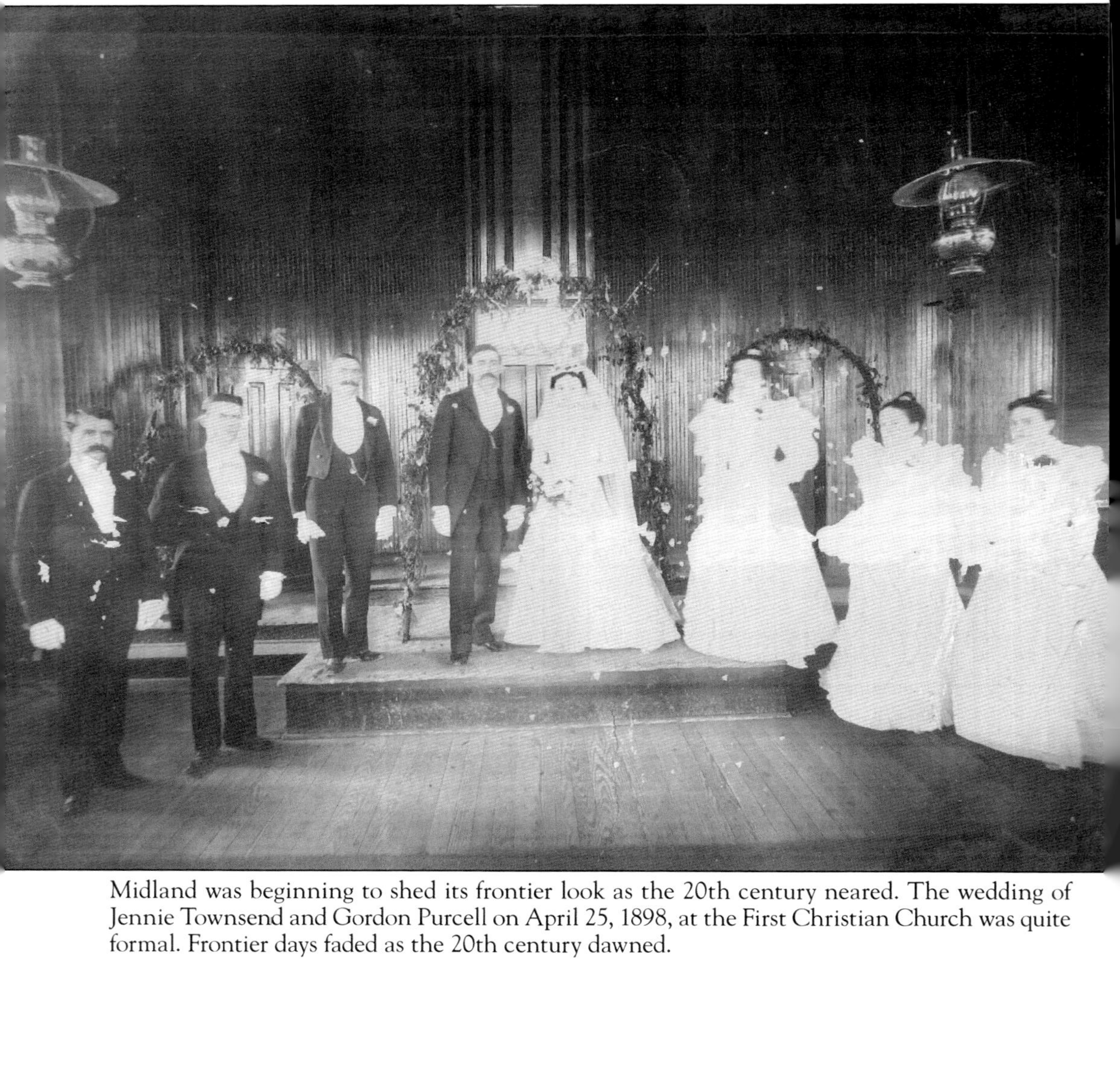

Midland was beginning to shed its frontier look as the 20th century neared. The wedding of Jennie Townsend and Gordon Purcell on April 25, 1898, at the First Christian Church was quite formal. Frontier days faded as the 20th century dawned.

Two

Windmill City in the Land of the High Sky

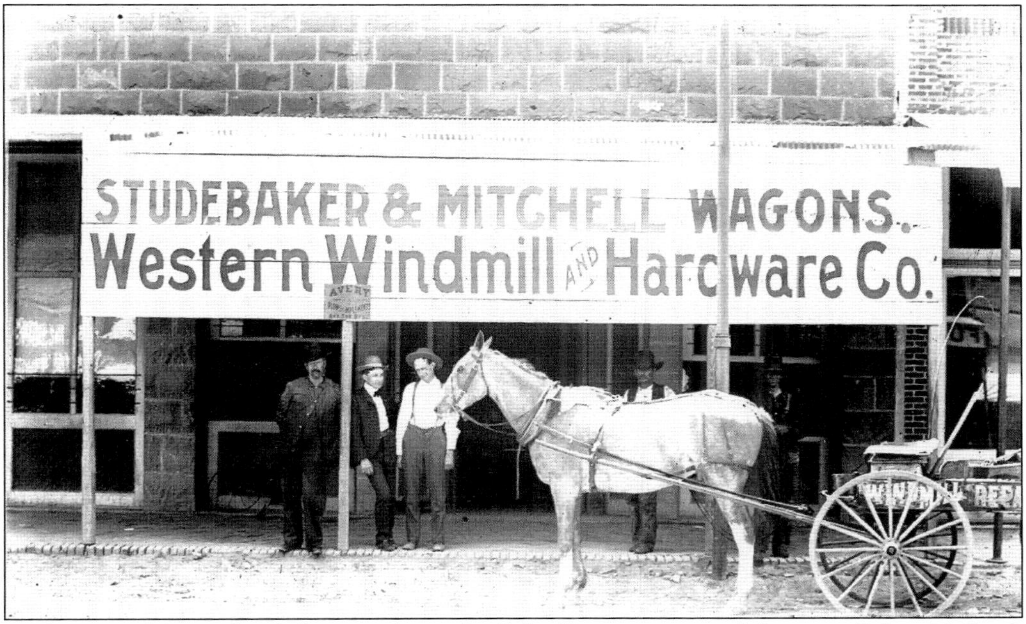

By the time of this undated photograph, windmills had become a critical element of life in Midland, but it had not happened overnight. The scarcity of water on the Llano challenged all forms of enterprise, from communities to cattle ranches. Nelson Morris tried wooden water tanks. The sun and wind warped them. When Herman Garrett erected his first windmill, a Star model from California like the others shipped in, it was unsuited to the arid climate and tough winds.

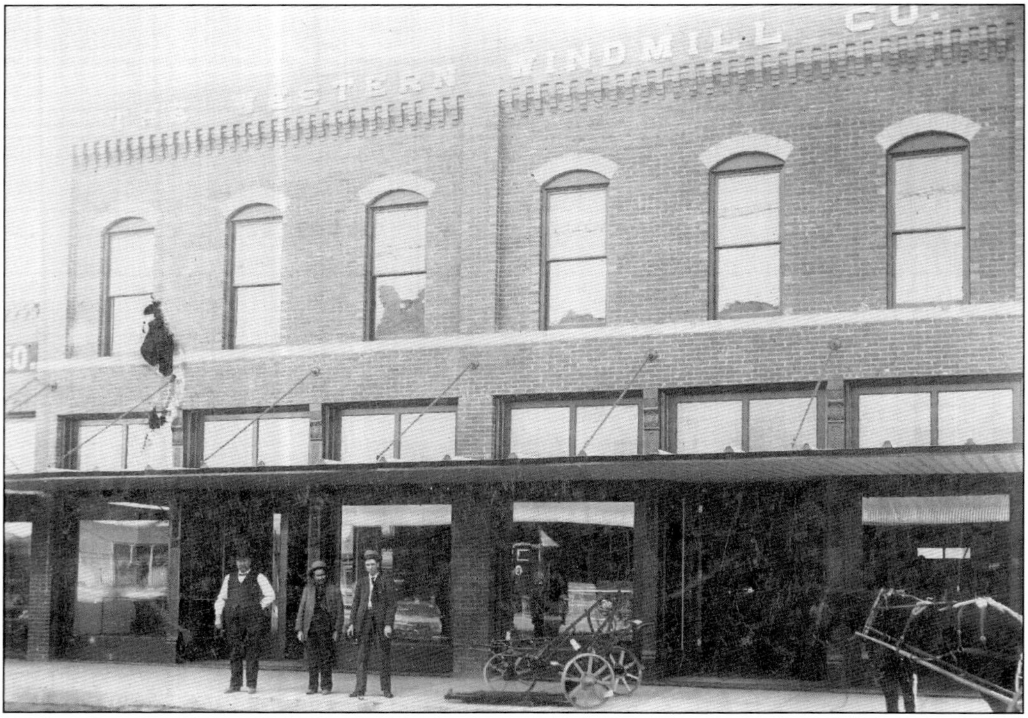

John Tolbert (left) clearly had a more prosperous Western Windmill Company by the time of this photograph (before 1909). Bill Oden, ranch hand for Francis Divers on the Pecos River, began to tinker with the mills. Many cowboys laughed at him. Henry Cummins did not. Between them, they produced windmills adapted to the Texas plains.

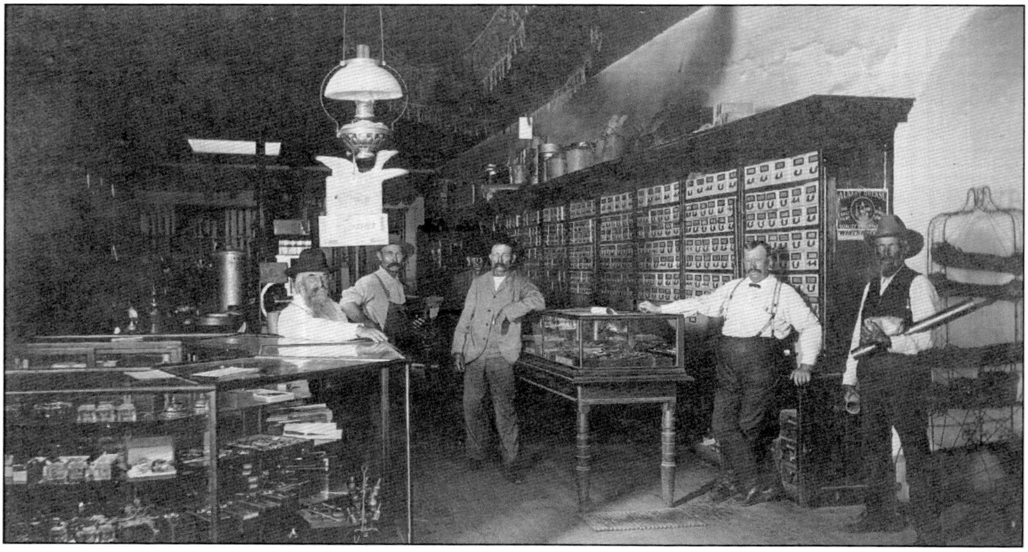

E. J. Mumford (left) and John Tolbert (second from right) visit with three windmill men inside the Western Windmill Company. With workable windmills available, the market exploded. Townspeople put them in their yards rather than hauling water from the town pumps. Every business added one. Midland became known as the "Windmill City."

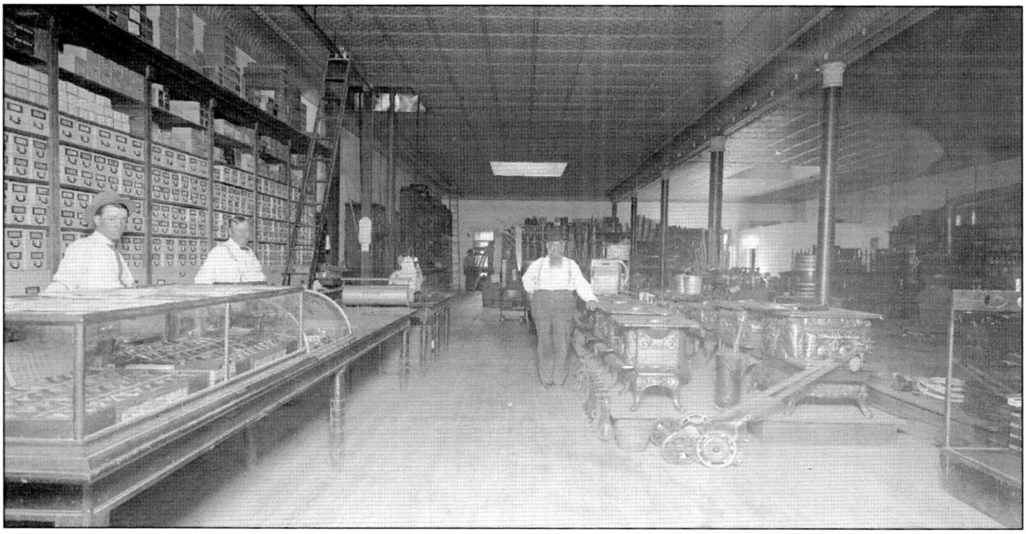

The increasing Progressive Era prosperity of Midland spurred the growth of businesses. Brick buildings began to replace wooden storefronts. Clerks Allen and John Tolbert (left) stand behind the counter. E. J. Mumford possessively rests a hand on his display of stoves.

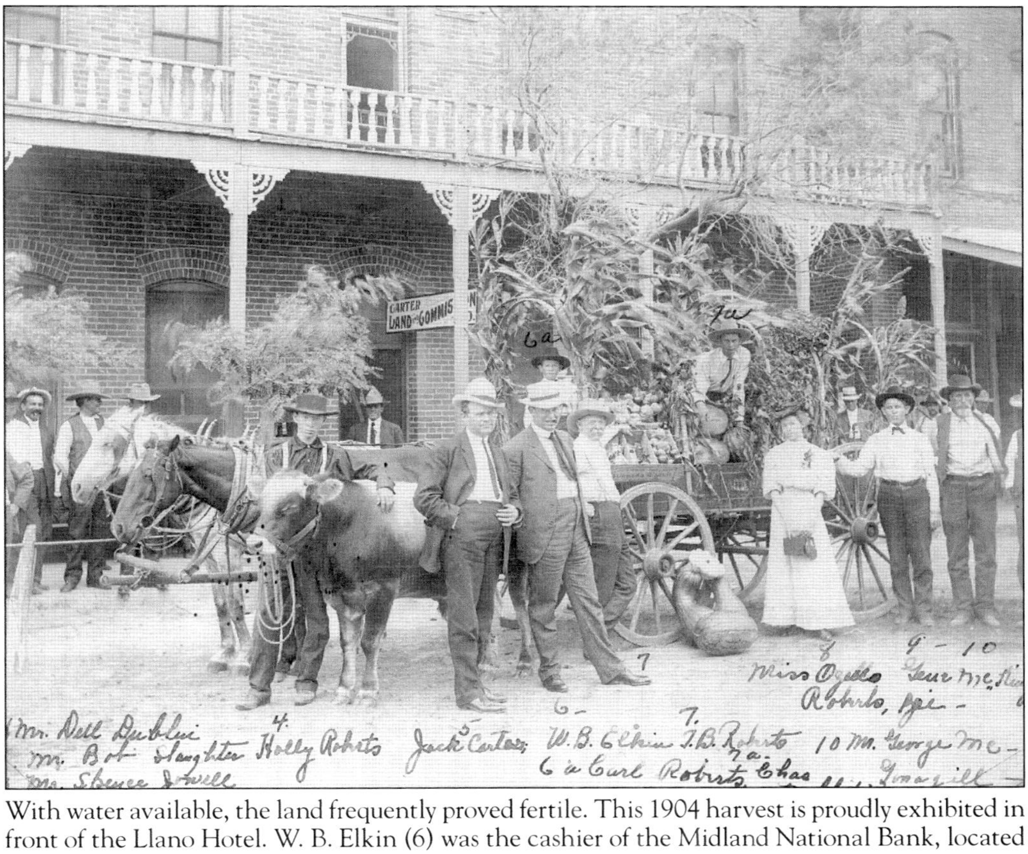

With water available, the land frequently proved fertile. This 1904 harvest is proudly exhibited in front of the Llano Hotel. W. B. Elkin (6) was the cashier of the Midland National Bank, located behind them in the Llano Hotel building.

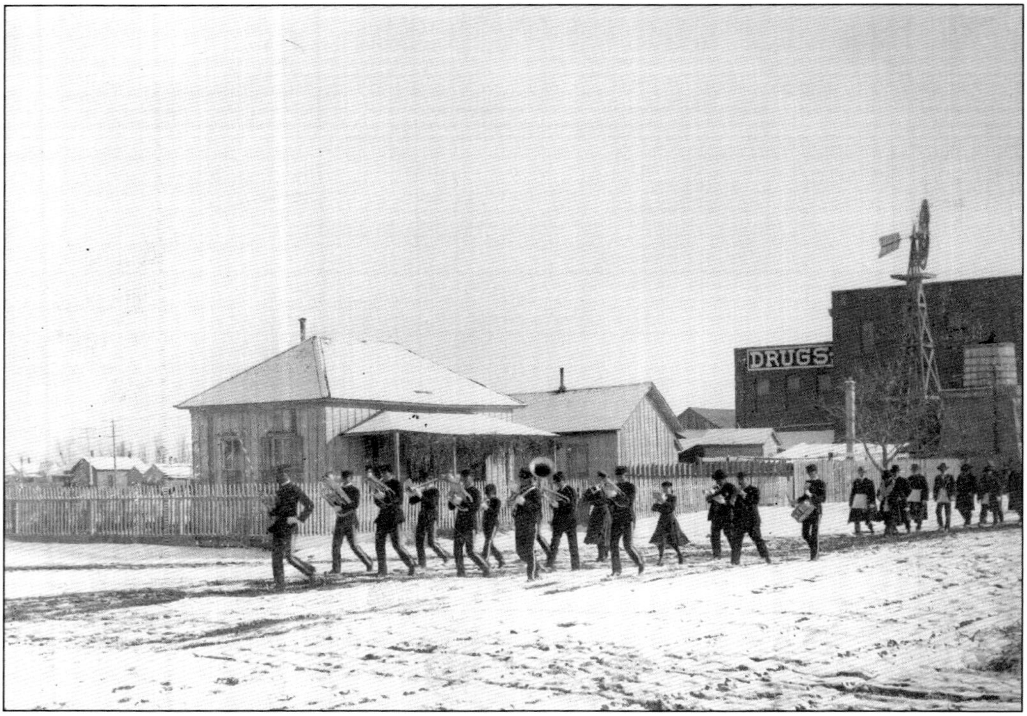

In the 1904 Masonic Parade, the band from neighboring Odessa, 20 miles west, came over to march. The Odessa band was the first organized in West Texas. Carl Beck was director, and Will Martin was president. The parade is headed west on Iowa (Wall) Street. Behind them are the A. W. Ellis Drug Store and the Llano Hotel and a windmill.

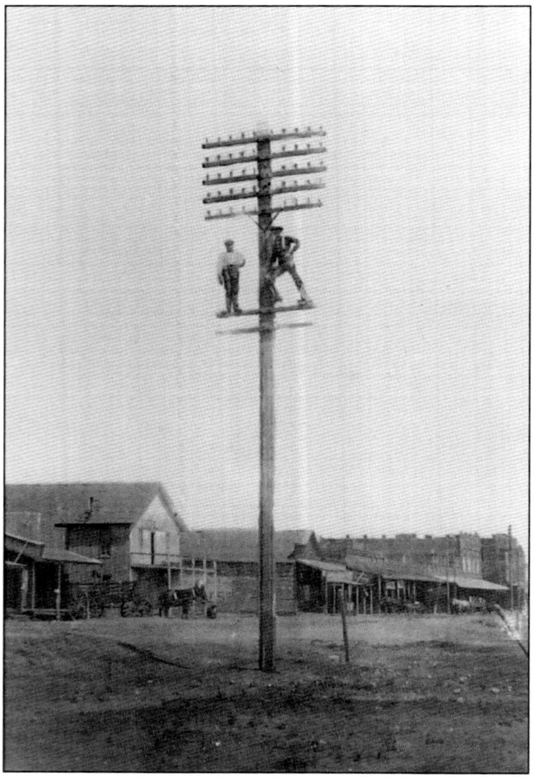

A couple of workers pose nonchalantly atop a telegraph pole in 1902. Modern communications helped link the growing community with the East. The Llano Hotel, now a brick structure, is on the far right. Next to it is the First National Bank Building.

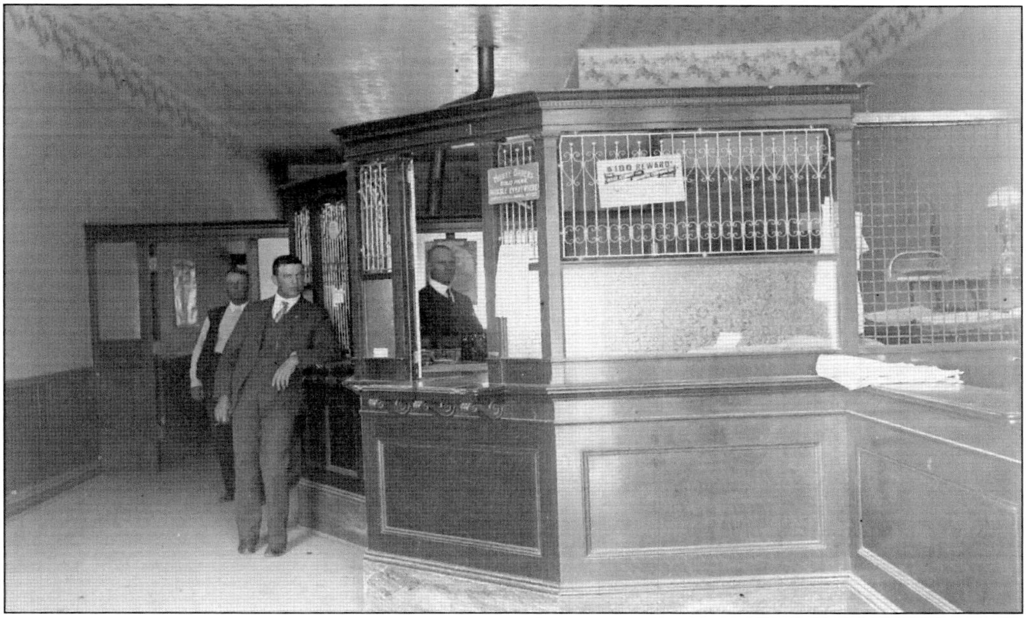

The Midland National was a transplant from Odessa. In 1903, Odessa National moved to Midland and changed its name. This photograph from around that time shows the bank lobby in the Llano Hotel. It was Midland's second major bank. Rancher John Scharbauer and Wilson and Giles Connell organized a private bank in 1888 that became the First National Bank of Midland in 1890. First National occupied the corner across the street from the Llano Hotel.

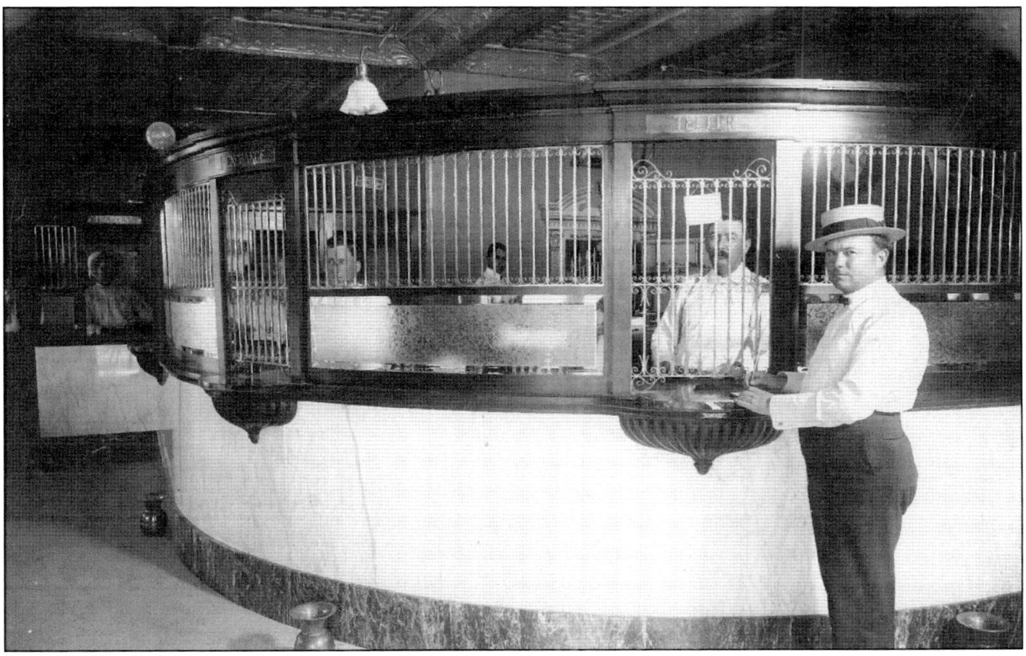

The 1909 Midland National Bank lobby exhibited a fancier look than at the bank's beginning. On the right are Dave Brunson, president (behind window), and Frank Elkin, vice president (straw hat). The two banks anchored Midland's position as the financial center of the region.

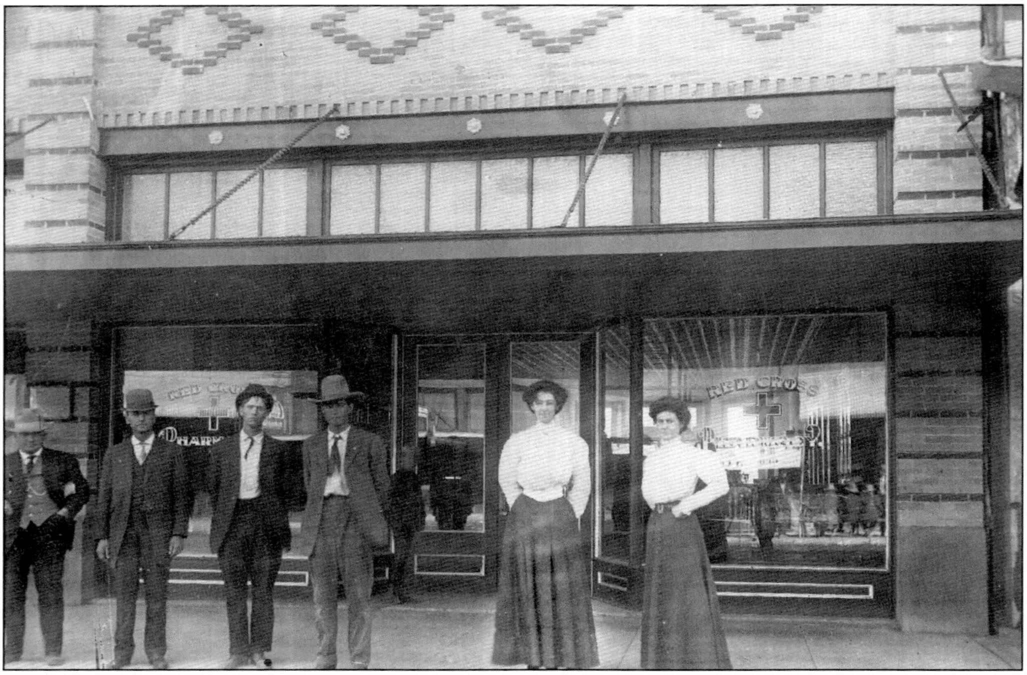

Maggie McCormick (one of the two women) poses along with Bert Ramsey, Speck Voliva, and others in front of the Red Cross Pharmacy on south Abilene Street. The Gibson Girl shirtwaists and the brick building place the photograph sometime in the opening decade of the 20th century.

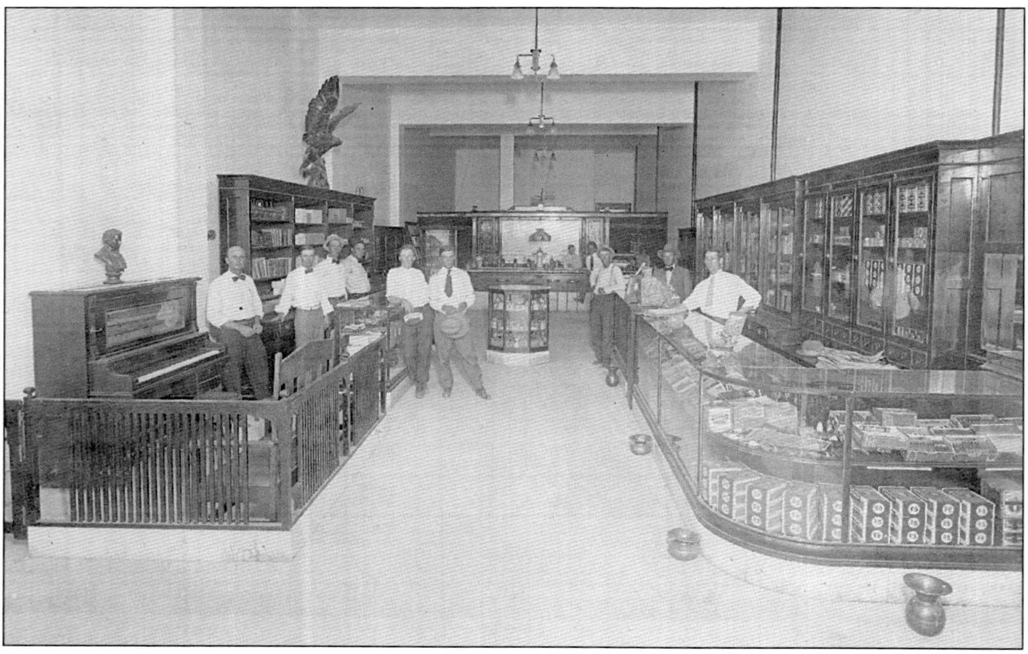

By 1905, Midland had at least five doctors. The interior of the Red Cross Pharmacy appears to have plenty of clerks and cases full of merchandise. It also had plenty of spittoons and, a bit incongruously, a piano.

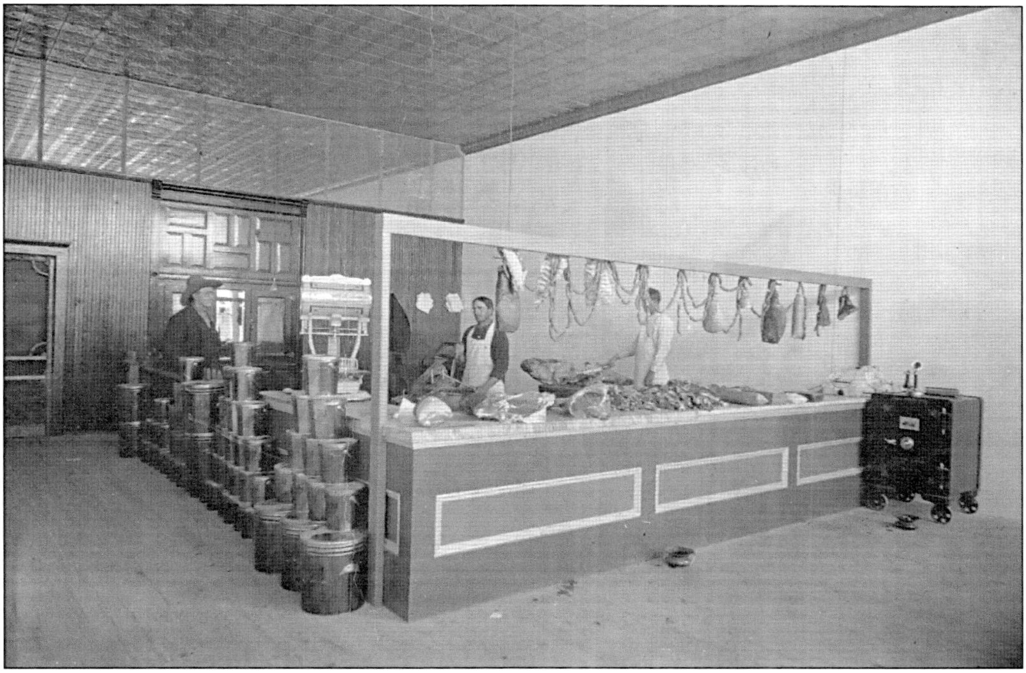

The City Meat Market on Main Street acquired its meat from area ranches such as the C. Behind the counter is butcher Ben Ethridge (left) and his son, Buster. The customer is not identified. At one time, Frank McCormick also owned the market.

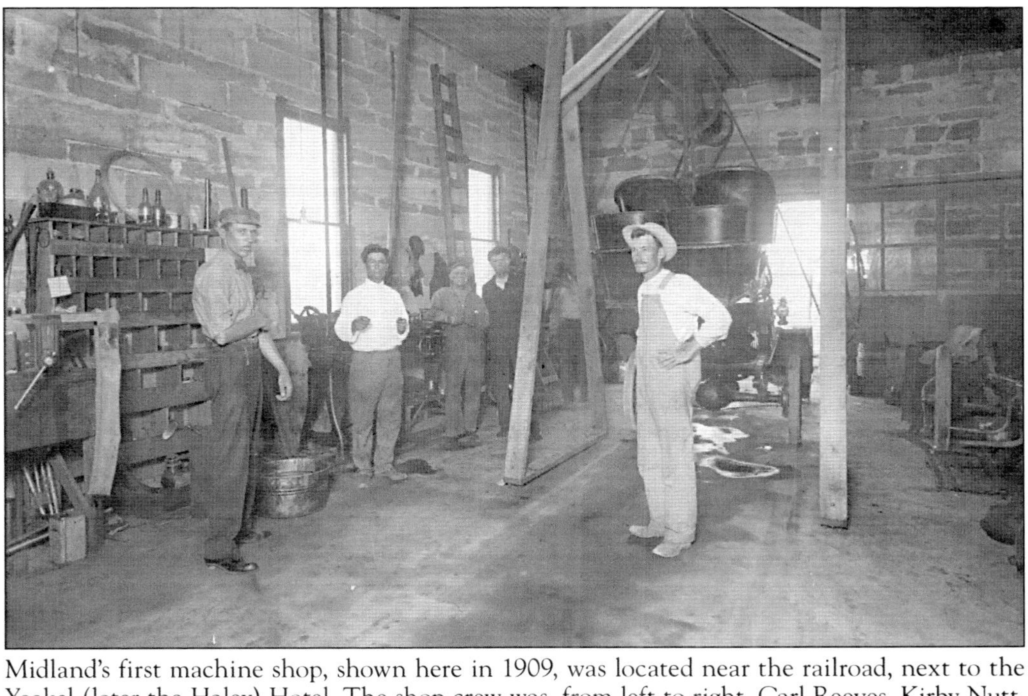

Midland's first machine shop, shown here in 1909, was located near the railroad, next to the Yeakel (later the Haley) Hotel. The shop crew was, from left to right, Carl Reeves, Kirby Nutt, John G. Peebles, Will Roller, unidentified, and Frank Hermann.

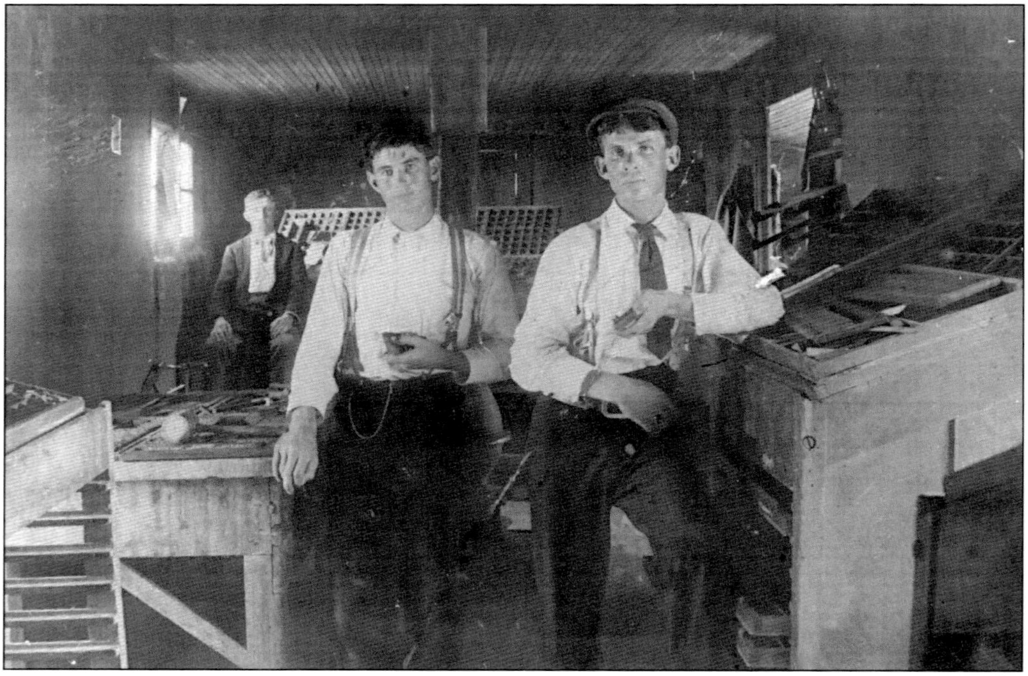

A number of weekly newspapers came and went like a West Texas rain, including the *Staked Plains*, Midland's first newspaper published by J. C. Rathbun around 1886. The *Midland Gazette* began in 1890. In this 1895 photograph, By Johnson and Bert Rawlins, with ink-smeared faces, pause in their work on a Washington handpress. Behind them is John Scharbauer's son, Clarence. The *Midland Livestock Reporter*, begun in the early 1890s, survived several name changes to become the current *Midland Reporter-Telegram*.

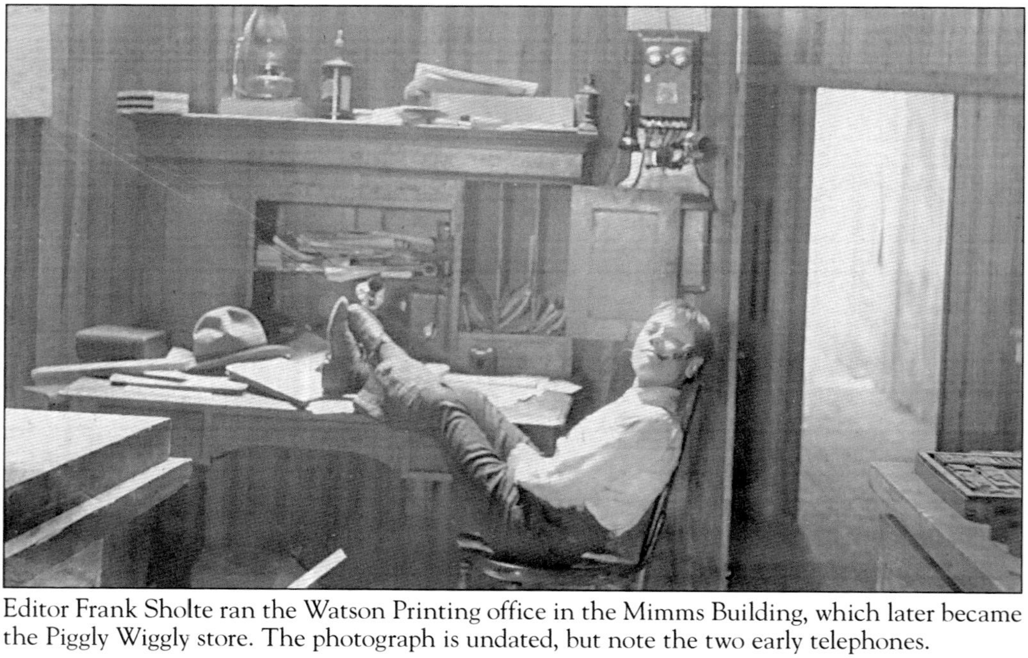

Editor Frank Sholte ran the Watson Printing office in the Mimms Building, which later became the Piggly Wiggly store. The photograph is undated, but note the two early telephones.

Along with new businesses, fine homes with more comfort and luxury also arose. Herman Garrett built a new residence on Big Spring Street in 1903. Zachariah Taylor Brown, another early sheep man, erected this house on North Weatherford Street in 1900. Successful in ranching and farming, Brown also went into the mercantile business with Frank Crowley and J. H. Barron. Complete with fireplaces, hardwood floors, and hued-glass windows, the house cost $2,800.

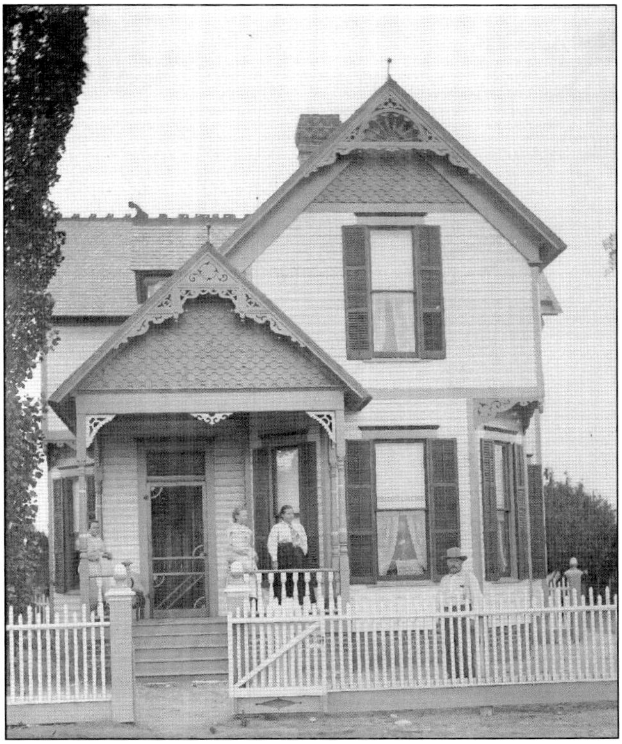

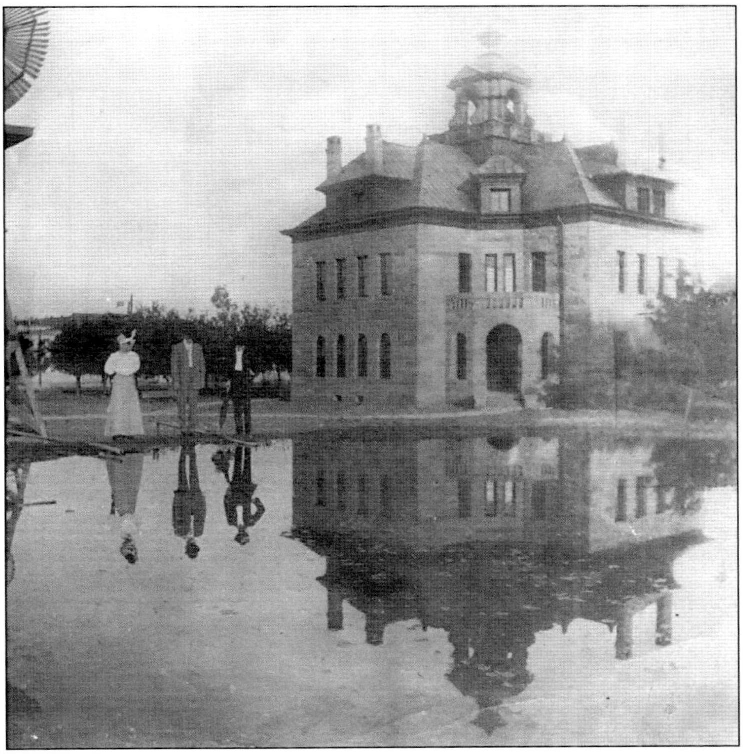

In 1905, Midland County built a new courthouse. The facility, constructed of Pecos Red Sandstone, stood three stories high. It was built at a cost of $30,000. For a time, a pond stood on the courthouse grounds. The tradition was to toss the bridegroom into the pond on his wedding day.

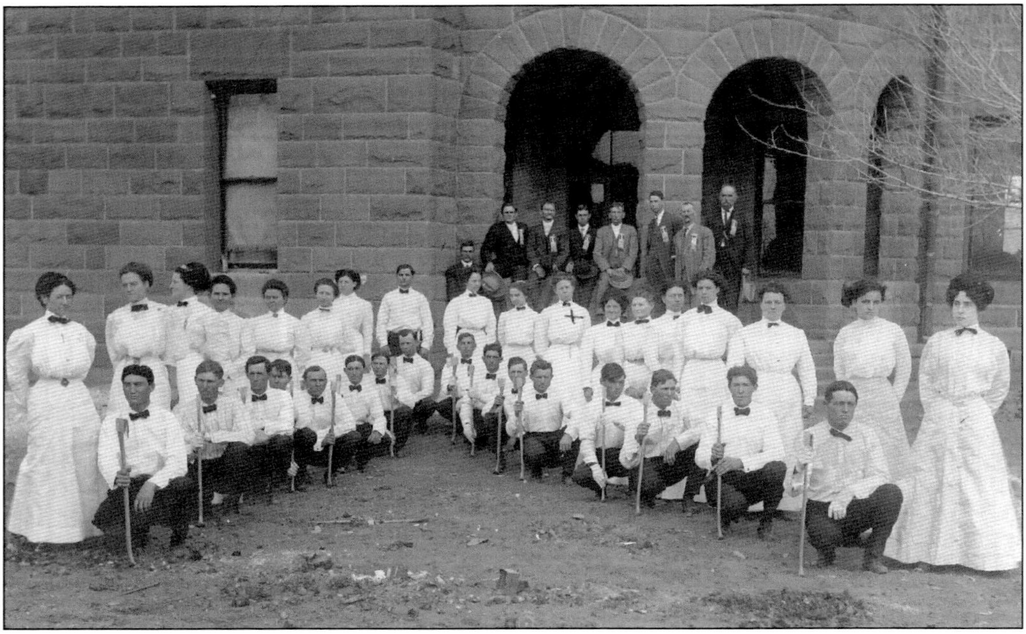

The courthouse became a popular spot for photographs, the sandstone columns and tier of steps providing a great backdrop for all types of groups. Here the Woodmen of the World and their wives pose at the courthouse. Founded in Nebraska in 1890, the Woodmen provided a fraternal organization that operated a private insurance company for its members. Before 1930, the Woodmen were also known for erecting distinctive tombstones shaped as tree stumps.

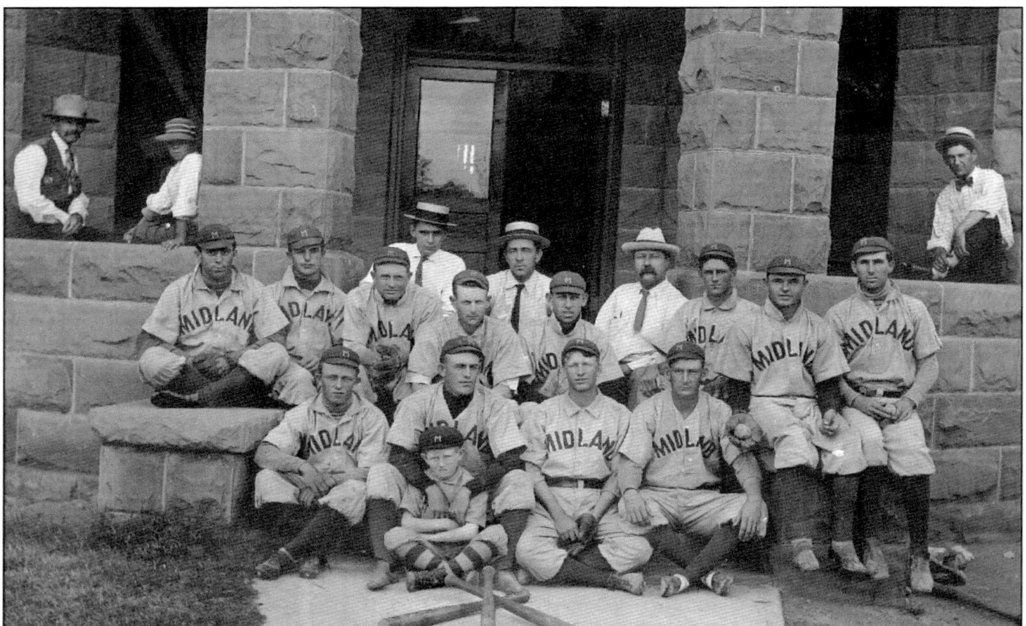

The Midland baseball team had their courthouse photograph taken on July 16, 1908. They played all comers and were reputed to be a good team.

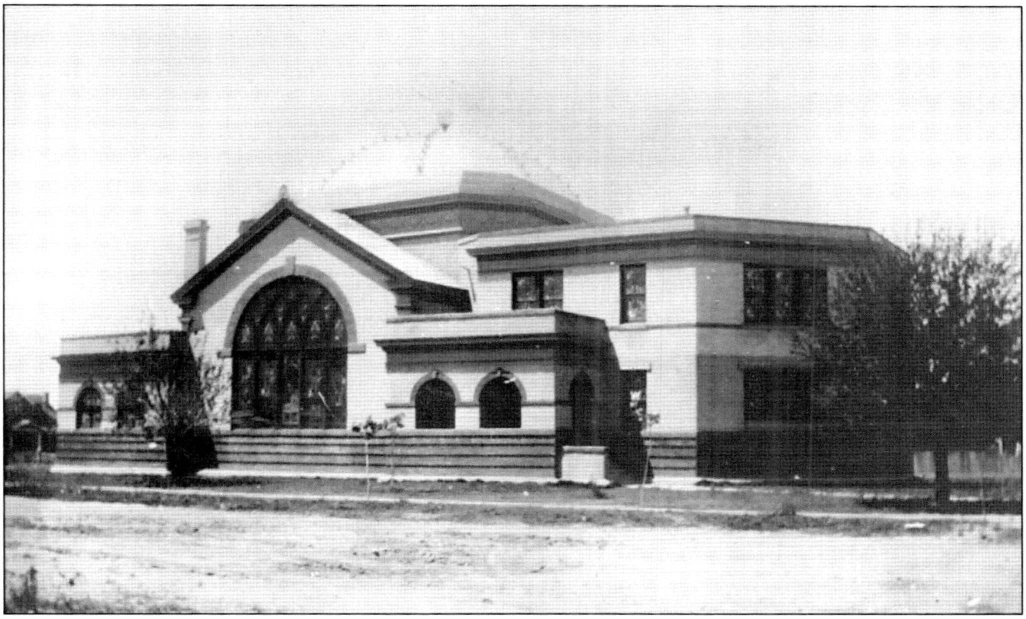

Religious institutions grew along with the young city. The Baptists organized in January 1886 with a congregation of 26. In 1892, they erected a prominent brick building on North Main and Illinois Streets under the leadership of their second pastor, Rev. Leander Millican, or "Brother Lallie." According to the First Baptist Web site, Brother Lallie was a cowboy preacher who lived and worked with ranchers and cowboys as part of his ministry. "He preached without a salary and carried a Bible in one saddle bag and a six-shooter in the other."

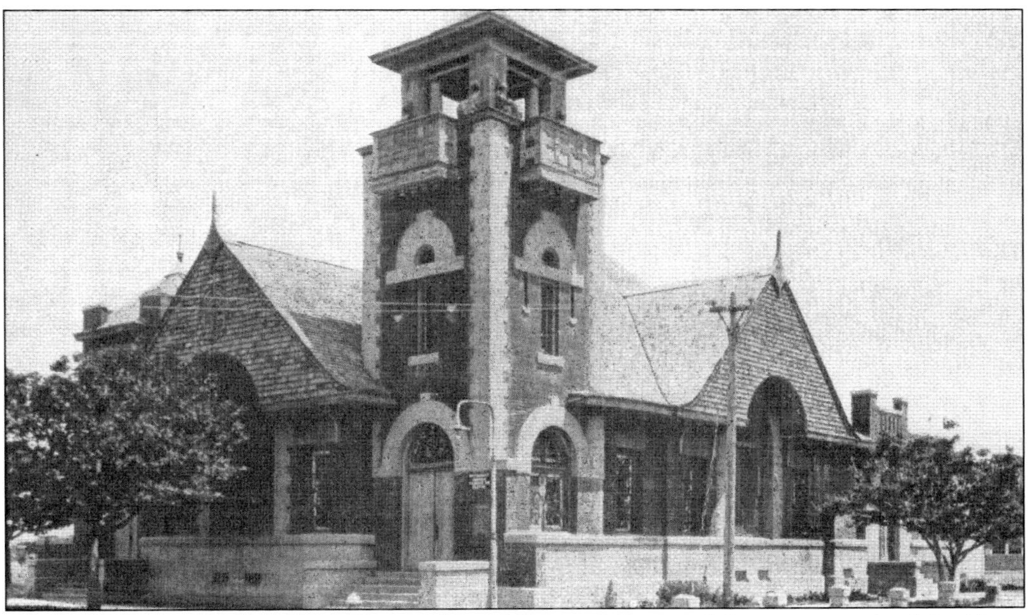

The Methodists moved north to Main and Baird Streets and erected their own new brick building, setting the cornerstone on Thanksgiving Day, November 28, 1907.

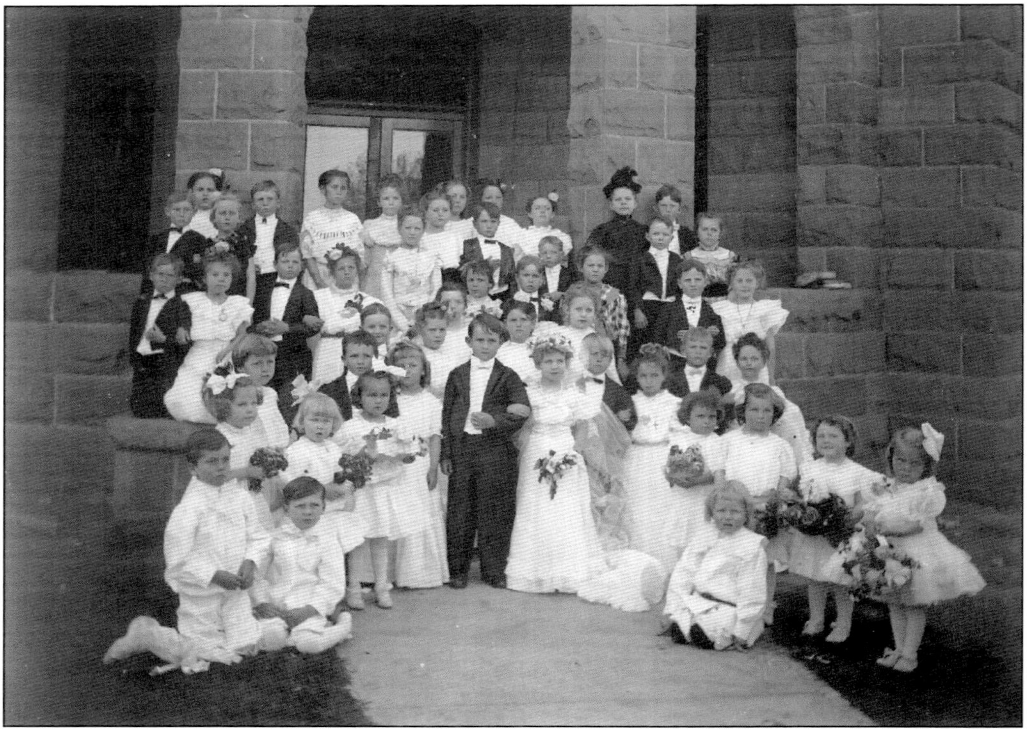

The Methodists also favored the courthouse photograph. In 1908, this entourage from a Tom Thumb wedding trooped over the two blocks for a picture. Tom Thumb weddings served as church fund-raisers; children dressed as the famed midget performer Gen. Tom Thumb, his bride, and the wedding party. The party seen here included Leona McCormick, daughter of Frank and Mollie McCormick. Some participants appear less enthusiastic than others.

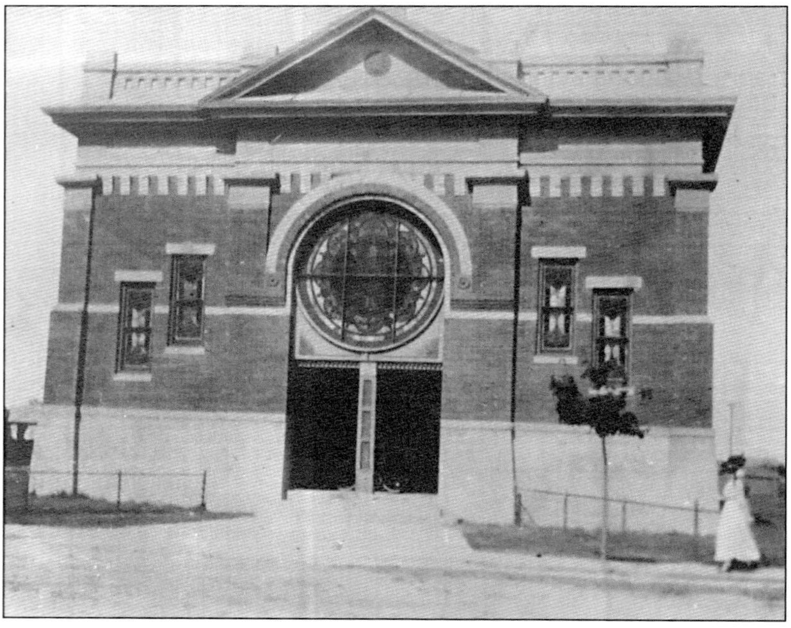

The First Christian Church was built in 1908 in the 300 block of North Loraine Street. Services were held in the courthouse during construction of the redbrick building. The building served the congregation for 42 years.

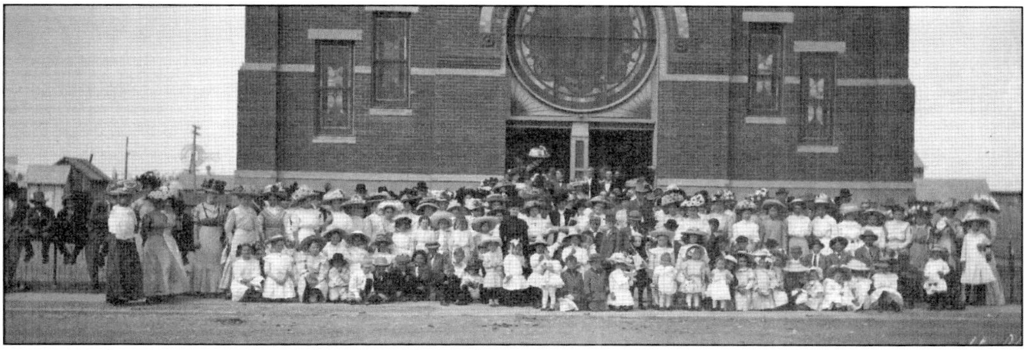

In 1910, the congregation stood proudly in front of the new church building. Daisies appear to have been the style for hats in Midland that year.

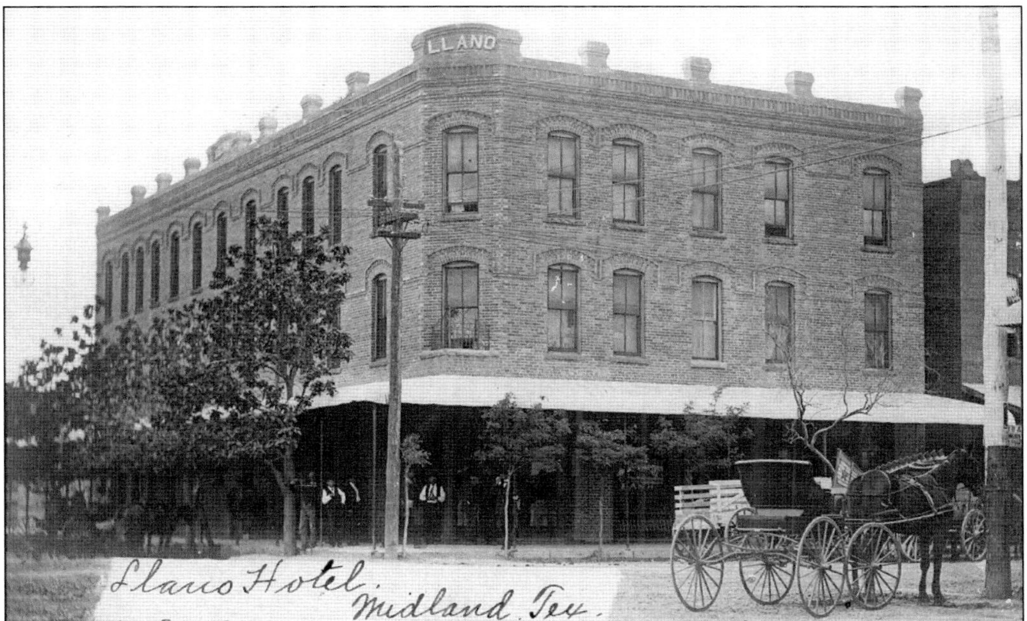

A Midland landmark underwent remodeling in 1907. Elza White, proprietor of the Llano Hotel, rebuilt it at a cost of $15,000. George Gray acquired the Llano in December 1908. This is a 1908 postcard from the City Drug Store. The Midland National Bank can be seen on the first floor.

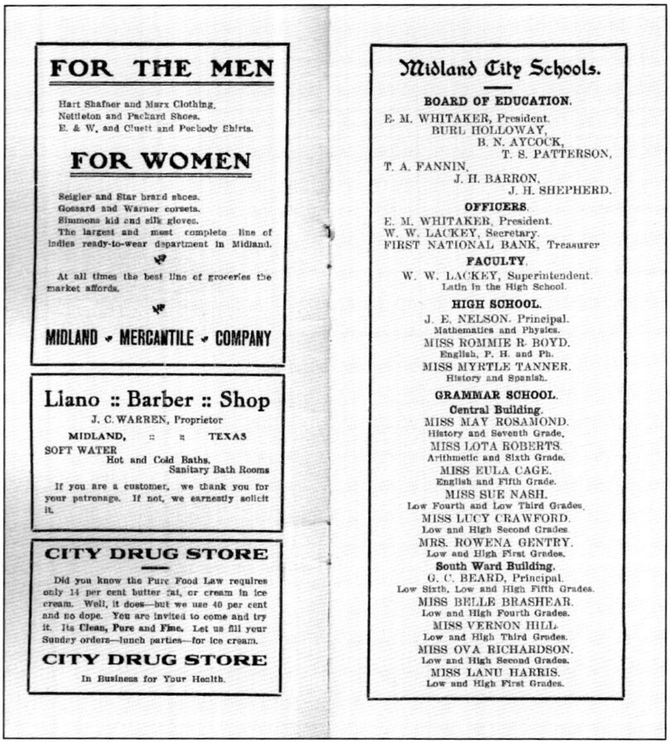

FOR THE MEN

Hart Shafner and Marx Clothing.
Nettleton and Packard Shoes.
E. & W. and Cluett and Peabody Shirts.

FOR WOMEN

Seigler and Star brand shoes.
Gossard and Warner corsets.
Simmons kid and silk gloves.
The largest and most complete line of ladies ready-to-wear department in Midland.

At all times the best line of groceries the market affords.

MIDLAND • MERCANTILE • COMPANY

Llano :: Barber :: Shop

J. C. WARREN, Proprietor

MIDLAND, :: :: TEXAS

SOFT WATER
Hot and Cold Baths.
Sanitary Bath Rooms

If you are a customer, we thank you for your patronage. If not, we earnestly solicit it.

CITY DRUG STORE

Did you know the Pure Food Law requires only 14 per cent butter fat, or cream in ice cream. Well, it does—but we use 40 per cent and no dope. You are invited to come and try it. Its Clean, Pure and Fine. Let us fill your Sunday orders—lunch parties—for ice cream.

CITY DRUG STORE

In Business for Your Health.

Midland City Schools.

BOARD OF EDUCATION.
E. M. WHITAKER, President.
BURL HOLLOWAY,
B. N. AYCOCK,
T. S. PATTERSON,
T. A. FANNIN,
J. H. BARRON,
J. H. SHEPHERD.

OFFICERS.
E. M. WHITAKER, President.
W. W. LACKEY, Secretary.
FIRST NATIONAL BANK, Treasurer

FACULTY.
W. W. LACKEY, Superintendent.
Latin in the High School.

HIGH SCHOOL.
J. E. NELSON, Principal.
Mathematics and Physics.
MISS ROMMIE R. BOYD.
English, P. H. and Ph.
MISS MYRTLE TANNER.
History and Spanish.

GRAMMAR SCHOOL.
Central Building.
MISS MAY ROSAMOND.
History and Seventh Grade.
MISS LOTA ROBERTS.
Arithmetic and Sixth Grade.
MISS EULA CAGE.
English and Fifth Grade.
MISS SUE NASH.
Low Fourth and Low Third Grades.
MISS LUCY CRAWFORD.
Low and High Second Grades.
MRS. ROWENA GENTRY.
Low and High First Grades.
South Ward Building.
G. C. BEARD, Principal.
Low Sixth, Low and High Fifth Grades.
MISS BELLE BRASHEAR.
Low and High Fourth Grades.
MISS VERNON HILL.
Low and High Third Grades.
MISS OVA RICHARDSON.
Low and High Second Grades.
MISS LANU HARRIS.
Low and High First Grades.

The Midland Independent School District organized in 1907. The first superintendent was W. W. Lackey. By the fall of 1911, when faculty received this booklet outlining a teachers' institute involving six days throughout the school year, the district had three campuses and over 500 students.

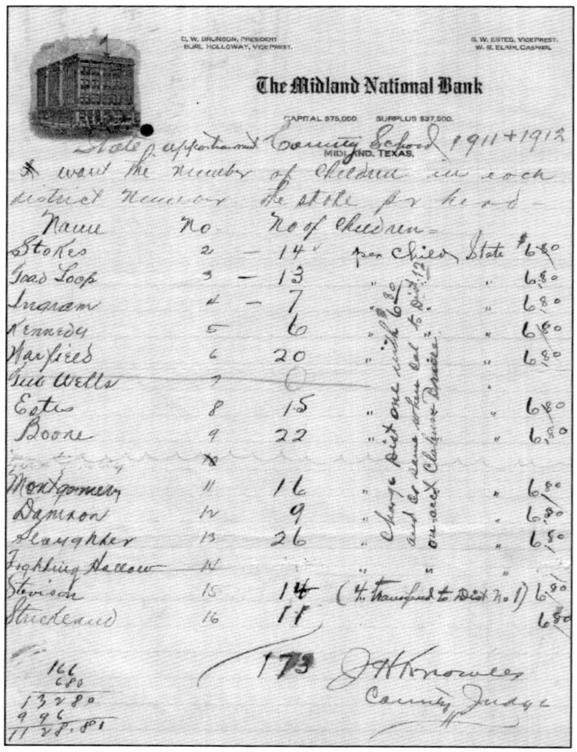

C. W. BRUNSON, PRESIDENT
BURL HOLLOWAY, VICE PREST.
G. W. ESTES, VICE PREST.
W. S. ELKIN, CASHIER

The Midland National Bank

CAPITAL $75,000 SURPLUS $37,500

MIDLAND, TEXAS.

State apportionment County School 1911+1912
I want the number of children in each district number the state per head

Name	No	No of children		
Stokes	2	14	per child State	$6.80
Toad Loop	3	13	"	6.80
Ingram	4	7	"	6.80
Kennedy	5	6	"	6.80
Mayfield	6	20	"	6.80
~~Sue Wells~~	7	0		
Estes	8	15	"	6.80
Boone	9	22	"	6.80
Montgomery	11	16	"	6.80
Damron	12	9	"	6.80
Slaughter	13	26	"	6.80
Fighting Hollow	14			
Stevisch	15	14 (4 transferred to Dist no 1)		6.80
Strickland	16	11		6.80

Charge dist one with 6.80 and same when out to dist 12 on acct Clabaugh Draw

173

J H Knowles
County Judge

166
680
13280
996
1128.80

Many children still lived outside Midland in small rural communities throughout the county. The State of Texas apportioned funds to help counties employ teachers for these rural schools. The Midland National Bank managed these accounts. In 1911, the State of Texas apportioned $6.80 "per head" for 173 children.

Girtha Hix, on this check, attested that she taught at the Stokes School in District Two in December 1909, for which she received a salary of $50. The Stokes School was located east of Midland. Like the other rural schools, it eventually closed (in 1929).

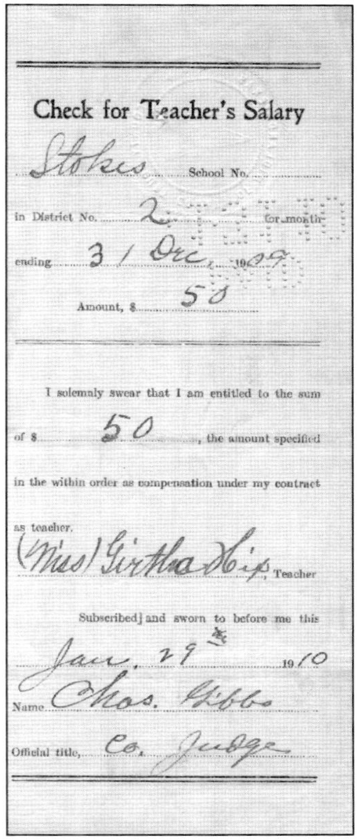

Check for Teacher's Salary

Stokes School No. ....

in District No. 2 for month

ending 3 / Dec, 1909

Amount, $ 50

I solemnly swear that I am entitled to the sum of $ 50, the amount specified in the within order as compensation under my contract as teacher.

(Miss) Girtha Hix, Teacher

Subscribed and sworn to before me this Jan. 29th 1910

Name Chas. Gibbs

Official title, Co. Judge

The city schools might be larger and the buildings now made of brick, but students remained students. They continued to express the same enthusiasm—or lack thereof—as those before them. The caption on this photograph reads only, "Jack's First Grade Class Midland Southside 1912." This time the girls are behind, the boys sit in front, and the class clown is in the middle.

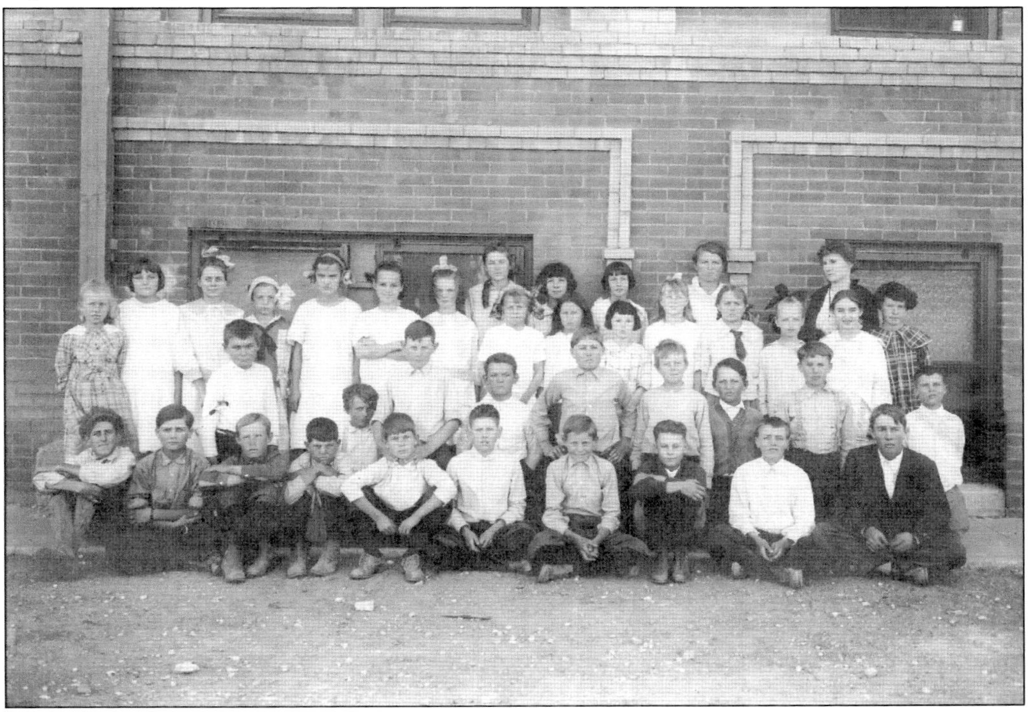

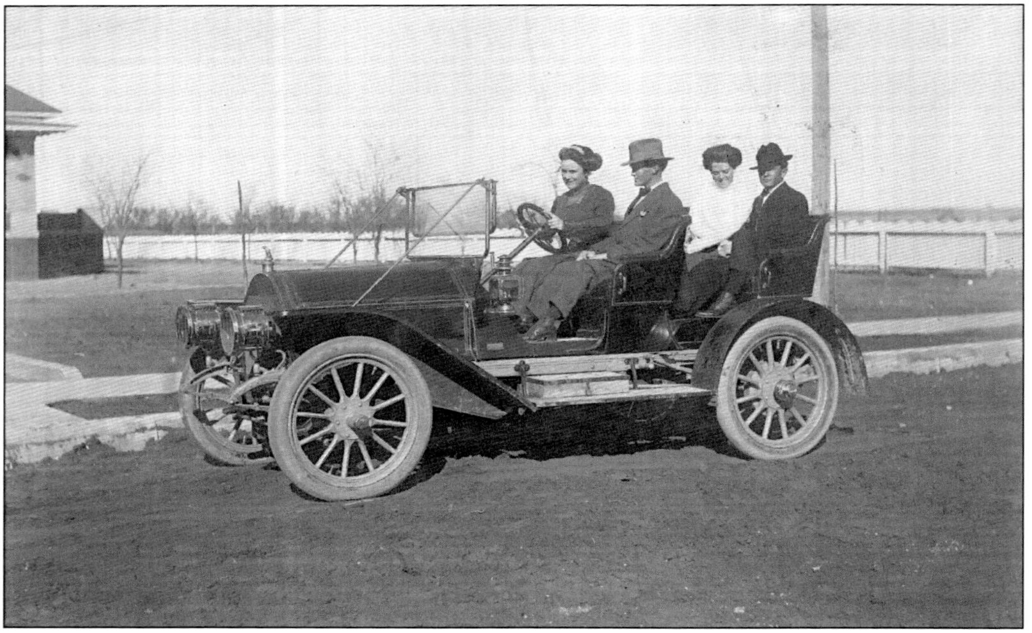

The early 1900s were a time of many transitions. Horses and buggies remained common, but the automobile had come to Midland. Mamie Cowden Rowe takes Elliot Cowden, Helen Ulmer, and Ellis Cowden for a ride. The steering wheel is on the right.

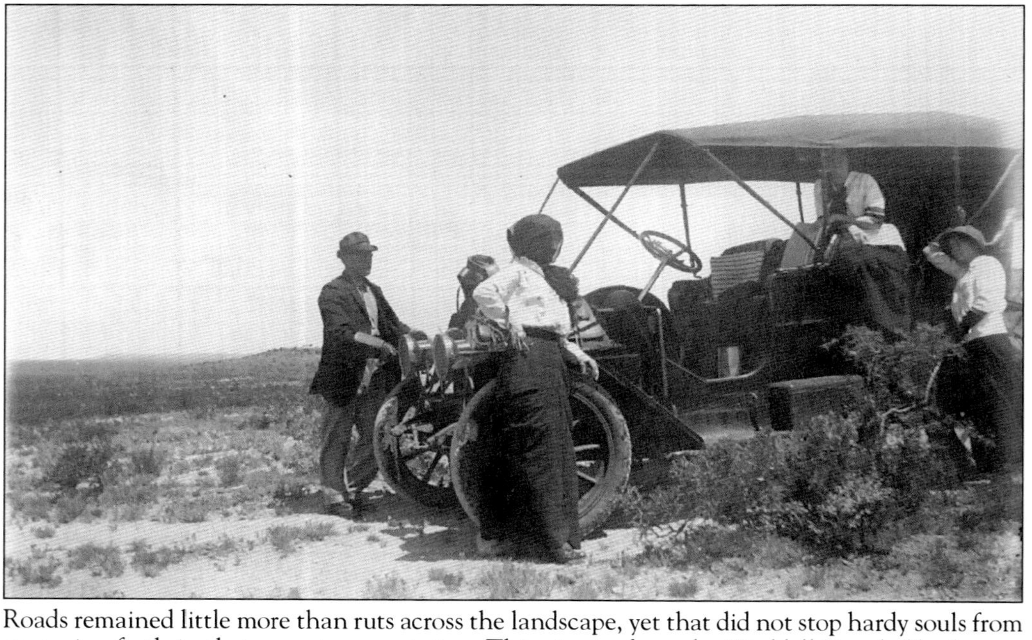

Roads remained little more than ruts across the landscape, yet that did not stop hardy souls from venturing forth in their new transportation. This picture from the Waddell Ranch files has no caption, but it appears the group has driven to a point on the "caprock" at the edge of the Llano Estacado. The view remains much the same today and calls to mind the words of Ten Bears, "I was born upon the prairie, where the wind blew free, and there was nothing to break the light of the sun."

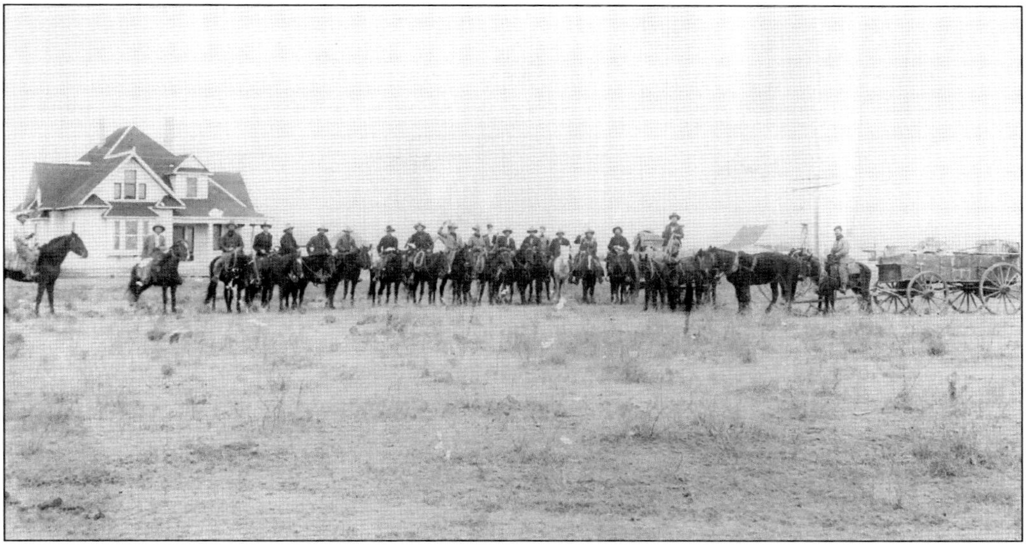

On the plains, the horse remained supreme. In March 1910, Elliott Cowden ran away to ride up the trail with 3,300 JAL steers in two herds—11 cowboys and a 100-horse remuda with each one—to be delivered to Mount Blanco on the northern plains. Cowden related, "We were caught in one of the worst storms I ever saw. The steers died like flies, 150 in one bad night. Even some saddle horses froze to death." The group made it to Mount Blanco, as shown here. Cowden was on the trail 31 days and came home with $31.

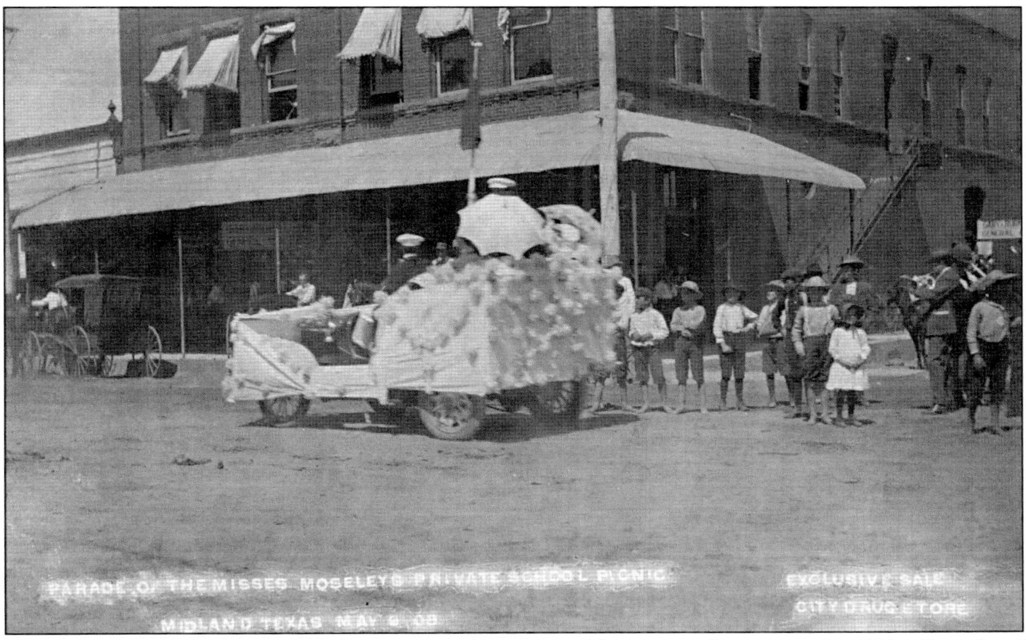

Horses, buggies, and automobiles coexisted comfortably, especially at parades. The Parade of the Misses took place on May 6, 1908. A cloth-covered auto, with misses under the umbrellas, passes the Gary and Burris General Merchandise Store. A horse and buggy is on the right. The caption reads, "The band was there, the auto looks like left-hand drive." Miller Studios took this photograph. The City Drug Store sold the postcards made from this image.

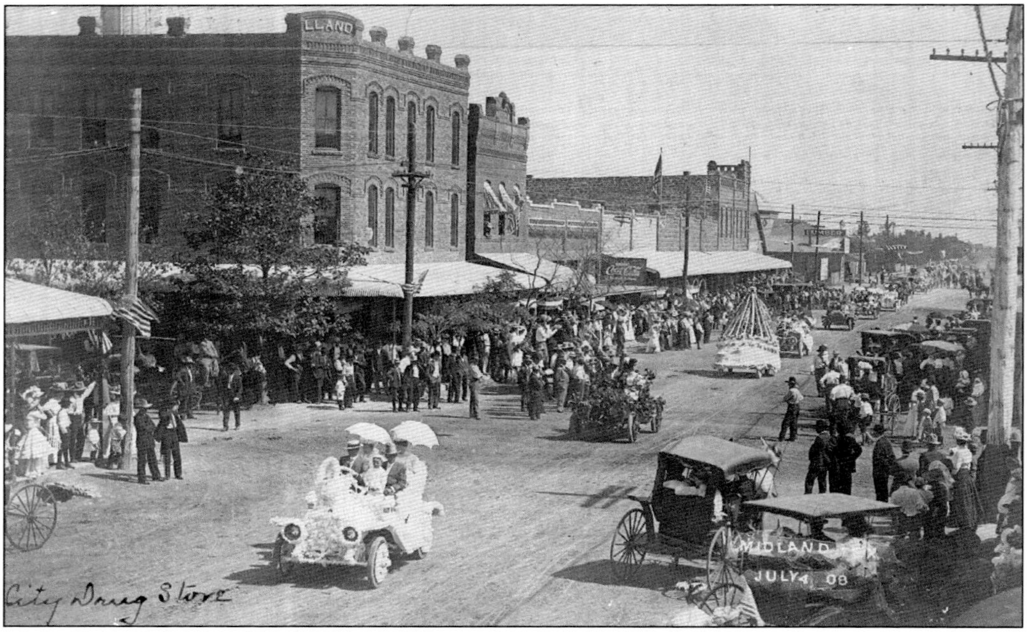

The Mosley School held another parade on July 4, 1908. The three Mosley sisters, Mary, Carrie, and Louise, college teachers from Tennessee, established the private school in 1905 on the corner of Big Spring and Tennessee Streets. Tuition was $4.25 per month. The misses' car has just passed the corner of Abilene (Main) and Iowa (Wall) Streets. The Llano Hotel is on the corner. A Coca-Cola sign marks the City Drug Store. The awning of the First National Bank is on the left.

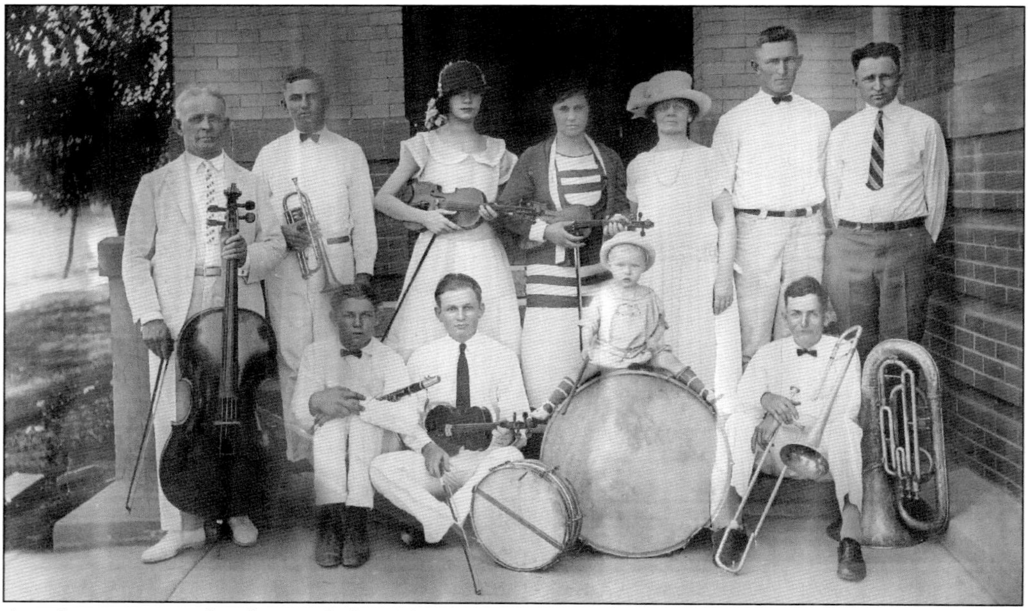

Another private school provided a different form of entertainment. Ned Watson (far left) and Lydia, his sister (in the white hat), organized the Watson School of Music in 1900 and operated it for more than a half-century. Here music students and perhaps faculty pose with their instruments, including a very young drummer.

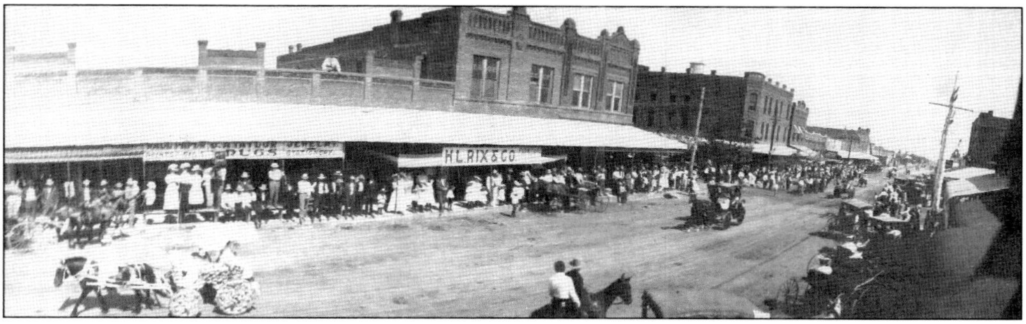

Horses still had their role in parades. This one is tentatively dated to 1909, but it appears to be the July 4, 1908, parade. The rebuilt Llano Hotel is right of center. The First National Bank is the large two-story building in the center. The H. L. Rix and Company Furniture Store would become Everybody's Store, which would feature dry goods.

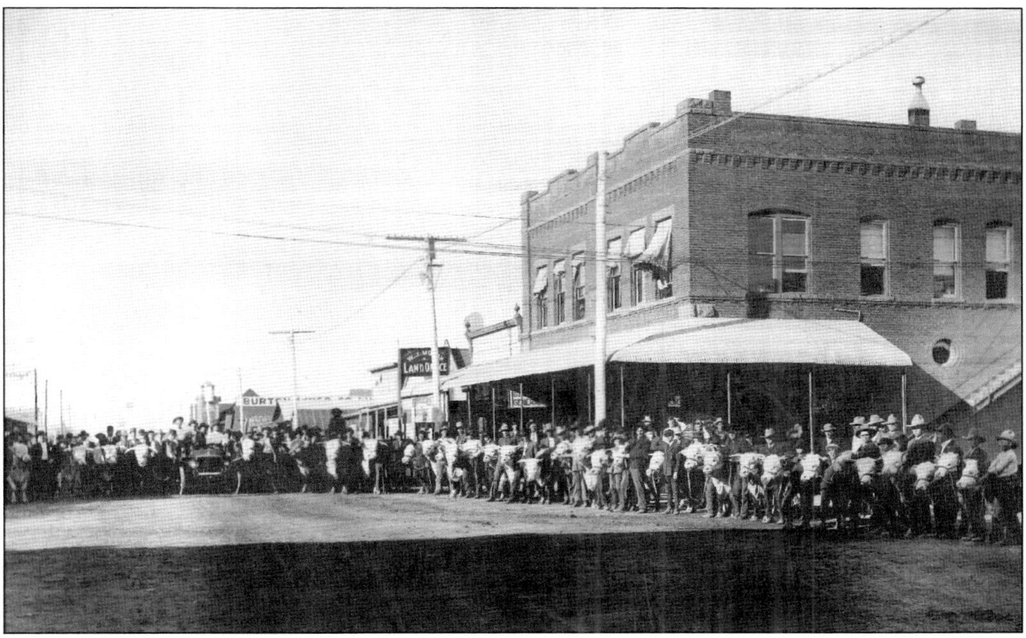

Parades were not the only entertainment. This scene is from a 1908 souvenir program for the Cowboy Carnival and Fine Stock Show. Hereford cattle line the street in front of the Gary and Burris General Merchandise Store. The Burton Lingo Lumber Company can be seen on the corner of the next block, with the tower of First Methodist Church just behind it.

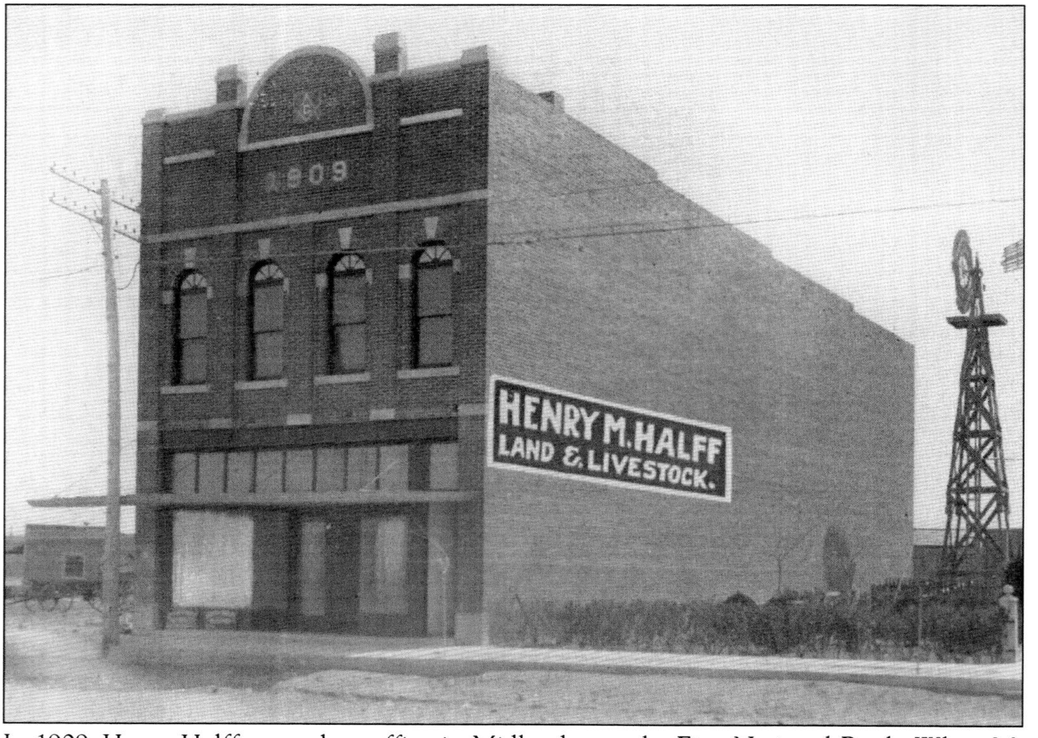

In 1909, Henry Halff opened an office in Midland near the First National Bank. When M. Halff died in 1902, his son, Henry, took over the extensive Quien Sabe and J. M. Ranches south of Midland. Henry quickly learned ranching and became a proponent of improving livestock bloodlines. Halff also began developing irrigated farms and opened his real estate company to help connect homesteaders with the new lands opened up by the state.

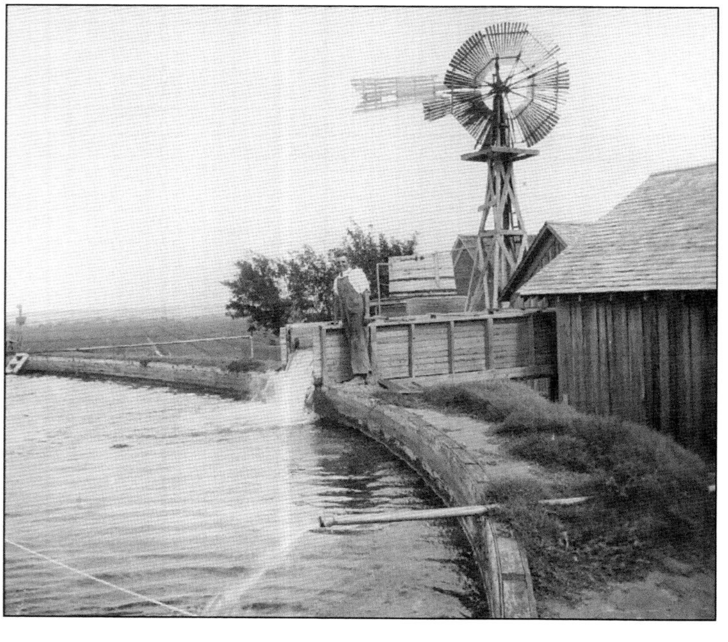

Beginning in 1908, Halff published several booklets promoting irrigation in Midland County. He claimed that 90 percent of the soil was arable, adding, "Water can be had anywhere without fail, at a depth ranging from 20 to 150 feet. The supply is practically inexhaustible." To prove his case, he built a pavilion at one of his water tanks east of Midland. Cloverdale became a popular swimming, dance, and picnic spot. This well, drilled in 1915, tested at 1,000 gallons per minute.

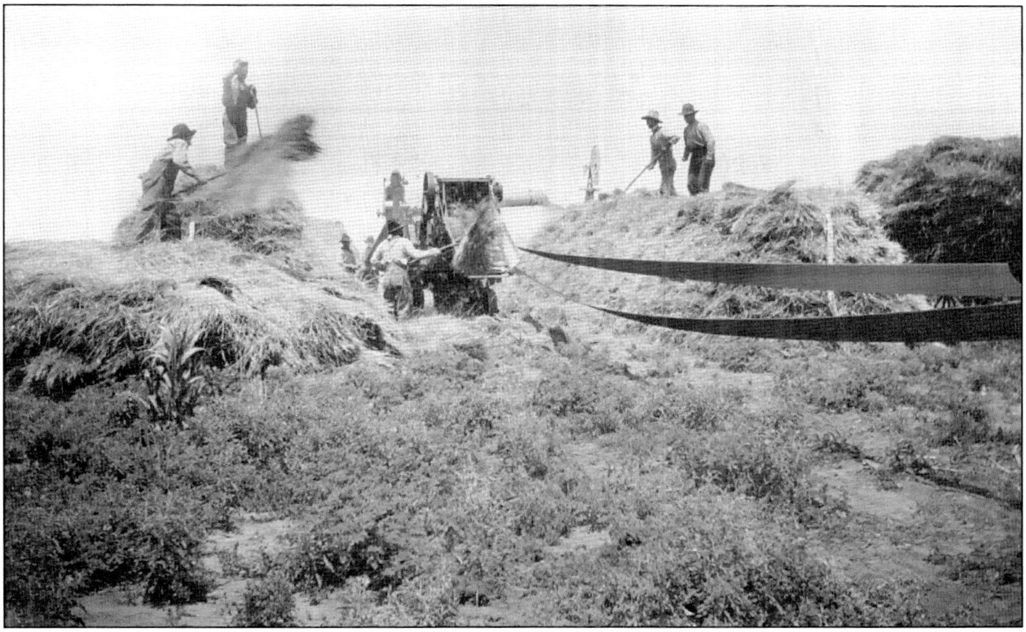

Halff's claims may have been a bit exaggerated, but the land was productive when water was available, as this photograph titled "Threshing Wheat at Red Top Hall Farms, 1916" demonstrates. While farming never gained the economic status of ranching, it did contribute significantly to the Midland economy for a time.

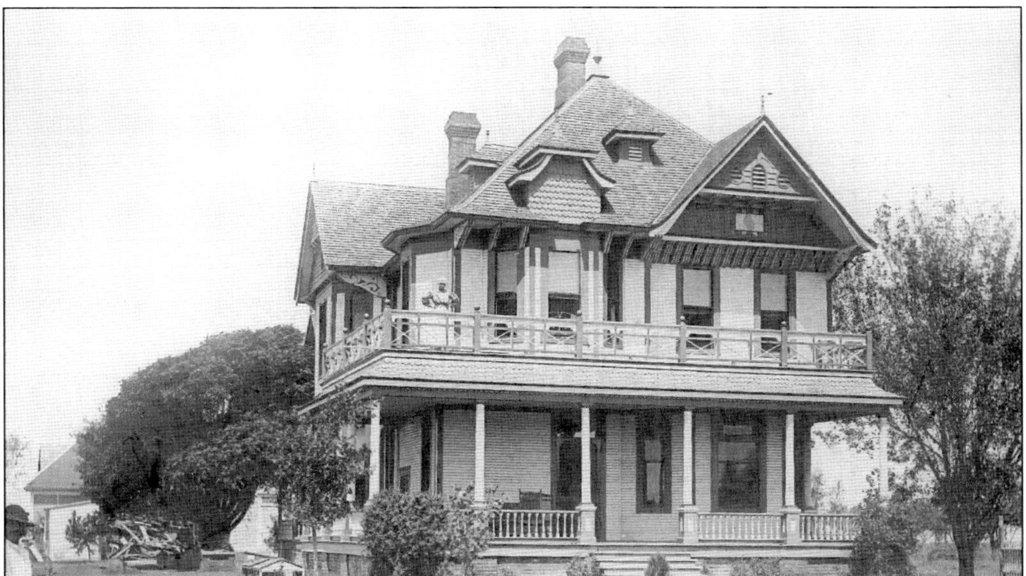

Henry Halff was an early advocate of soil and water conservation and scientific farming. His Midland home, pictured here, demonstrated the success of his ventures. Halff also imported racehorses to breed with native quarter horses because he believed they would produce high-quality polo ponies. Halff organized a polo team that competed across the United States and in international matches.

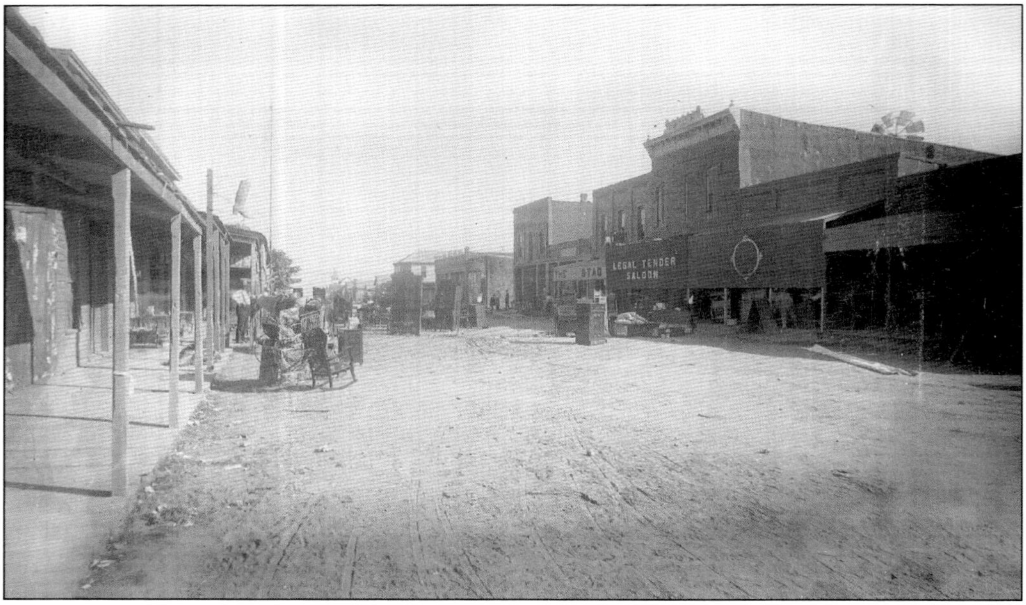

As buildings in downtown Midland grew more numerous, hazards increased. There were several serious fires between 1900 and 1910. In this undated photograph (before 1907) residents have carried furniture and other possessions into the center of Abilene (Main) Street after a fire to assess the damage. The Legal Tender Saloon (on the right) opened in 1896. After Midland went "dry" in the early 1900s, the Legal Tender relocated to El Paso, then to Juarez with the establishment of Prohibition.

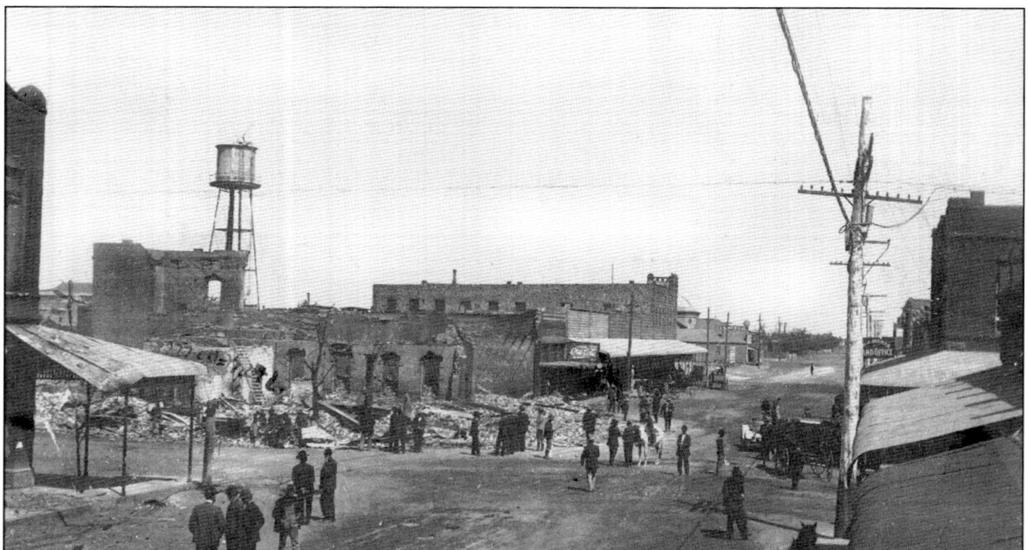

On the night of April 8, 1909, a devastating fire swept through the center of town. Before it was extinguished much of downtown was rubble and smoldering ruins. This image centers on the intersection of Abilene and Iowa Streets. The fire originated in the Llano Hotel, marked by the pile of rubble (center). The City Grocery also perished (the arches and columns). The City Drug Store survived (Coca-Cola sign) as did the Dorsey Barber Shop and Bath House and the post office.

The exact cause of the fire has been lost. A strong breeze blowing from the north carried the fire across Iowa Street to the First National Bank Building. By early morning, it too was a smoldering shell, all the interior gone. The fire swept down the block, consuming business after business.

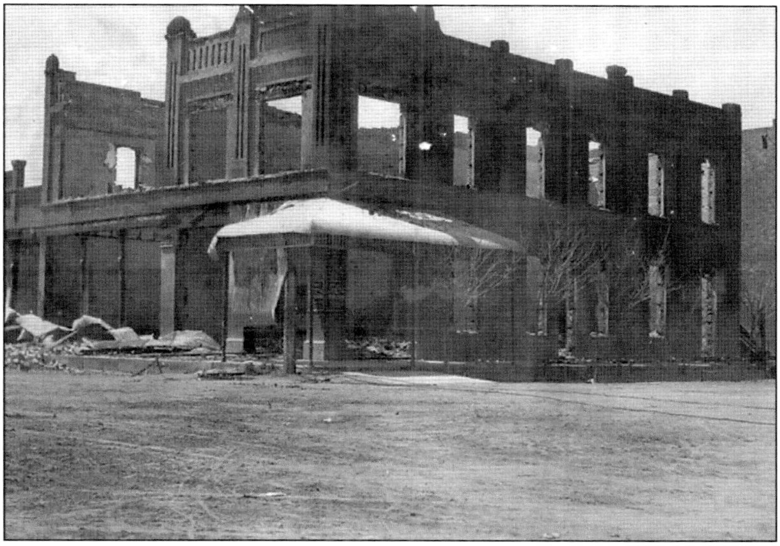

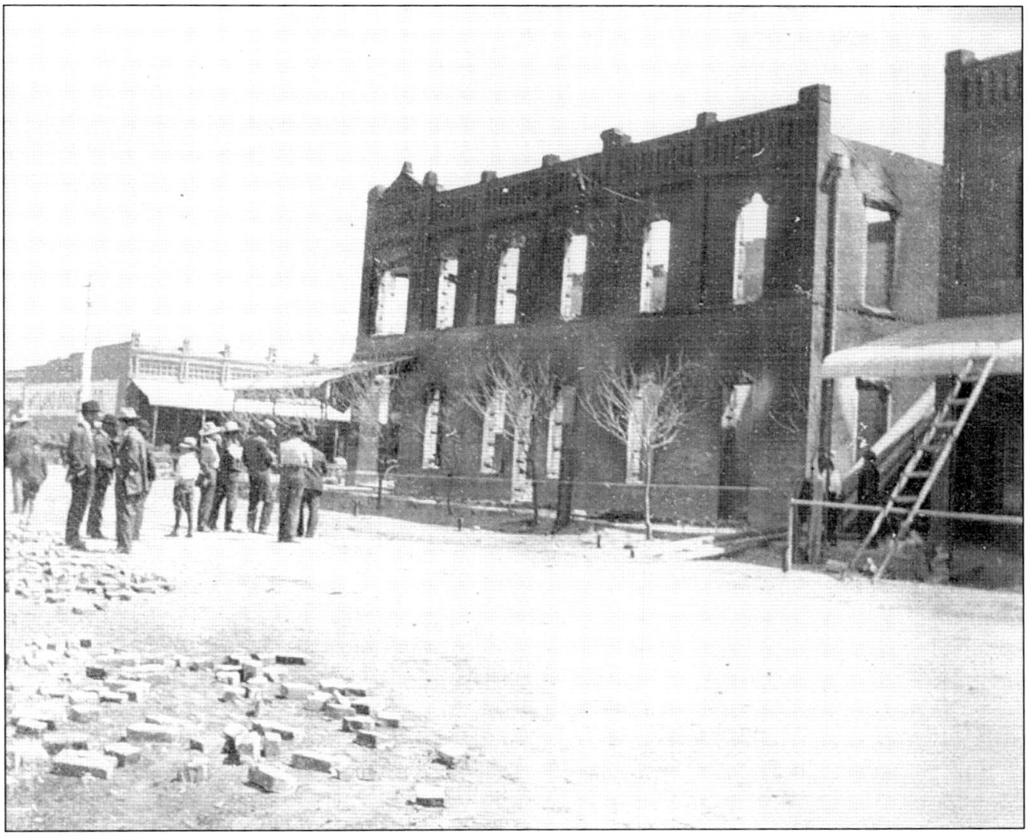

According to the records of the Midland Masonic Lodge, a fire destroyed the Lodge Hall at 3:00 a.m. on April 9, 1909. The hall occupied the second floor of the First National Bank Building (on the right). The total destruction of both of Midland's major financial institutions contributed to this fire's notoriety as "the greatest fire in Midland's history."

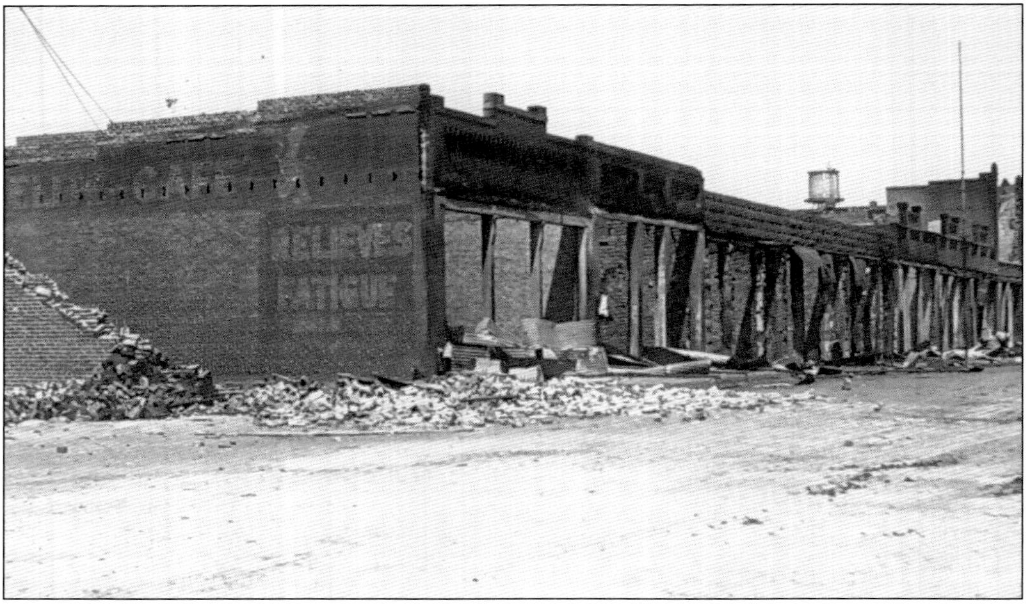

The fire burned south along the west side of Abilene Street, gutting the 100 block. The First National Bank can be seen on the far right. Next door were the ruins of Everybody's Clothing Store. A line of bricks held up by charred columns was all that remained of the C. A. Taylor Drug Company. An old sign, the Elite Café, was revealed when the adjacent building crumbled into fragmented walls and piles of brick.

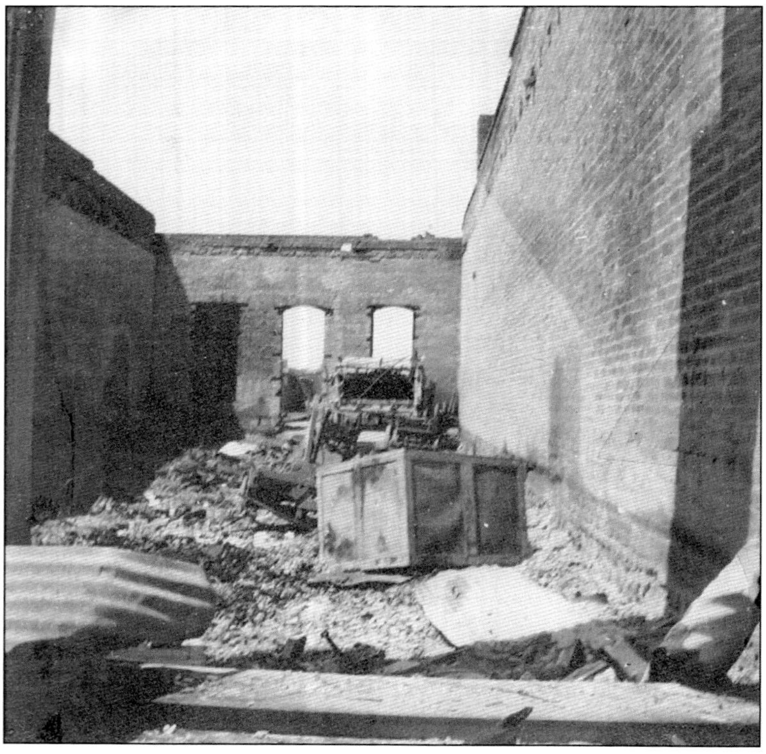

All the interior floors, walls, and ceilings were completely gone. This building contained some larger equipment that did not burn. In front might be a safe or vault. The back item may be some sort of printing press. The *Examiner* was published from the Francis Land Company office in the 100 block of South Abilene. This could be that office.

The fire became a watershed point in Midland's history. Midland's third mayor, J. A. Haley, worked to implement changes. Several downtown structures were condemned. In October 1909, the Midland City Council held a bond election to create the first city waterworks. Views such as this along the back of North Abilene Street helped bond supporters sell their cause.

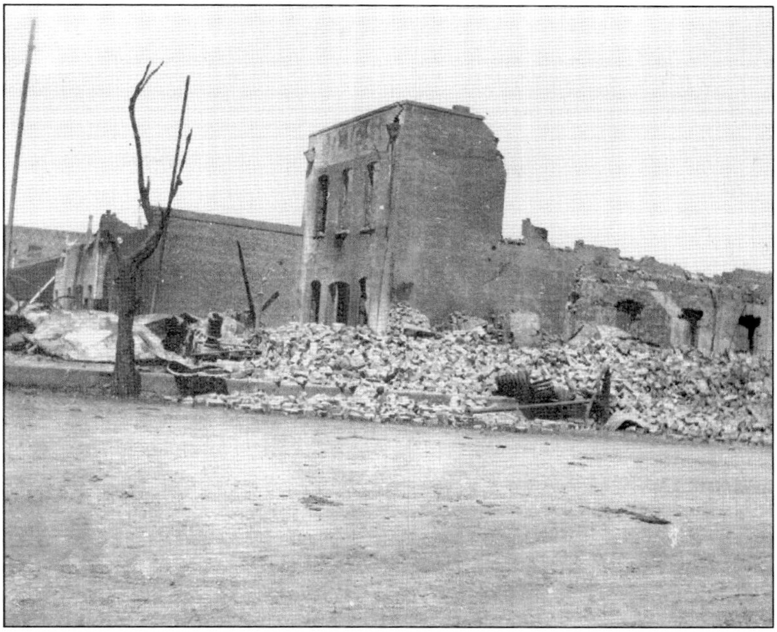

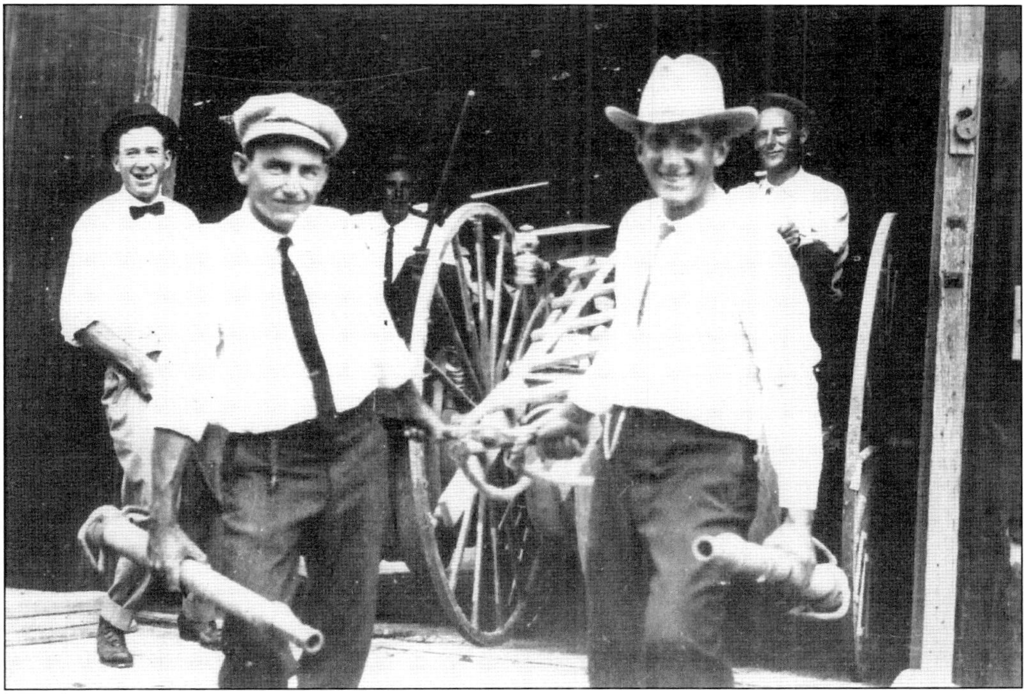

The Midland Volunteer Fire Department also organized in 1909 and purchased a hand-pull engine. The 1910 crew included are, from left to right, Lonnie McCormick, Frank Prothro, unidentified (in back), Luther Tidwell, and Fred Barber. In December 1910, another fire struck the downtown area, this time spreading along the east side of the 100 block of Abilene Street. One life was lost and several buildings were destroyed, but a quick response by the fire department utilizing the new water system halted the fire's further spread.

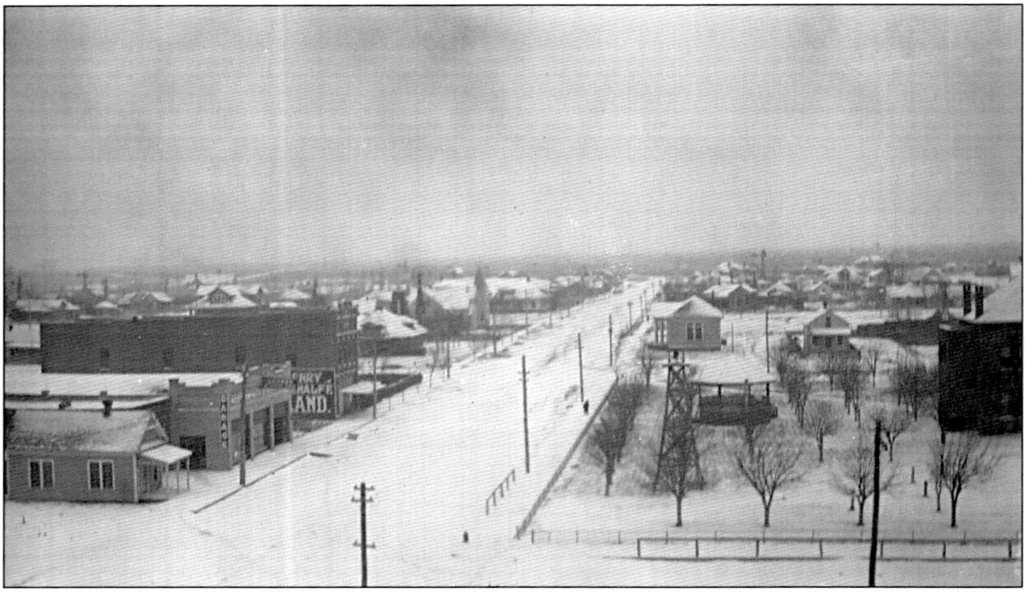

A more peaceful portrait of c. 1910 Midland comes from these four photographs. On a cold, wintery day, someone climbed atop the Llano Hotel and took pictures of a quiet, snow-covered Midland. Without a specific date, it is impossible to determine if this is before or after the 1909 fire. This view west along Iowa (Wall) Street shows part of the Midland County Courthouse on the right. The pond is gone. A gazebo has been added. Across the street is Henry Halff's real estate office, built in 1909.

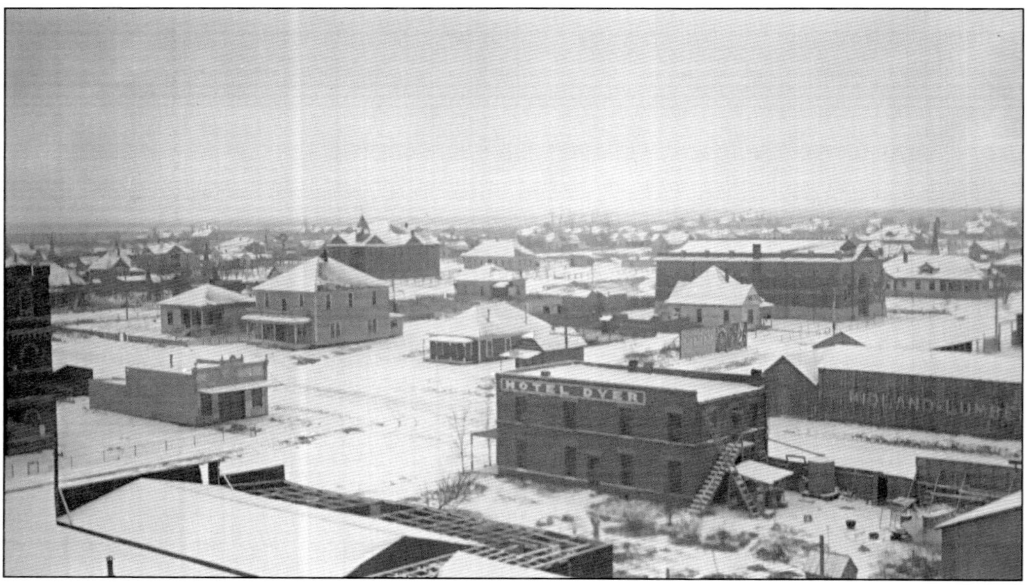

Viewed looking northwest, Windmill City appears deserted. One corner of the county jail is on the left edge of the photograph. In the center background is the North Ward School. Right of center is the First Christian Church. In the center foreground is the Hotel Dyer. In all four photographs, windmills become shadowy images standing beside homes and businesses.

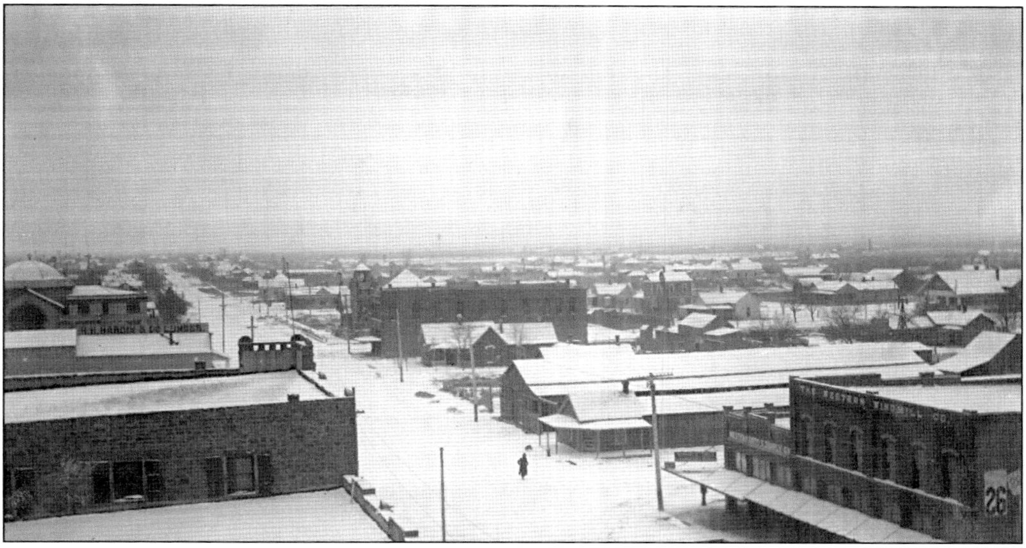

A solitary soul walks along Abilene (Main) Street, which stretches north onto the Llano. In the lower right corner stands the Western Windmill Company. Just right of center is the tower of the First Methodist Church. Across the street the round dome of First Baptist Church can be seen.

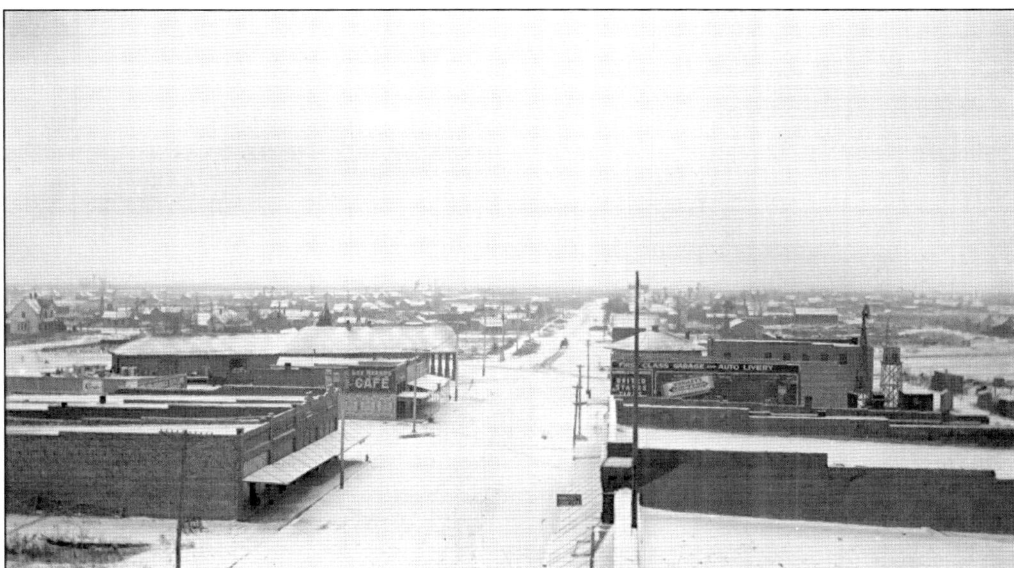

Looking south, the railroad tracks lie buried beneath the snow. On the left is the Midland Depot, just behind Lee Heard's Café. Across the street are the First Class Garage and Auto Livery (with the Wrigley's Doublemint sign). Behind the garage is the Yeakel Hotel, with its own windmill and water tank.

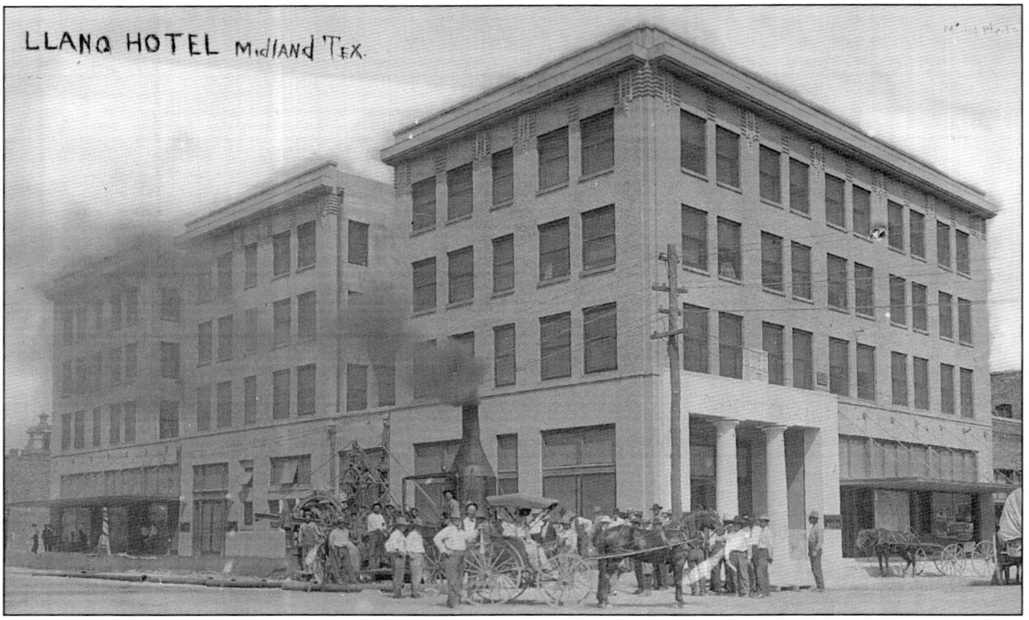

Downtown Midland recovered rapidly from the 1909 fire. The Llano Hotel was rebuilt and back in operation with an entirely new look in 1910. The horses and buggies in this photograph appear almost incongruous beside the powerful ditching machine. This may be part of the development of the new city water system. The Midland National Bank, with its new imposing columns and lobby, remained in the Llano Building.

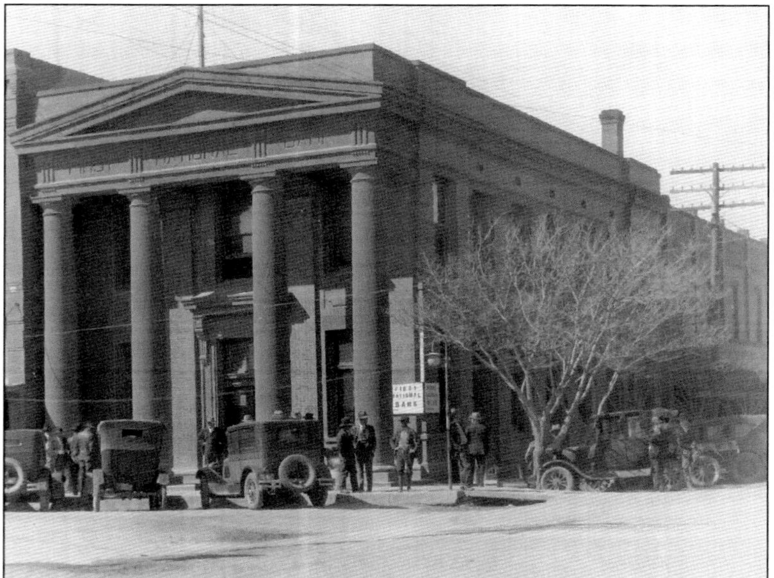

Across the street, the First National Bank was also rebuilt by 1910. A Greek Revival porch completely changed the bank's look. After the 1910 fire, merchants placed numerous advertisements in the *Midland Reporter* promising "to rebuild and reopen better than ever." The First National Bank announced it had $600,000 in resources and a surplus of $100,000.

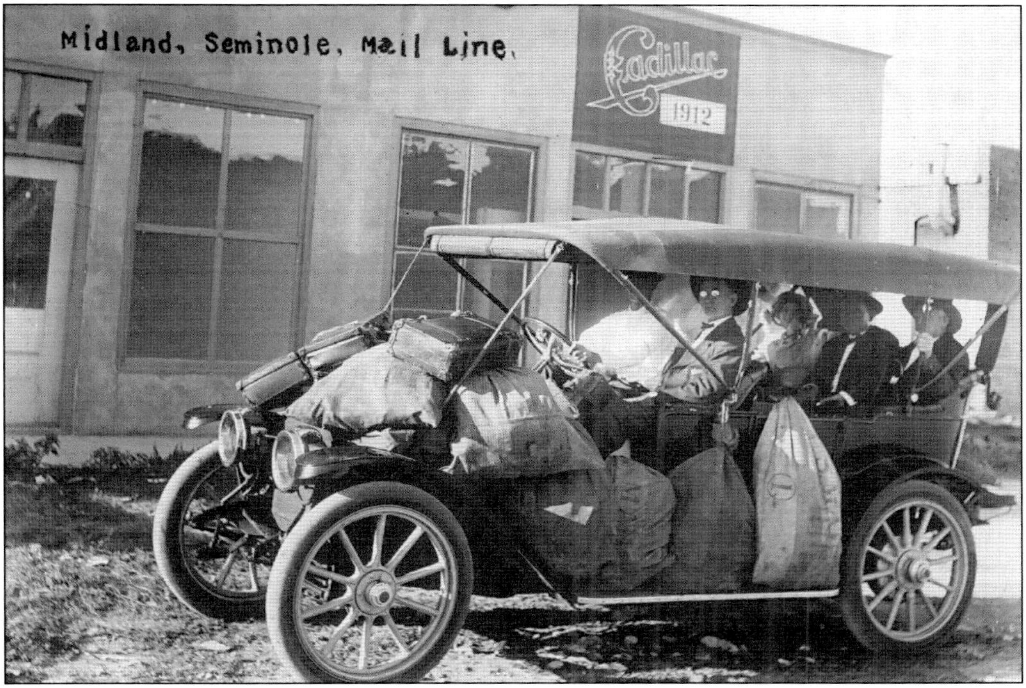

The combination of Western spirit and Progressive Era optimism launched Midland into the second decade of the 20th century. New adventures and new enterprises marked the decade. Not all would succeed. The Spaulding brothers began the Midland to Seminole Mail Line in 1910 and operated it until 1915.

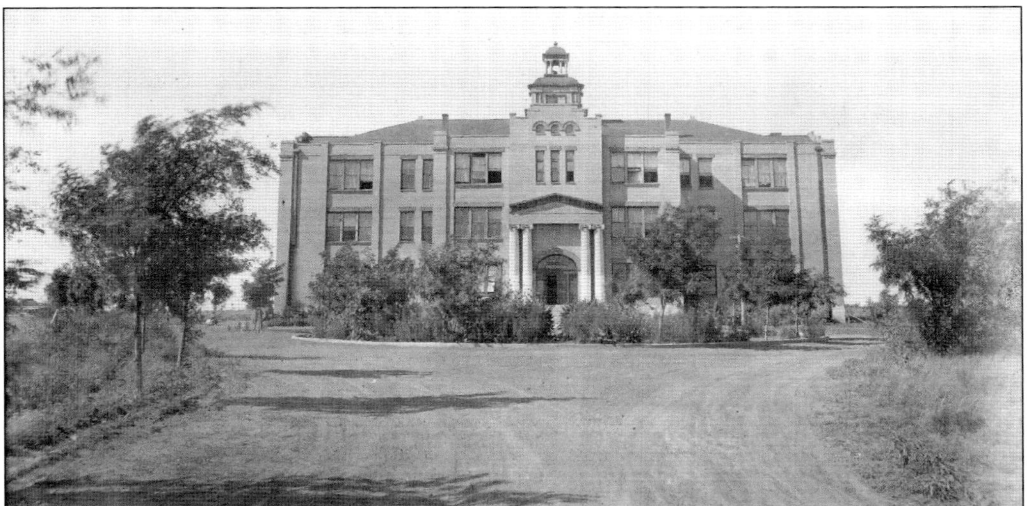

In 1908, the trustees of Texas Christian University sought to establish a junior college in west or southwest Texas. Midland became their choice. In 1909, Midland pioneers H. N. and Lucy Garrett donated land for the college 1.5 miles west of the courthouse. Midland Christian College opened in September 1910 with 107 students. S. J. Rives was the first president. The three-story brick building had stone trimmings and Corinthian columns at the front and side entrances. The first two floors were offices and classrooms, and the third floor provided dormitory accommodations.

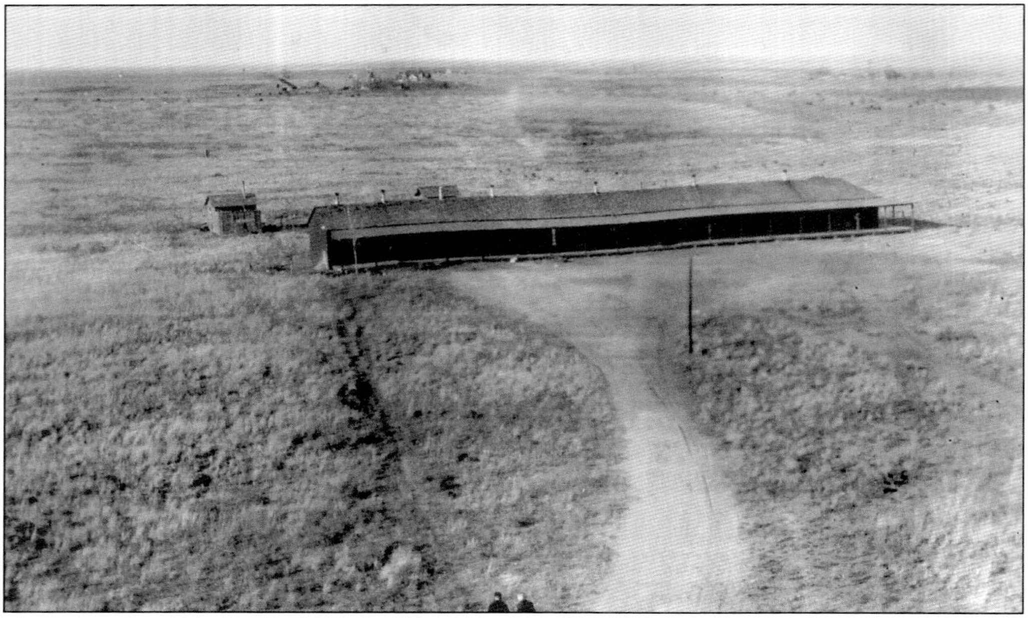

The dormitory floor of Midland College was originally intended to be coed; however, the boys were soon moved to a long one-story building constructed on the north side of the campus. It was quickly dubbed "The Dog House." (Courtesy of the Nita Stewart Haley Memorial Library, Midland, Texas.)

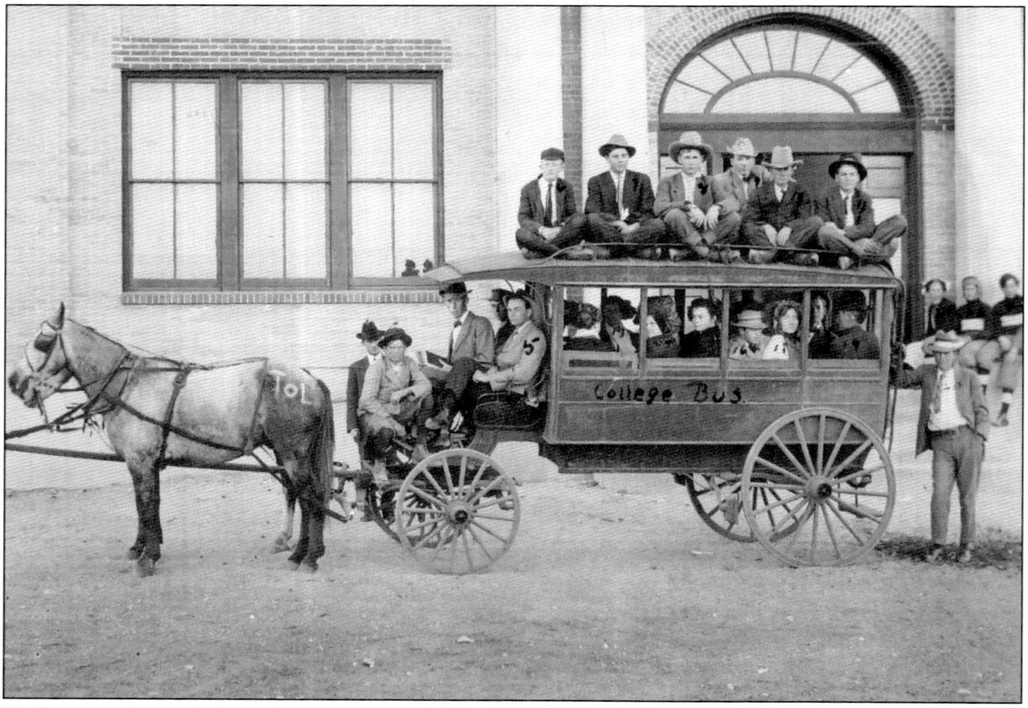

College students did not have to worry about the trek from the college into town. The college bus, pulled by the faithful Tol, provided transportation.

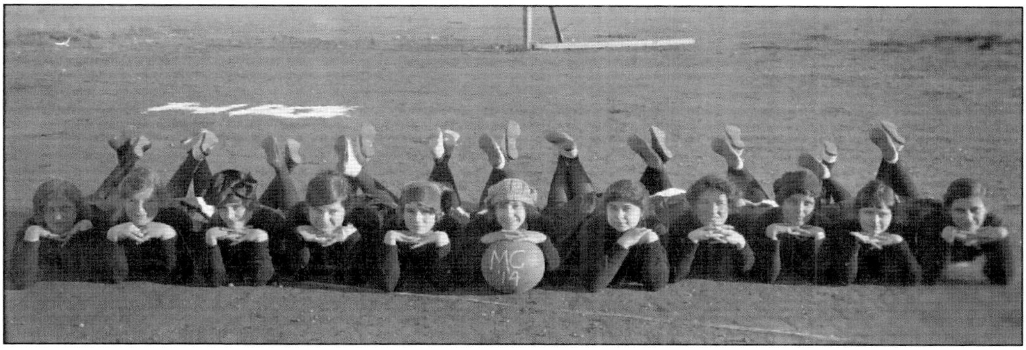

The Midland College trustees believed a healthy body was a prerequisite to a healthy mind, so the college developed a full athletic program. This is the 1914 girls' basketball team. Seen here, from left to right, are Elrie Carson, Eunice Allen, Bessye Cowden, Lula Elkins, Bessie Garrett, unidentified, Ethel Johnson, unidentified, Annie Mae Ingrum, Mary Wadley, and Lorena Allen.

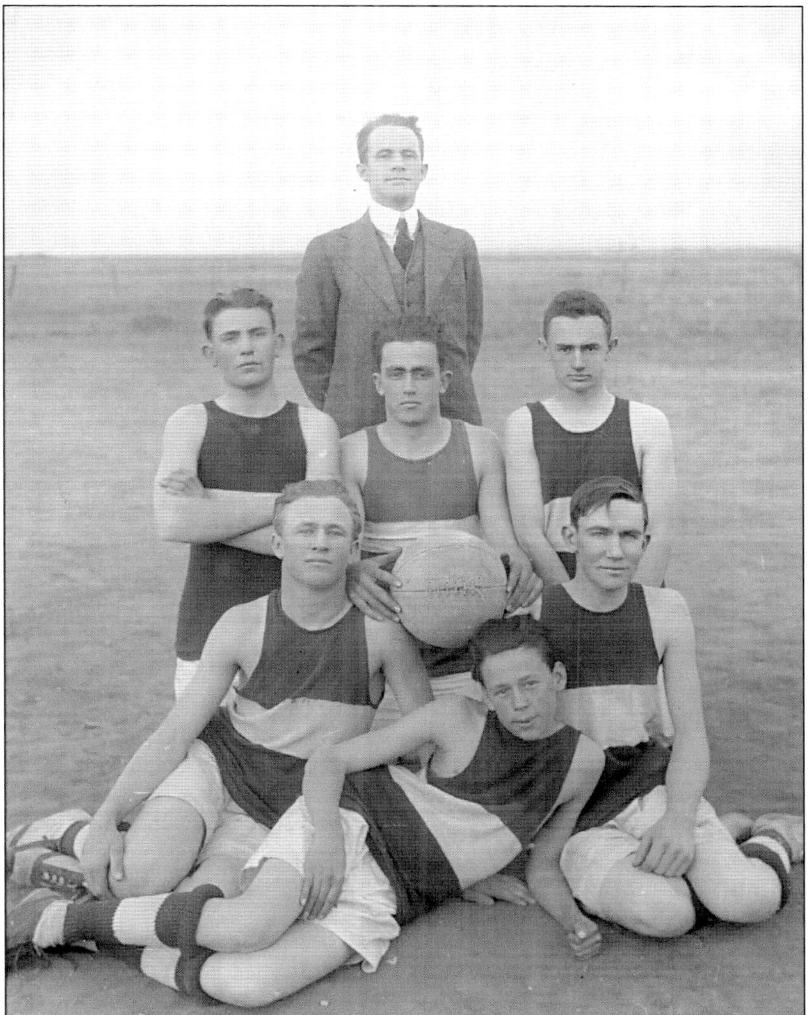

The names of the 1916 men's basketball team have been lost, but their confident spirit, seen here as they pose with their coach on the dirt basketball court, remains. In addition to basketball, the college fielded football, baseball, and tennis teams.

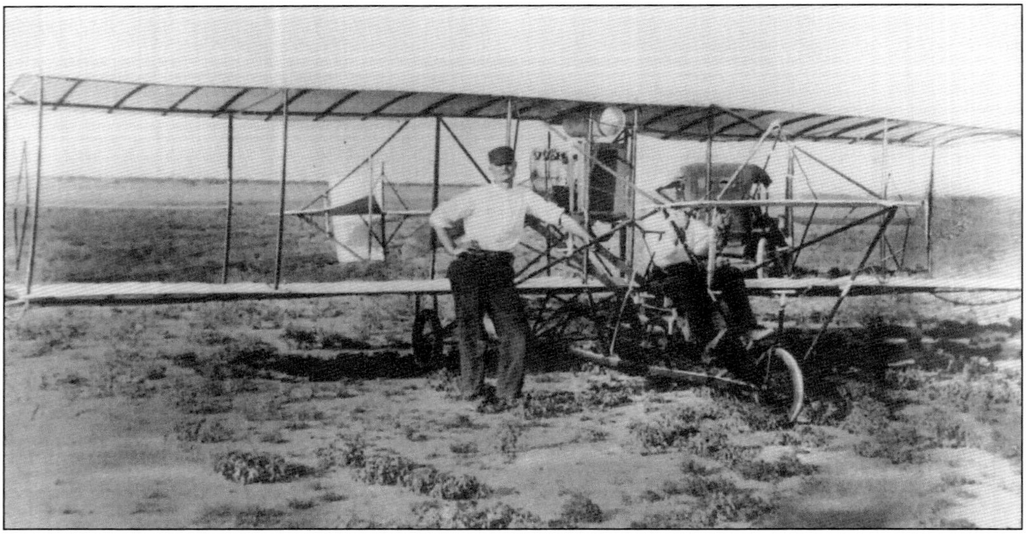

In 1911, blacksmith John Pliska (left) embarked on a highly unique venture. Inspired by Robert Fowler's November 1911 visit in his Wright Flyer II, Pliska set out to build his own airplane. He shared his plans with local auto mechanic Gray Coggin (right), and together they constructed the first airplane built *and* flown in Texas. They built the plane in Pliska's shop, using the simplest machinery. (Courtesy of the Midland Historical Museum Collection.)

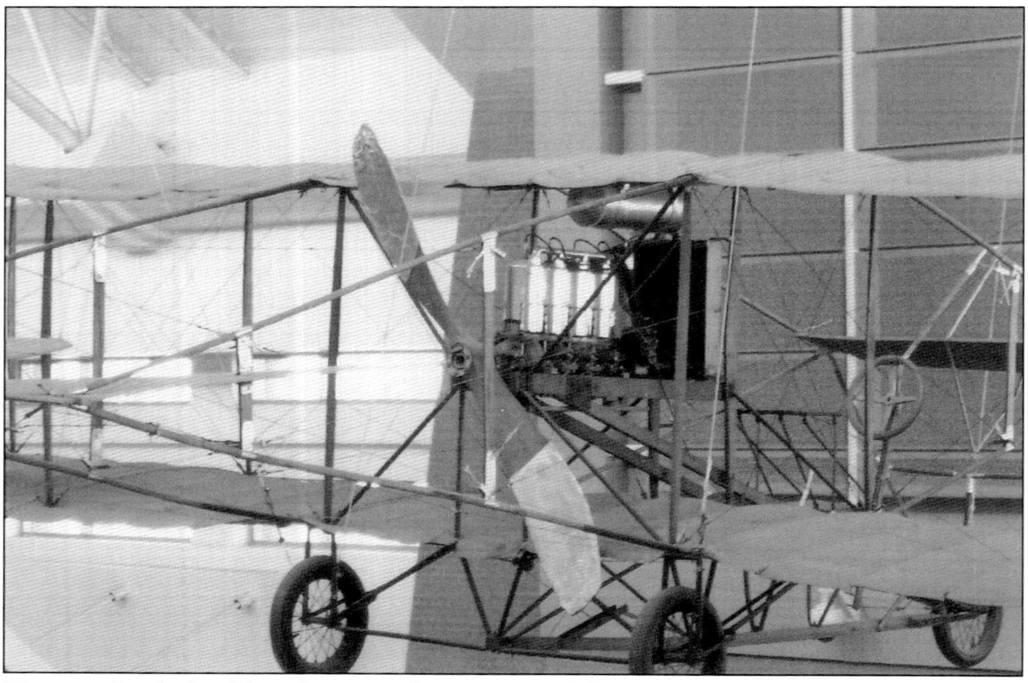

To get to Sandusky, Ohio, for an airplane engine, Pliska and Coggin hired on with the Texas and Pacific Railway, unloading cattle at pens every 300 miles. They found an engine at Roberts Motor Company, the first manufacturer to build motors specifically for airplane use. The four-cylinder, 165-pound engine generated 50 horsepower and ran on fuel shipped from New York City. (Photograph by author.)

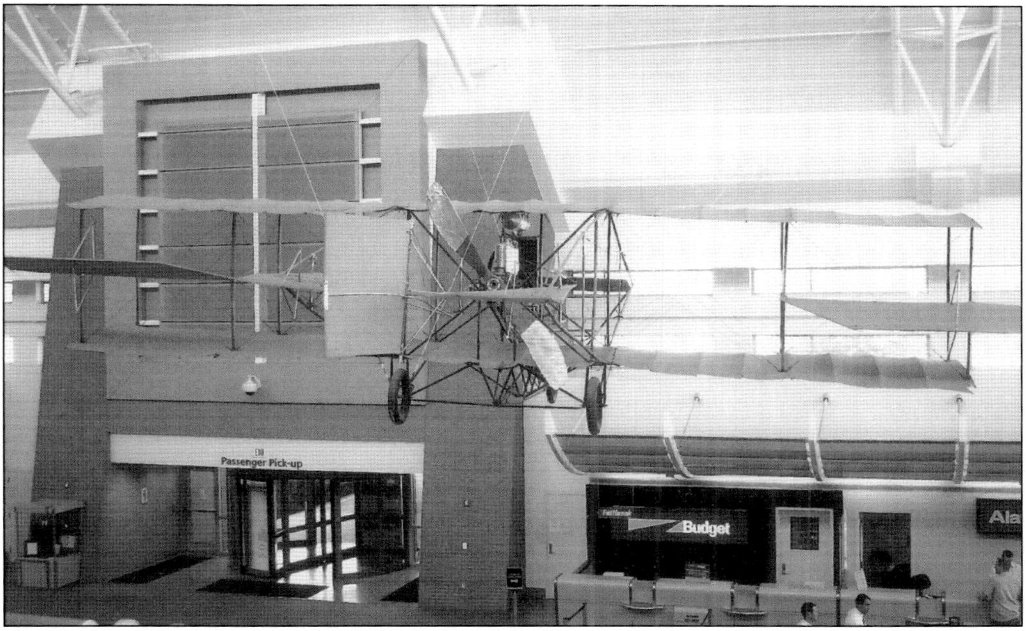

The wings were covered in canvas, shellacked to provide more lift. Piano wire formed the guy wires. Couplings were built from metal in the blacksmith shop. They made the propeller by gluing pieces of straight wood together, then forming a curved surface by hand with a knife and rasp. In early flights, the prop was "damaged by encountering mesquite and other brush." A metal sheath was laced to the ends of the blades, creating the first metal-tipped propeller. (Photograph by author.)

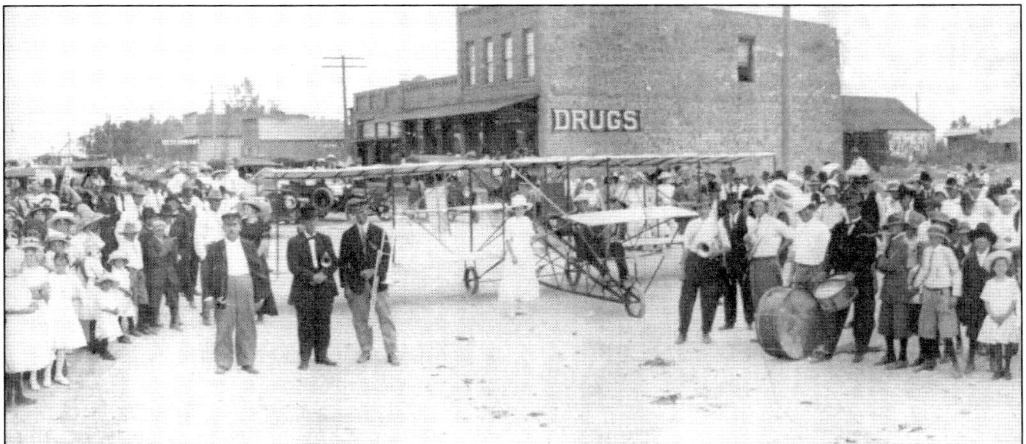

The first flights took place in spring of 1912 in a dry lake bed north of Midland and covered about a quarter of a mile. With refinements, they reached 2 miles at Henry Halff's polo grounds. On July 4, 1912, Pliska and Coggin agreed to an exhibition in neighboring Odessa, shown here in this segment from a panorama. Cowboys in for the day helped clear the road of mesquite; however, the hot, dry afternoon air provided inadequate lift. Despite several attempts, they never got airborne. The cowboys wanted their money back. Pliska took the airplane home and stored it in his shop. When the shop was dismantled 50 years later, the plane was rediscovered. It now hangs in the Midland International Airport—one of a kind. (Courtesy of the Permian Historical Society Archives.)

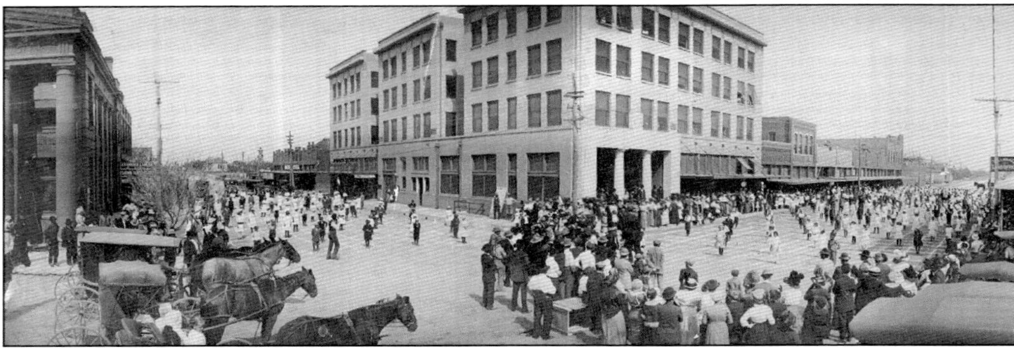

Midland remained the region's social center. On San Jacinto Day, April 1914, Midland schoolchildren demonstrate an exercise drill, with the Llano Hotel and Midland National Bank as a backdrop.

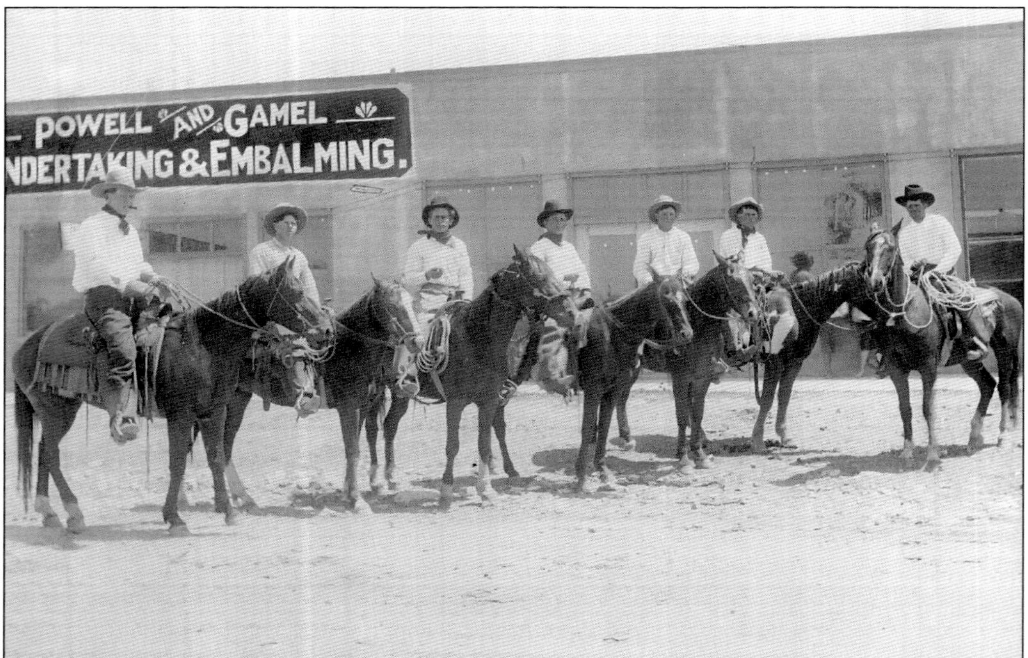

Local cowboys like these riders from the Quien Sabe still came into town for rodeos and parades. (Did they pause accidentally or intentionally in front of the Powell and Gamel Funeral Parlor?) Seen here, from left to right, are Ben Driver, Fred Truelove, Raby Preston, Gill Haynes, Jas Curry, Bob Preston, and Cleo Gaither.

Midland was home to one of the first professional rodeo cowboys. Clay McGonagill came to West Texas when he was four. Working on ranches in West Texas, New Mexico, and Arizona as a young man, he became an excellent bronco rider and steer roper. As the sport of rodeo evolved, McGonagill became a superstar. After the 1904 San Antonio rodeo, women tore his vest off for a souvenir. McGonagill competed throughout the United States and Mexico until he was crippled when his horse stepped in a hole and threw him. He died in 1921 when he accidentally grabbed an electric wire while hauling hay.

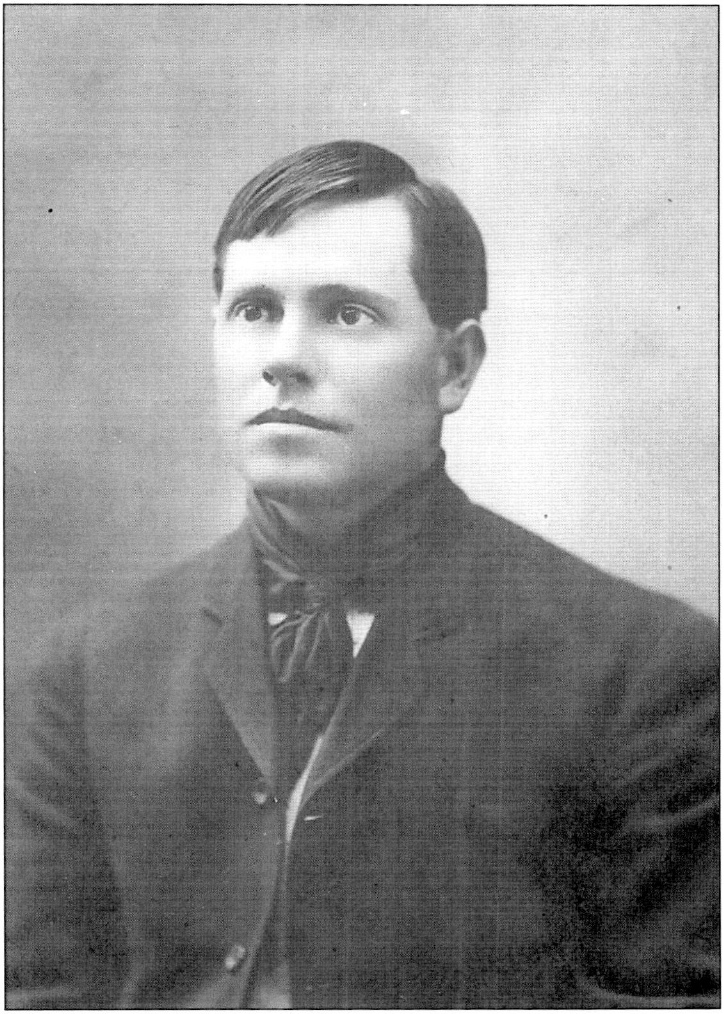

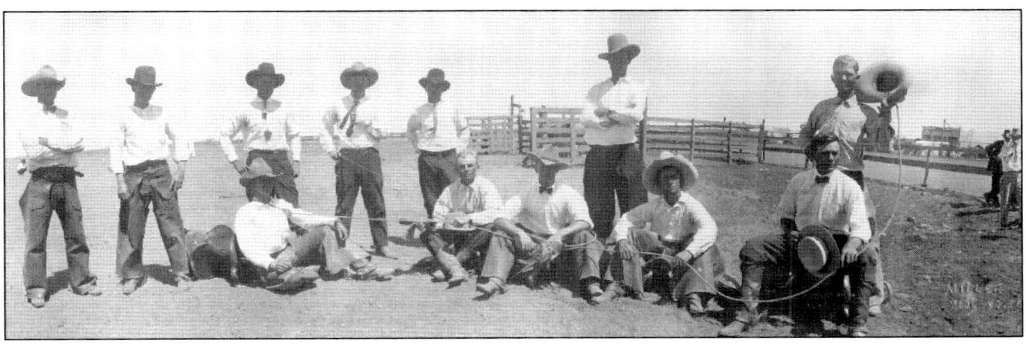

Cowboy competitions also continued as important events. This group of bronco riders competed at the Midland County Fair in September 1914. From left to right are (seated) Ed Cole, Allen Holder, John Dublin, Tar Dillard, and Jerd Wooten; (standing) Sam "Scissors" Nix, Jewel Kenney, Ed Stokeley, Len (Red) Driver, Jim Kenney, Fisher Pollard, and Charlie Blackburn. John Dublin won first prize on a saddle made by R. C. Caubla.

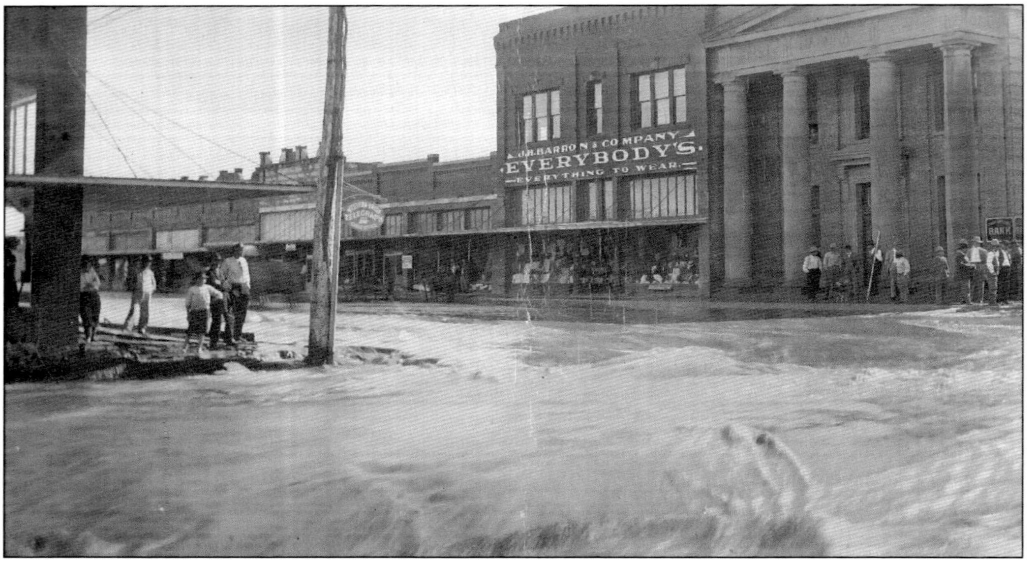

Prosperity or no, disasters still struck Midland from time to time. Though the town stood on the relatively flat Llano, torrential rains could overflow the arroyos and draws cutting across the area and flood Midland streets, as shown here in April 1914. Though often brief, floods nonetheless caused considerable damage.

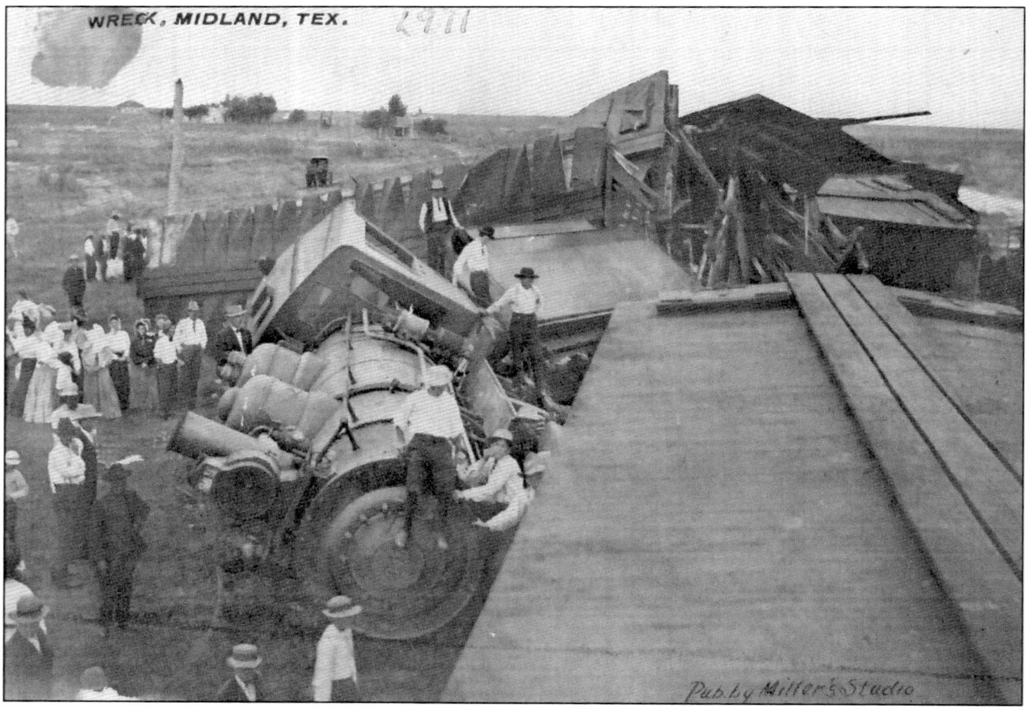

Train wrecks were not common, but when they occurred, they first drew out the town's more heroic residents and then the merely curious. Though the dates on some old photographs are suspect, the 1911 date on this image is most likely correct; records show that the Texas and Pacific locomotive No. 349, seen here on its side, was built in 1906.

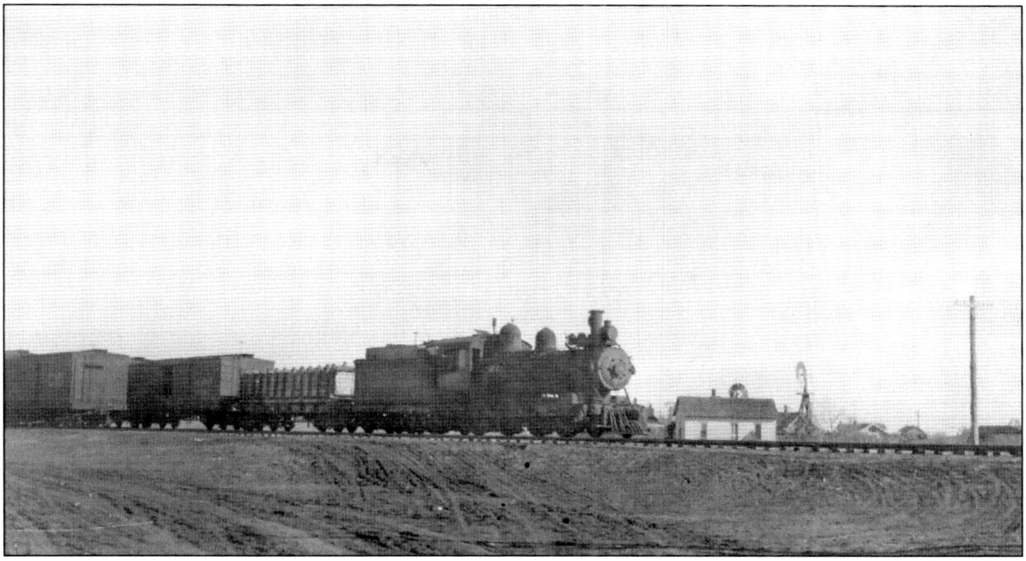

Midland had a second railroad for a time. In 1915, David Faskin Sr. began the Midland and Northwestern Railroad, which ran 65 miles north to Seminole. Designed for shipping cattle, the railroad also carried passengers. Ranches along the route required fencing across the right of way to keep their stock in place, so the train made frequent stops to open and close the gates. The drought of 1916–1918 broke with a series of downpours that damaged the tracks, and the enterprise was abandoned in 1921.

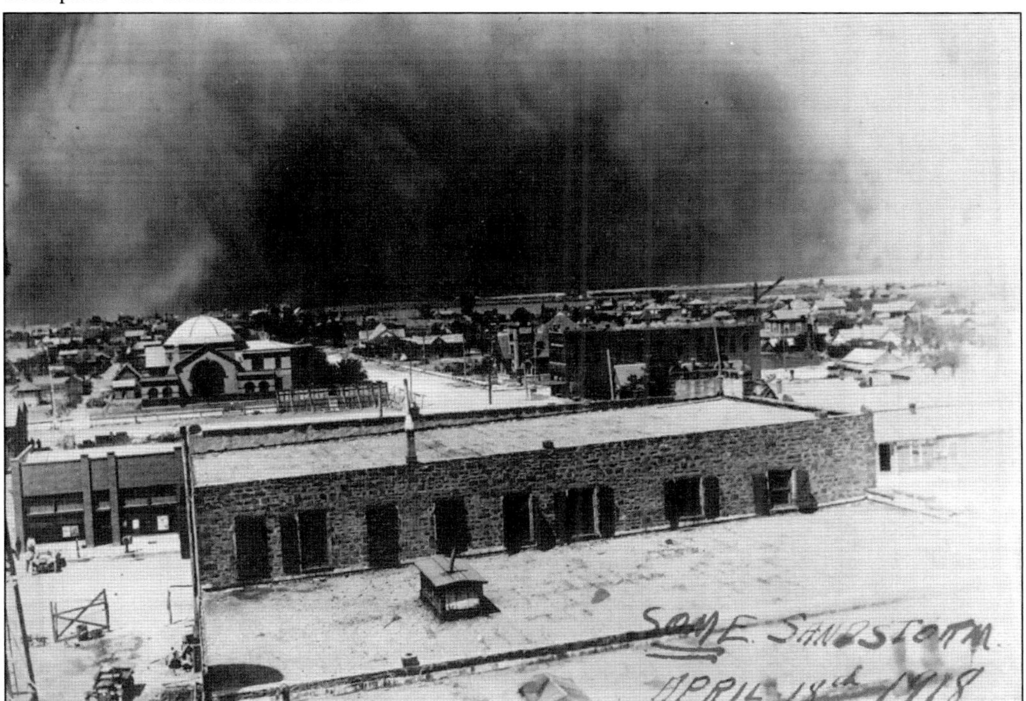

Sandstorms remained a hazard, especially in times of drought. As more farming loosened the topsoil, they could grow huge, dark, and threatening, as seen in this image dated April 18, 1918.

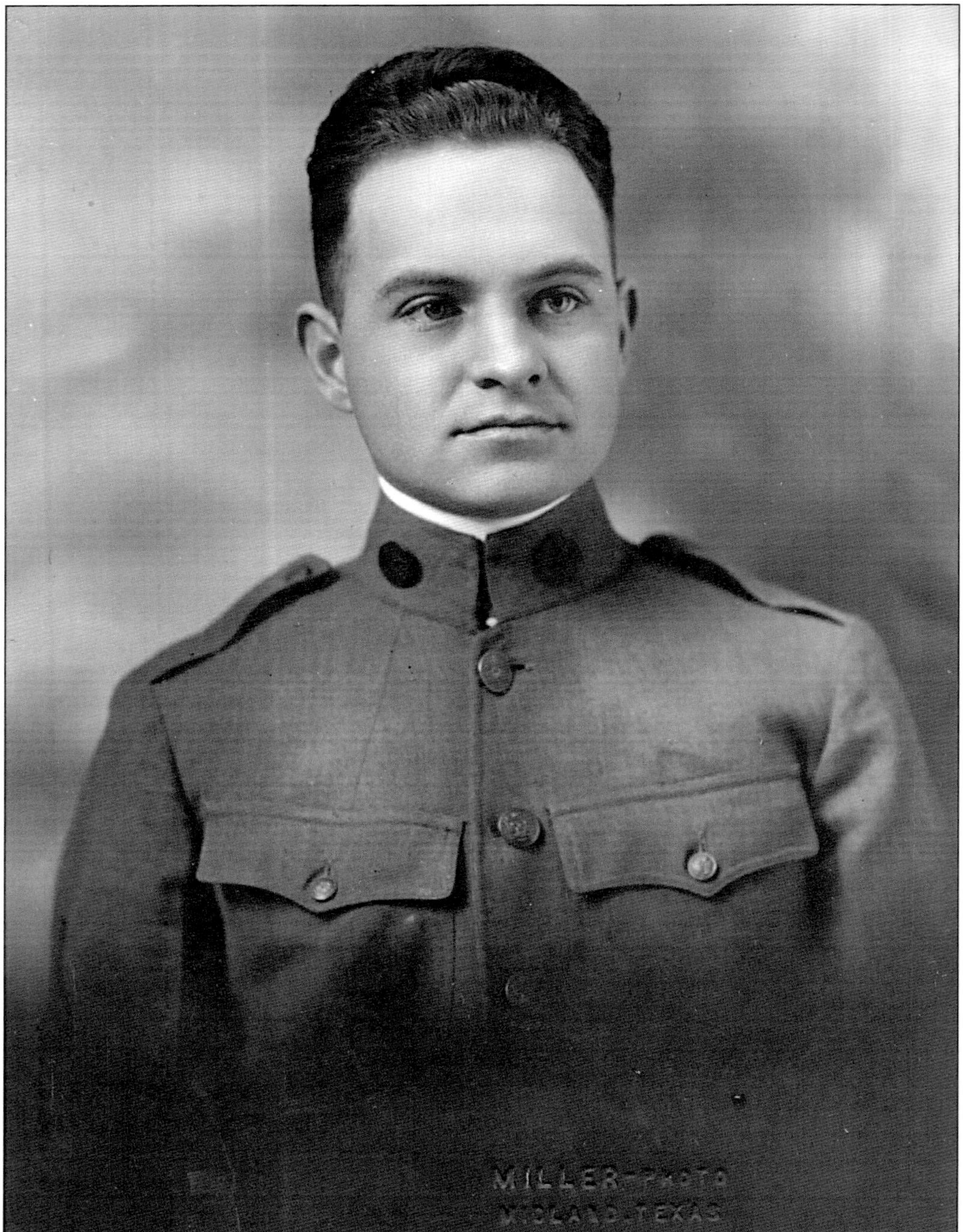

As the decade drew to a close, America was drawn into World War I and young Midlanders enlisted in the cause. One was George Dee McCormick, shown here in his uniform. The son of Frank and Mollie McCormick, George was born in Midland in 1896. He graduated from Midland High School and Midland Christian College. After his discharge, George returned home to become part of Midland's shift from "Windmill City" to a petroleum financial center.

Three

Big Dreams in the Permian Basin

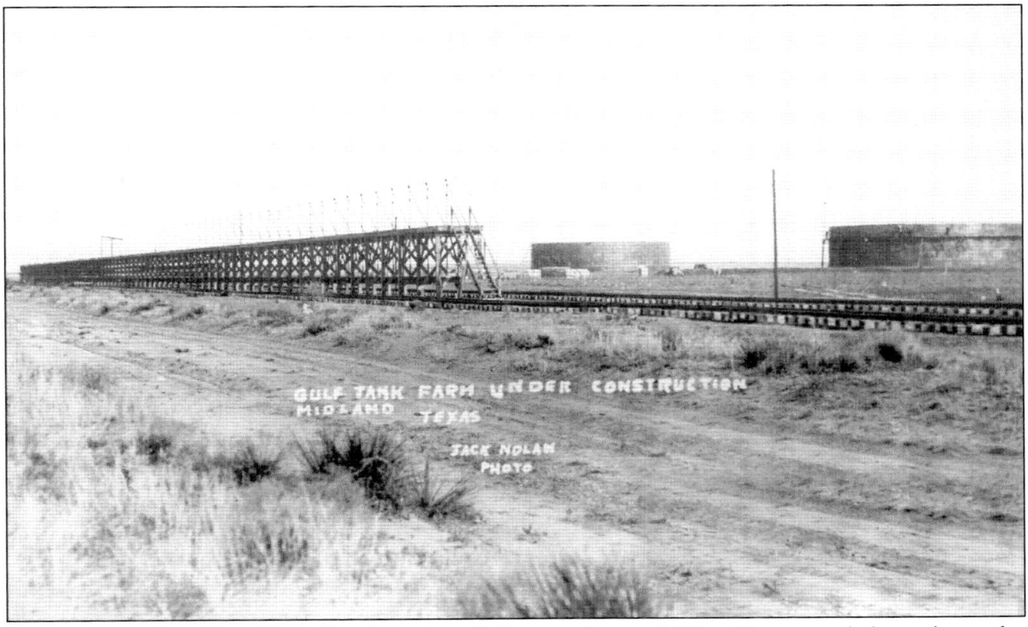

On May 29, 1923, the Santa Rita No. 1 well forever changed West Texas, and throughout the 1920s, the discovery of several additional large oil fields in the region fueled Midland's growth, even though there was no oil production within the county for decades. Instead, the city took advantage of its highway and rail connections. The Midland Chamber of Commerce, begun in 1924, encouraged oil companies to choose Midland as their regional administrative center. In 1926, Gulf Oil constructed a large tank farm beside the railroad to the east of town. (Courtesy of the Permian Historical Society Archives.)

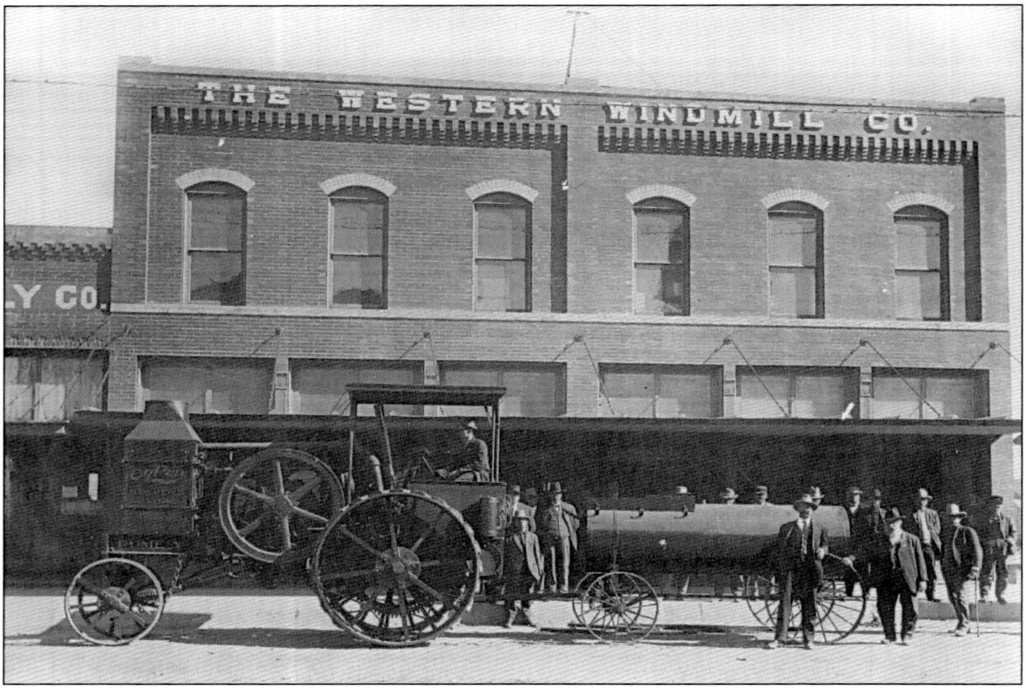

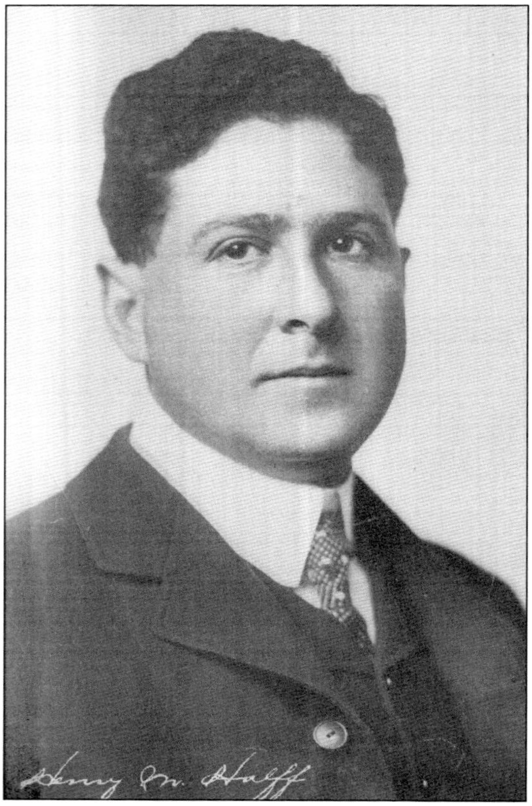

The decade saw many changes besides oil. Some things remained. Though drought drove many to leave, promoters like Henry Halff continued to be Midland boosters. He purchased a Rumilly Oil Pull tractor to help mechanize his farms and to improve roads. He brought it to town on several occasions. Here a group collects in front of the Western Windmill Company. The plow assembly shown on the cover is hitched to the Halff's tractor.

Henry Halff, shown here in a portrait from his 1914 promotional booklet, continued to spend thousands to improve his stock in cattle, polo ponies, swine, and chickens. He hired W. B. Starr as an early-day private version of a county agent to assist him as well as any others who sought agricultural advice. When he died in 1933, Halff's estate spread across four Texas counties and its eventual economic success vindicated his vision.

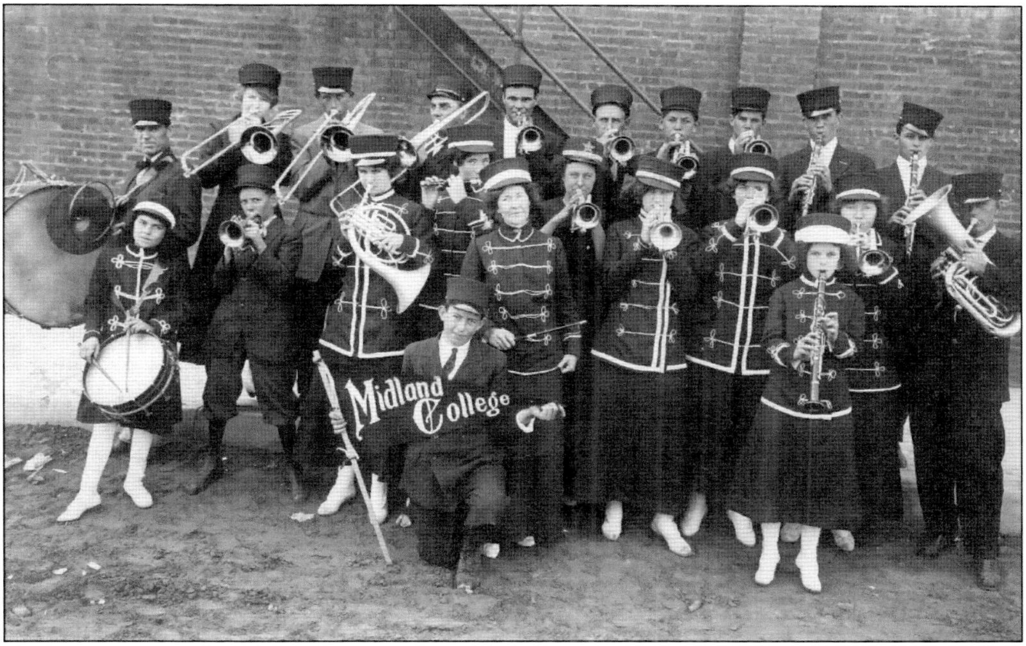

Some things did not last. Midland Christian College became a victim of the hard times after 1918, eventually closing its Midland facility in 1921. Several classes of students had passed through its doors, participating in a variety of programs, including the Midland College Band, pictured here sometime between 1915 and 1920.

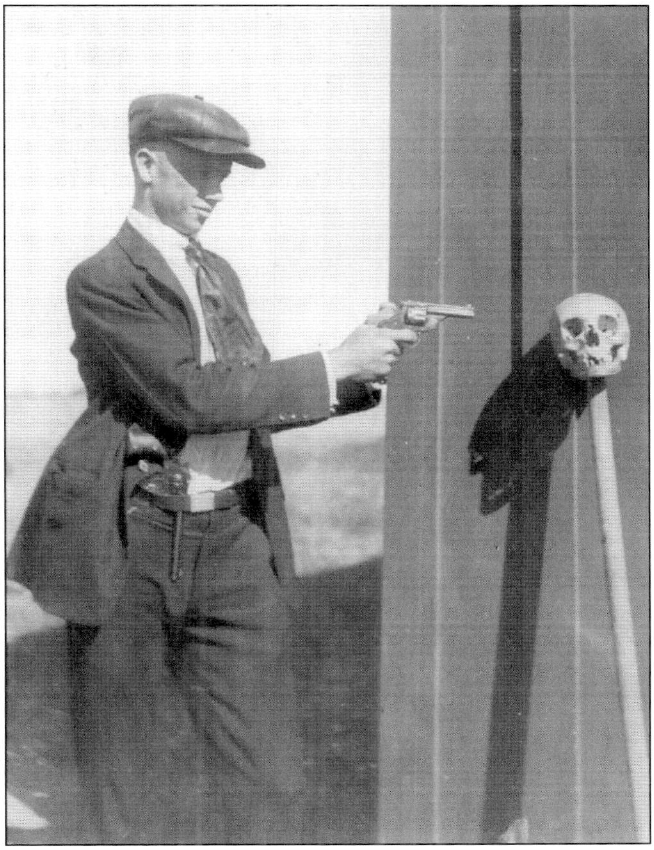

One student near the end of its history left a record of life at the college. J. Evetts Haley poses rakishly with pistols and a skull mounted on a pole. The strange props were apparently part of the paraphernalia of "The Apache Blood Boilers, the Mystic Society of 1920–21." Haley took a number of photographs of his year at Midland College. (Courtesy of the Nita Stewart Haley Memorial Library, Midland, Texas.)

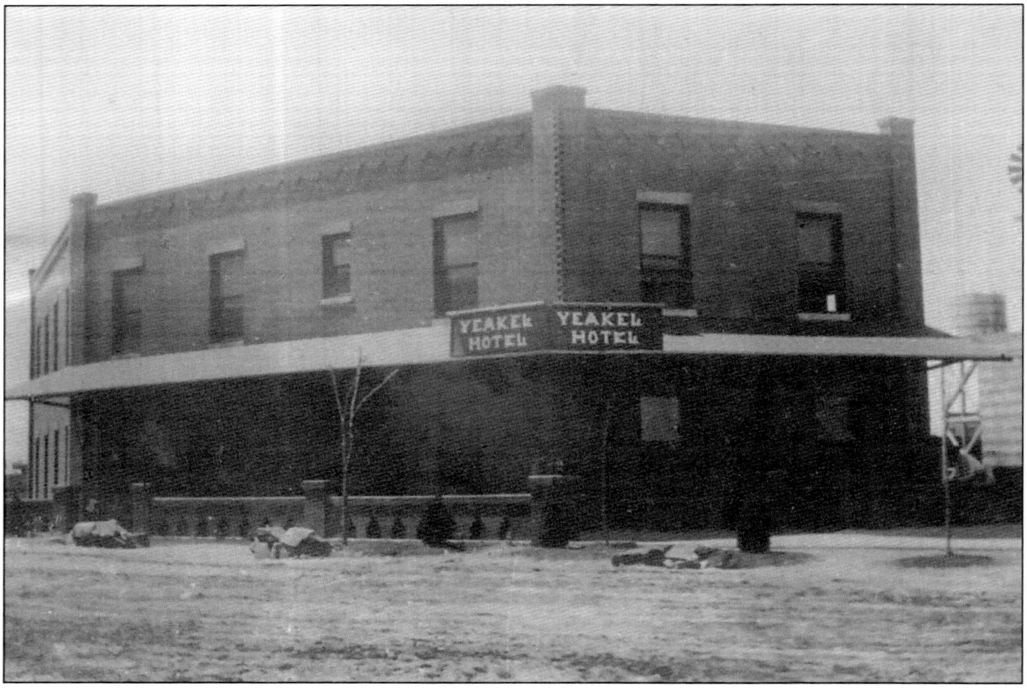

Haley came from a pioneer ranching family that relocated to Midland in 1907. His father, John, bought land in Midland County, where he was president of Midland Hardware Company and served as mayor in 1910. His mother, Julia, cooked at the Llano Hotel. In 1920, they bought the Yeakel Hotel (shown here) beside the railroad and renamed it the Haley.

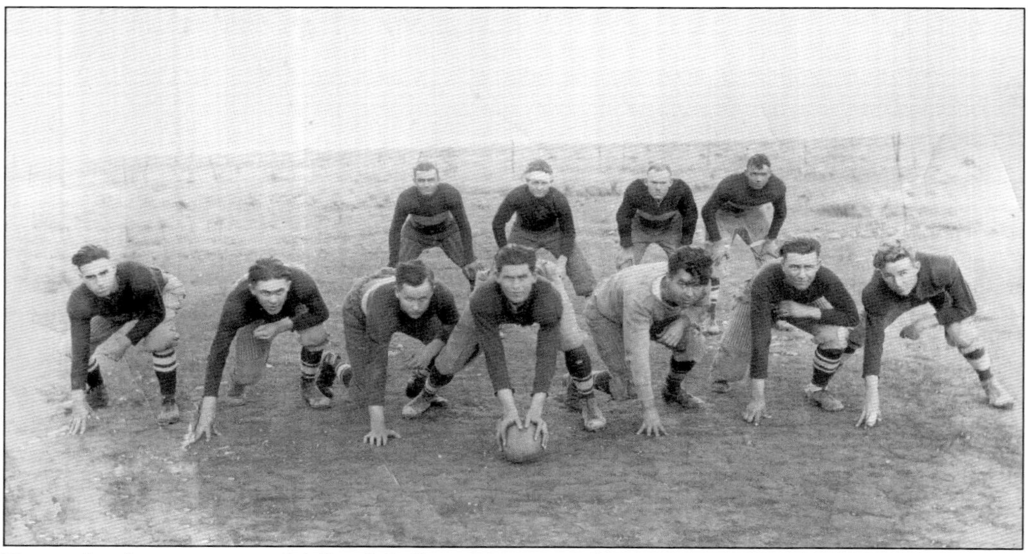

During his first semester at Midland College, J. Evetts Haley was a good student and played football well. He was awarded a football letter and elected captain of the team for the next season. Had the college not fallen into hard financial times, Haley might have had more of an athletic career. The caption indicates this is the 1921 team. None of the players are identified. (Courtesy of the Nita Stewart Haley Memorial Library, Midland, Texas.)

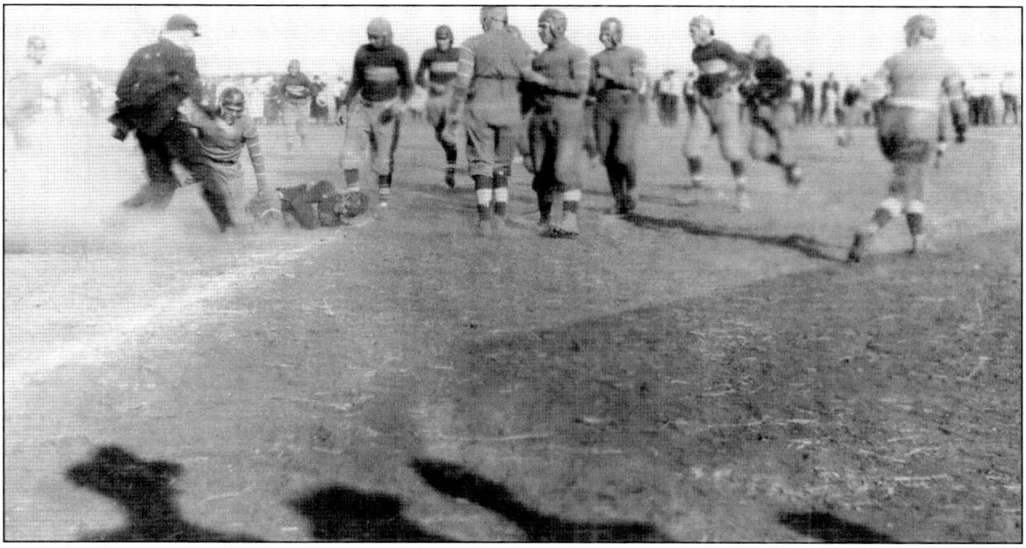

Haley's photograph album of his time at Midland College includes a rare action shot of a football game. While there is no date, no team identifications, and no score, the photograph does provide a graphic picture of the rugged nature of the game played on a packed-dirt field. (Courtesy of the Nita Stewart Haley Memorial Library, Midland, Texas.)

SEASON'S RECORD

Midland	0	Colorado	13

DISTRICT GAMES

Midland	51	Stanton	0
Midland	46	Odessa	0
Midland	13	Alpine	6
Midland	7	Odessa	6
Midland	51	Stanton	0
Midland	13	Pecos	6
Midland	13	Pecos	6

SECTIONAL CHAMPIONSHIP GAME

Midland	46	Ft. Stockton	0

BI-DISTRICT GAME

Midland	7	Sweetwater	19
	247		56

BULLDOGS '27

Archer, Joseph "Shot Gun"	Right Tackle
Brunson, D. W. "Dub"	Center
Fleenor, Dennis "Sandy"	Right Half
Fleenor, Robert "Bob"	Left Guard
Fryar, Harvey "Honorable Mention"	Quarter
King, Lynch "Dad"	Left Tackle
Long, Rex "Rexall"	Right Guard
Morgan, Glen "Bill"	Left End
Morgan, Ronald "Morgue"	Fullback
Orson, Wilton "London"	Left Guard
Paddock, Henry "Paddy"	Right Tackle
Pinnell, Dorsie "Ham"	Right Guard
Ray, Earl "Virgil"	Left Guard
Sowell, Rae "Rachael"	Center
Strawn, Alvie "Monk"	Left Half
Whitmire, Harwell "Little Man"	Left End
Whitmire, Witzel "Big Man"	Right End
Woody, Maurice "Woody"	Fullback

Menu

WHISTLE

ROASTED STANTON

SCALLOPED ODESSA — BROWNED COLORADO

MASHED ALPINE — CREAMED PECOS

SALTY SWEETWATER — STUFFED FT. STOCKTON

BUTTERED BULLDOGS

PERFECTION CHAMPIONS

BRICK SHIFLETT — ANGEL SEARCY

MINT KING

Program

Toastmaster	John Will Dorsey
To the Team	Barron Wadley
Response	Lynch King, Captain
To the Coaches	Alvie Strawn
Responses	D. D. Shiflett H. Clay Searcy, Jr.
To Our Superintendent	Ronald Morgan
Response	W. W. Lackey
To Our School Board	Henry Paddock
Response	Hon. B. Frank Haag
To the Pep Squad	D. W. Brunson
Response	Emily Flanigan
To Our Boosters	Rae Sowell
Response	Charles C. Watson

Announcement of Awards.

Music, interspersed.

Football was important in the public schools as well. The Midland High School football team had a great year in 1927, going undefeated and winning the bi-district championship over Sweetwater. No opponent scored more than six points on the team. Only the game with Odessa was close. The school celebrated with a special banquet. The meal selection included a humorous "menu" of defeated teams.

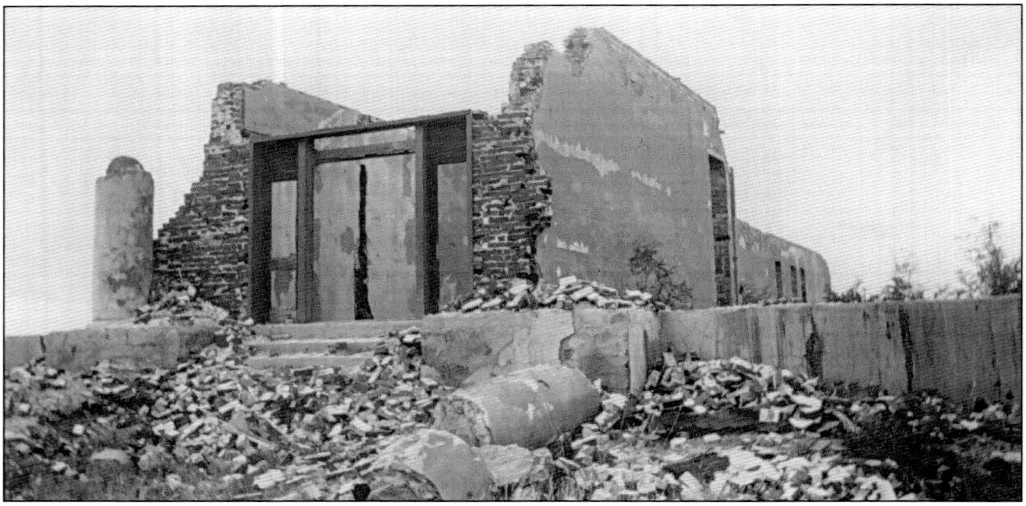

Haley, at his mother's urging, transferred to West Texas State at Canyon, Texas. The tough financial circumstances finally forced Midland Christian College to close it doors in the spring of 1921. The building fell into ruin. All that remains is a historical marker placed on the site in 1971. Midland would not have a college again until 1972, when Midland College was established as an independent junior college.

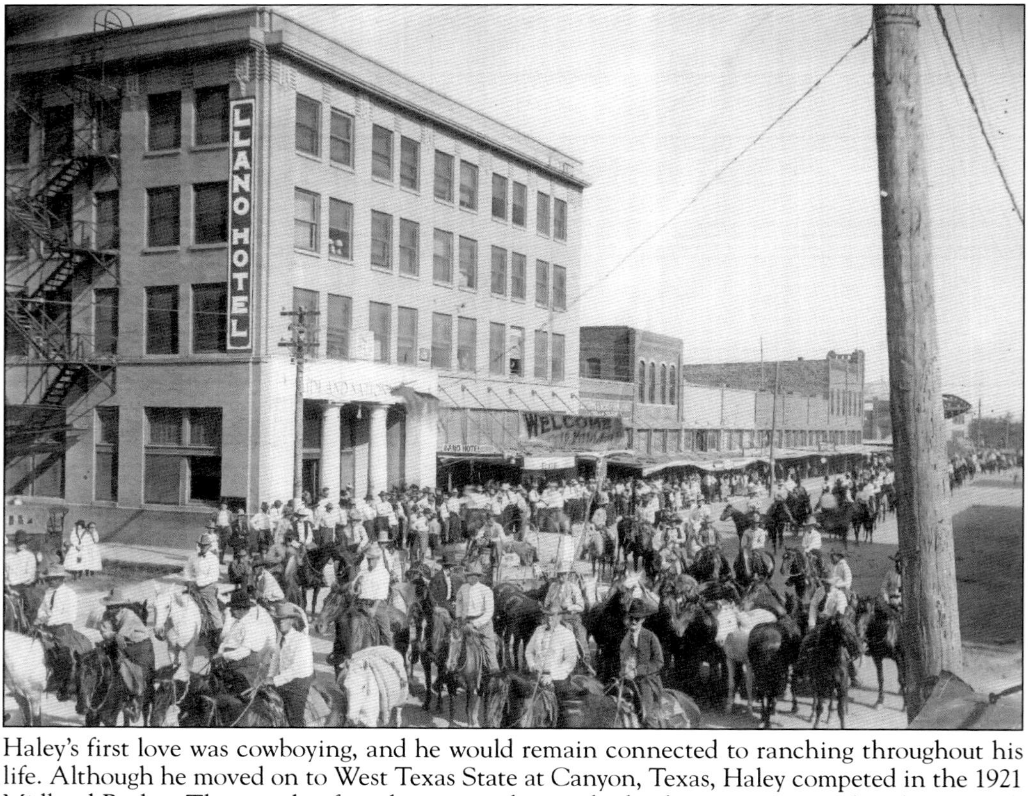

Haley's first love was cowboying, and he would remain connected to ranching throughout his life. Although he moved on to West Texas State at Canyon, Texas, Haley competed in the 1921 Midland Rodeo. The parade of cowboys, complete with chuck wagon, passes the Llano Hotel. (Courtesy of the Nita Stewart Haley Memorial Library, Midland, Texas.)

Many of the names in the old photographs are lost. This 1922 Rodeo program provides a list of several of the famous cowboys who thrilled audiences at the annual Rodeo and Barbecue. Some of the prominent names included are Foy Proctor, Spence Jowell, C. F. Cowden, Ellis Cowden, and Guy Cowden.

RODEO PROGRAM

TUESDAY, SEPTEMBER 5, 1922

10:30 a. m.—CALF BRANDING CONTEST. 1st prize, $100; 2nd, $75; 3rd, $50; 4th, $25. Following are the entries:

1 Elmer Jones
2 Ray Adams
3 Louis Jones
4 Young Lee
5 Foy Proctor
6 Porter Fancher
7 Aubrey Harrell
8 Ben Dublin
9 Ellis Cowden
10 Bert Weir
11 Roy Jennings
12 Jess Thorn
13 Jess York
14 Barney Hopkins
[illegible] B. Tinnin
16 Emmet Buck
17 Bob Crosby
18 Jim Coffey
19 Richard Merchant
20 Bill Wyche
21 Bill Gates
22 Geo. Daniels
23 Bill McCullough
24 John Collins
25 B. DeGraftenreid
26 Spence Jowell
27 Woody Tullous
28 J. V. O'Neal
29 Tom Sandifer
30 Robert White
31 Jess Moseley
32 Sam Kelton
33 John Ramsell
34 John Dublin
35 Myrl Dublin
36 Allen Holder
37 Add Eddins
38 C. F. Cowden
39 A. B. Cooksey
40 Doak Heard
41 Will Nix
42 Milt Good

Barbecue at Noon, Free to Everybody

1:00 p. m. BREAKAWAY CONTEST. 1st prize, $100; 2nd, $75; 3rd, $50; 4th, $25. Following are the entries:

1 Buck Bryant
2 B. DeGraftenreid
3 Allen Connell
4 Sam Kelton
5 John Ramsell
6 John Dublin
7 Myrl Jowell
8 Allen Holder
9 Add Eddins
10 C. F. Cowden
11 Ben Dunn
12 A. B. Cooksey
13 Will Nix
14 Geo. Daniels
15 Chas. King
16 Nay Styles
17 Elmer Jones
18 Frank Knight
19 A. B. Tinnin
20 Porter Foncher
21 Louis Jones
22 J. Ellis Cowden
23 Doak Heard
24 Bert Weir
25 Roy Jennings
26 Bob Crosby
27 Forest King
28 Louis Byers
29 Bill Van Huss
30 Guy Cowden
31 Young Lee
32 Aubrey Harrell
33 Kirby Nutt
34 [illegible] Buck
35 Bill Gates
36 Milt Good
37 Bug Means
38 John Collins
39 Jess Slaughter
40 Spencer Jowell
41 Woody Tullous
42 J. D. Christy
43 Rey Parks
44 Jim Coffey
45 Jess York
46 Ben Dublin
47 Barney Hopkins
48 Richard Merchant
49 Bill Wyche
50 Leslie Floyd
51
52 Lane Duprèe
53 Jess Moseley
54 D. Wilburn
55 Paschal Odom

2:00 p. m. STEER RIDING. 1st prize, $35; 2nd, $15; 3rd, $10. Entries to be announced.

3:00 p. m. BRONCO RIDING CONTEST. 1st prize, $50; 2nd, $30; 3rd, $20; $100 Saddle to highest average for the three days. Following entries:

1. Norman Woody on Sheler Lewis Sorrel.
2. Checker Bernard on Speckle Back.
3. Shag [illegible] on Schnaubert Horse.
4. Wildcat Bill on Rene Cocky.
5. Wilber Snyder on Bryant Blue
6. Arthur Schnaubert on Van Huss Brown.
7. Doke Heard on Bay H. Pony.
8. Billie Wyche on Bay H. Pony.
9. Fred Alvord on Bay Z X Pony.
10. Dodge Hammett on Scharbauer Horse.

Some things improved; among them was fire protection. In 1916, the Midland Fire Department replaced the hand-pull engine with their first fire truck. Ordered on December 29, 1916, from the La France Company, the truck arrived on June 22, 1917. The engine cost $5,800.

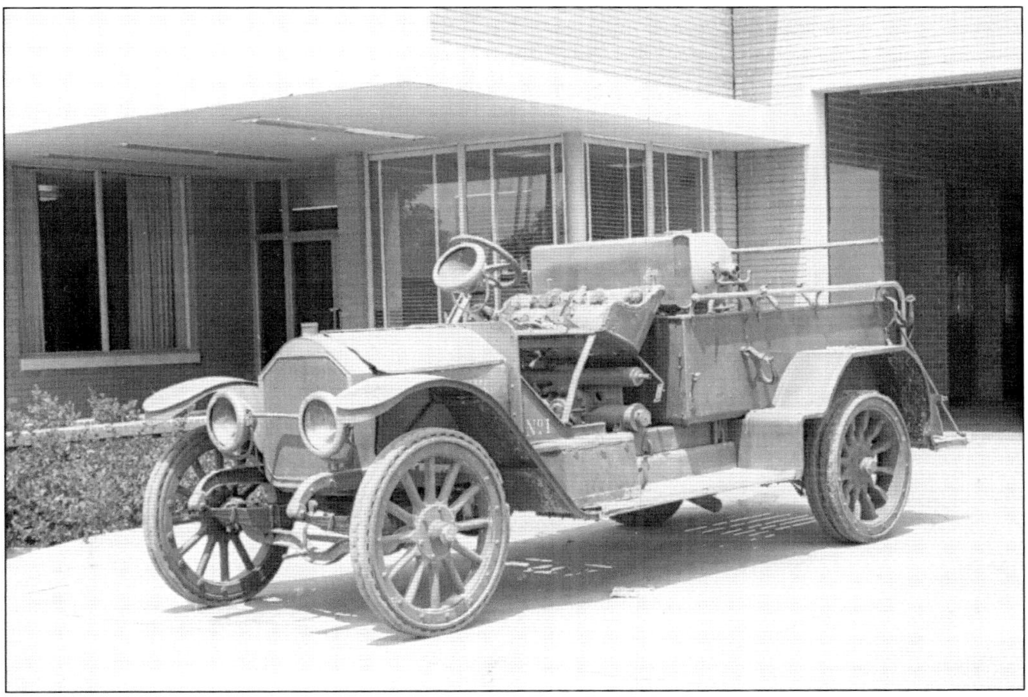

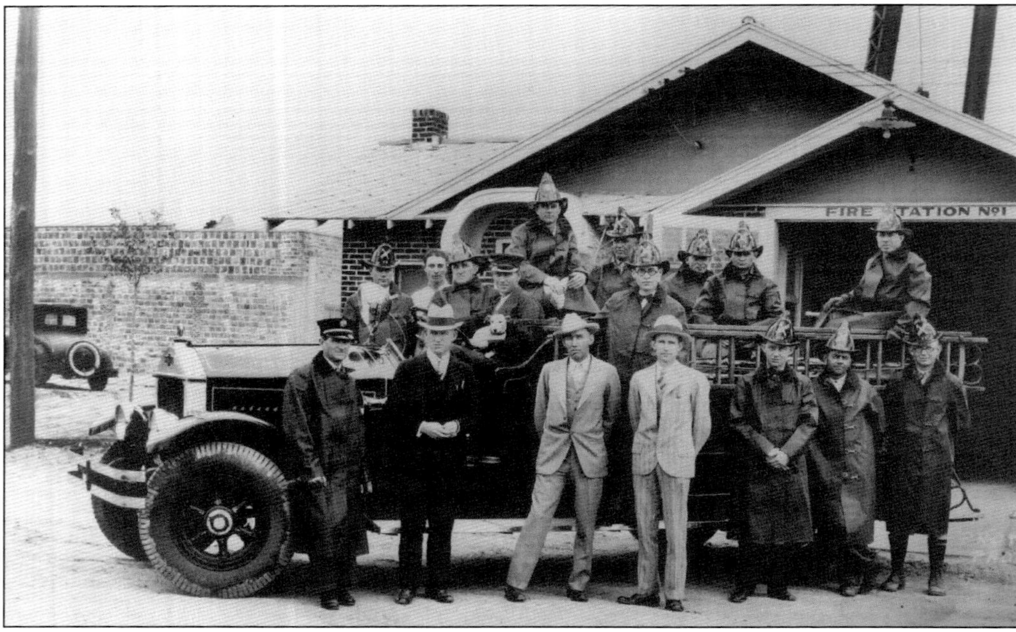

In 1928, the fire department purchased a new La France Fire Engine. It was christened Old No. Two. Those identified from the Old No. Two crew are, from left to right, (first row) Frank Prothro (fire chief), B. Frank Haag (mayor 1925–1929), A. J. Gates (city manager), J. C. Hudman (city secretary), Jerry Phillips, Goody Shroder, and Red Polier as well as other members of the Midland Volunteer Fire Department in the fire truck.

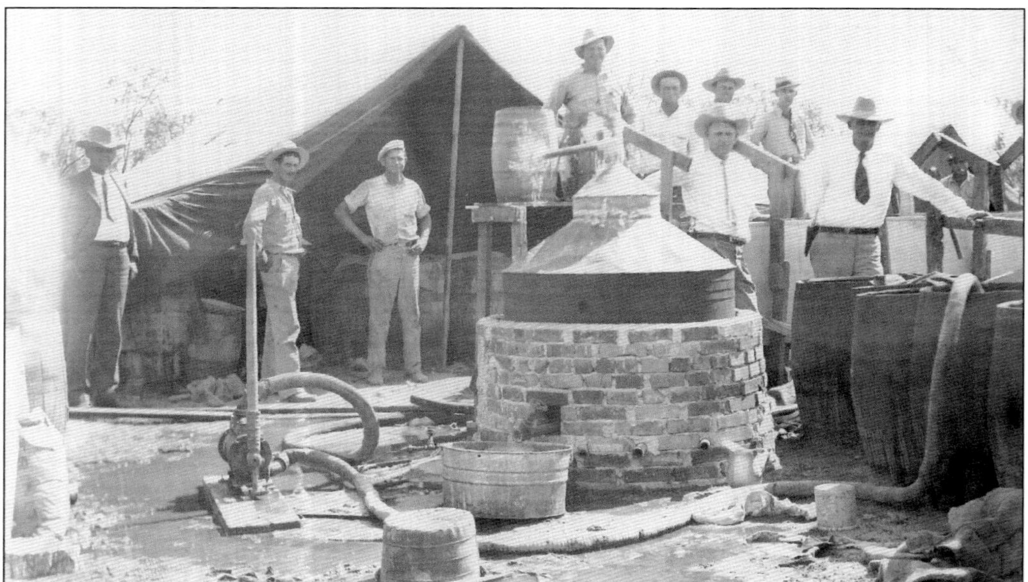

Some new problems emerged. Prohibition began after World War I. Though alcohol became illegal, demand did not completely cease and Midland was not immune to moonshiners. Sheriff Audie Francis (far left) and Bud Estes (far right) raided this whiskey still in 1923. Several still operations were shut down during the decade.

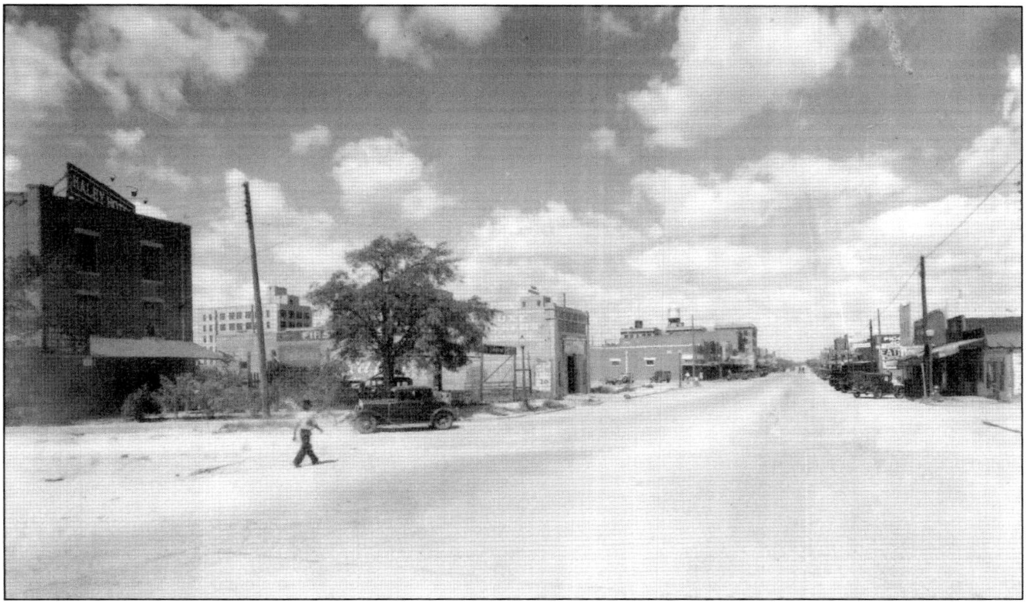

In the 1920s, oil brought the greatest changes to the Midland economy and skyline. While oil fields arose around the area, Midland County had no production. What it had was the ability to connect production, companies, and customers. Along with the railroad, Midland lay on the nation's first true interstate highway. In 1920, Texas Highway 1 became a segment of the Bankhead Highway from Washington, D.C., to San Diego, California. The "Broadway of America" linked Midland's Main Street (shown here in the late 1920s) to the rest of the nation.

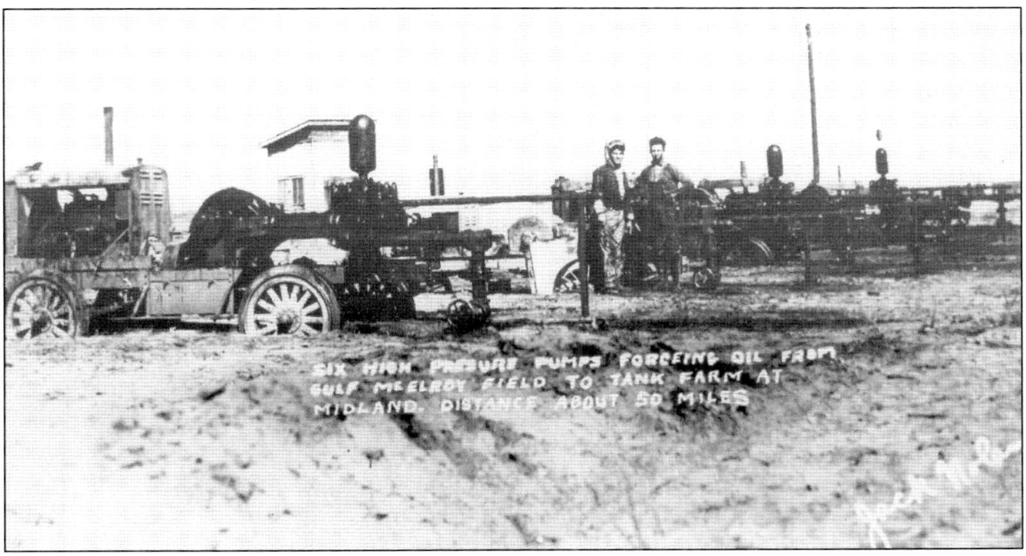

Oil production in the Permian Basin increased rapidly. In 1926, it reached 14 million barrels. The following year it was over 51 million. The Gulf Tank Farm provided a collection point for its Permian Basin fields. Their McElroy Field was southwest of Midland. Oil flowed to Midland through pipelines that formed a spidery network across the landscape. High-pressure pumps like these (seen here in 1926) pushed the oil to its destination. (Courtesy of the Permian Historical Society Archives.)

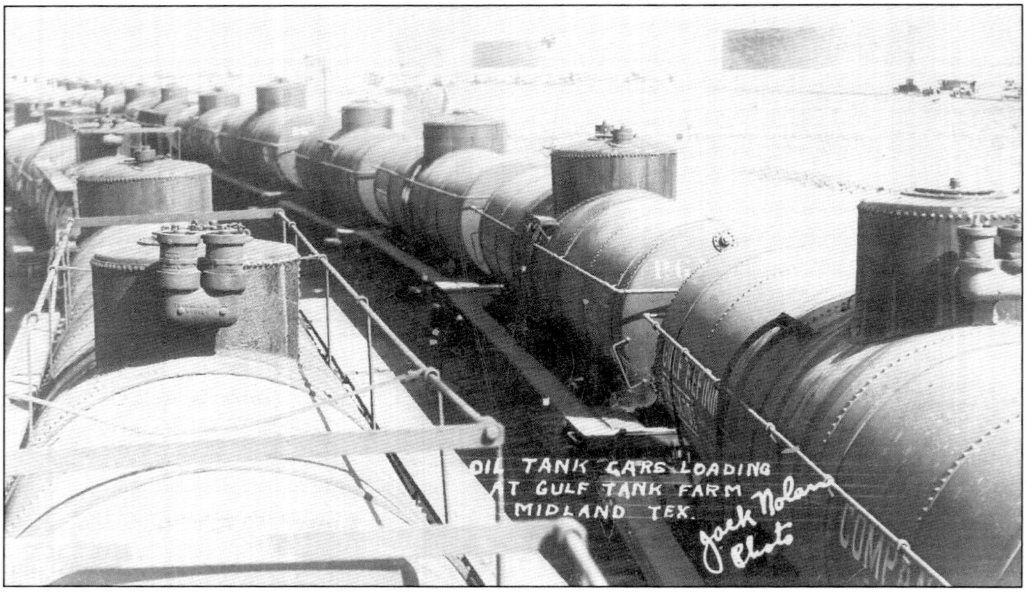

Oil arrived at the large metal tank facilities in Midland to be held until it was loaded into railroad cars and shipped east to refineries. The refined products provided fuel for the rapidly growing automobile industry. Some of these products returned to Midland to help drive further exploration and development. (Courtesy of the Permian Historical Society Archives.)

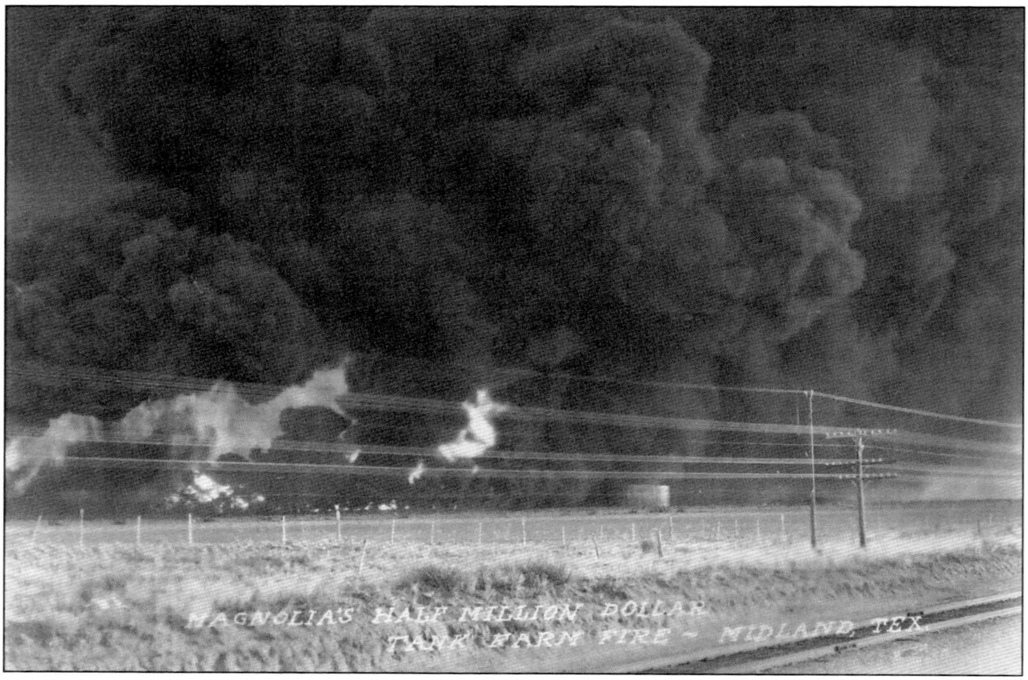

Not all oil projects moved smoothly. On August 17, 1928, a major fire damaged the Magnolia Tank Farm, captured in this photograph. The next month, Magnolia began construction on five new storage tanks. In January 1929, a boiler explosion rocked the tank farm, resulting in several injuries and deaths.

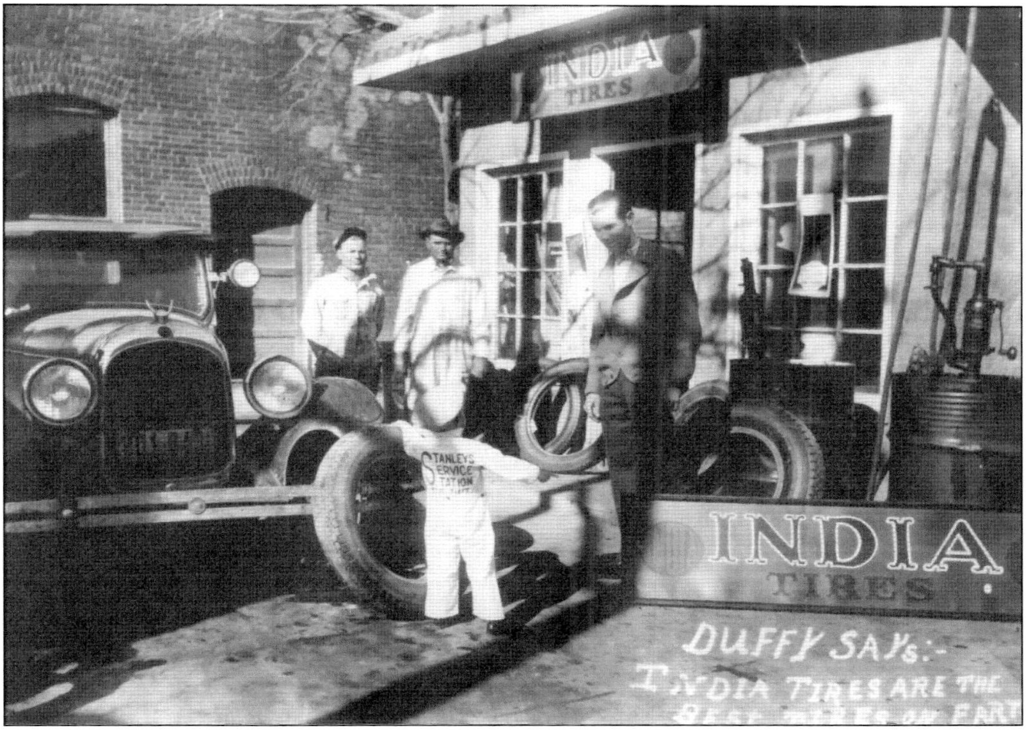

Several oil companies had offices in Midland by 1927. Gulf was the first to establish a district office, followed by Tidal Oil and independent contractors Gibson and Johnson. That same year, Midland's first service station opened. The Ever Ready Filling Station located at the corner of Wall and Colorado Streets provided gasoline and service to local customers and travelers on the Bankhead Highway. The caption on this postcard reads as follows: "Duffy says India Tires are the best tires on earth."

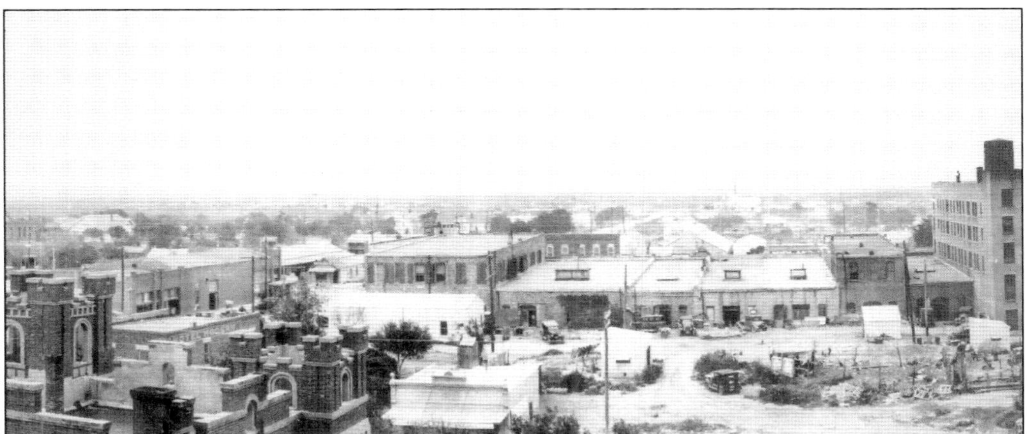

A July 1, 1927, article in the *Midland Reporter and Gazette* enumerated "four big sources of income" that made Midland "business good." These included cattle, farming, and tourist traffic. The fourth—oil—would benefit from providing hotel facilities, offices, and various luxuries and necessities. An aggressive construction program began. A 1927 panorama begins with a view of North Main Street, which shows little change.

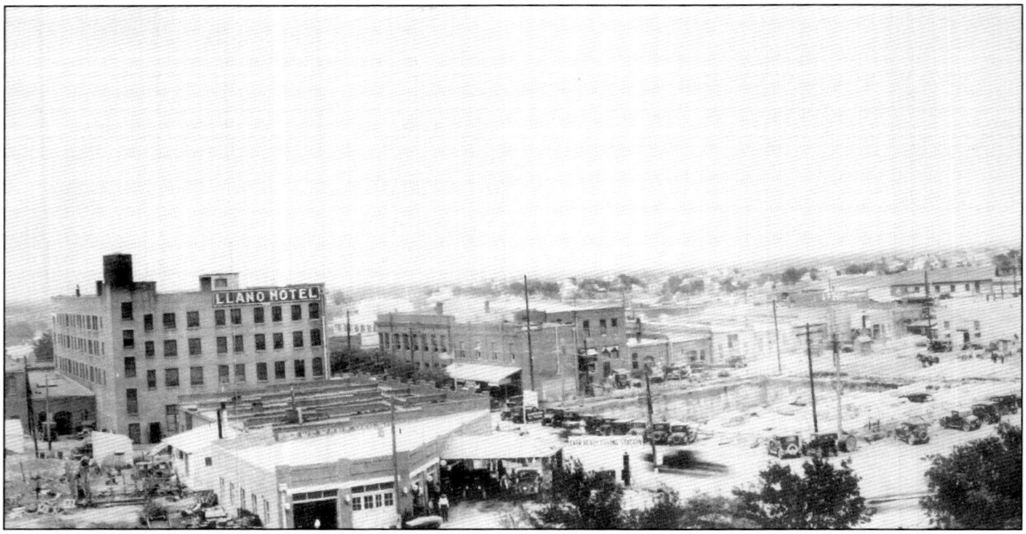

As the photographer from atop the courthouse panned toward the west, the changes became more evident. The Llano Hotel remains a prominent landmark. A large hole in the center marks the beginnings of the Scharbauer Hotel, a $200,000 project begun by Clarence Scharbauer. The hotel would stand six stories high and contain 150 rooms. In 1930, the hotel added a 100-room wing.

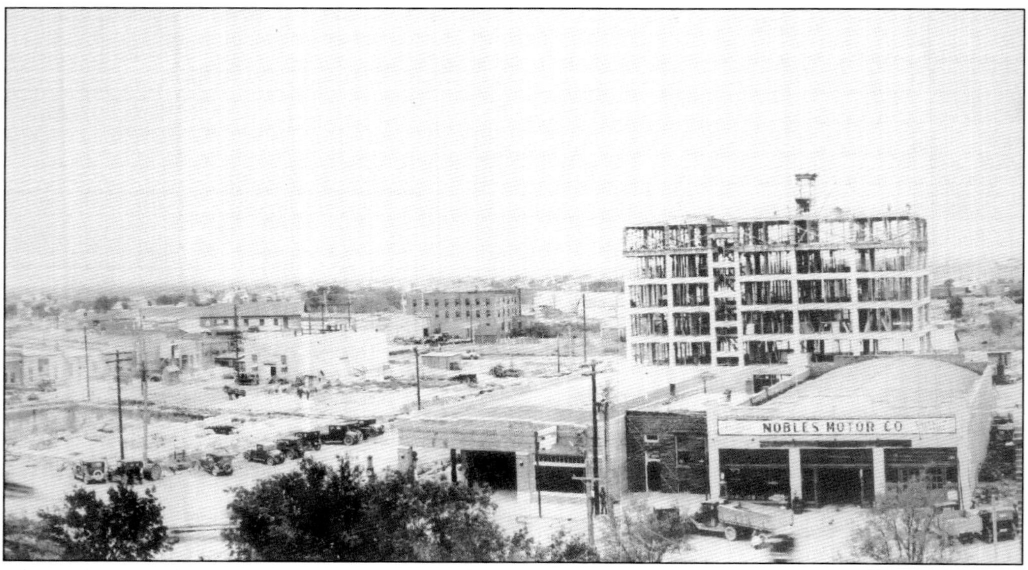

The right end of the panorama shows the skeleton of the Thomas Building. Dr. John Thomas, who had come to Midland in 1905, erected this six-story structure with a 25-bed hospital on the top floor. Thomas reported that oil-related businessmen had leased "every square inch of the building since the blueprints were drawn."

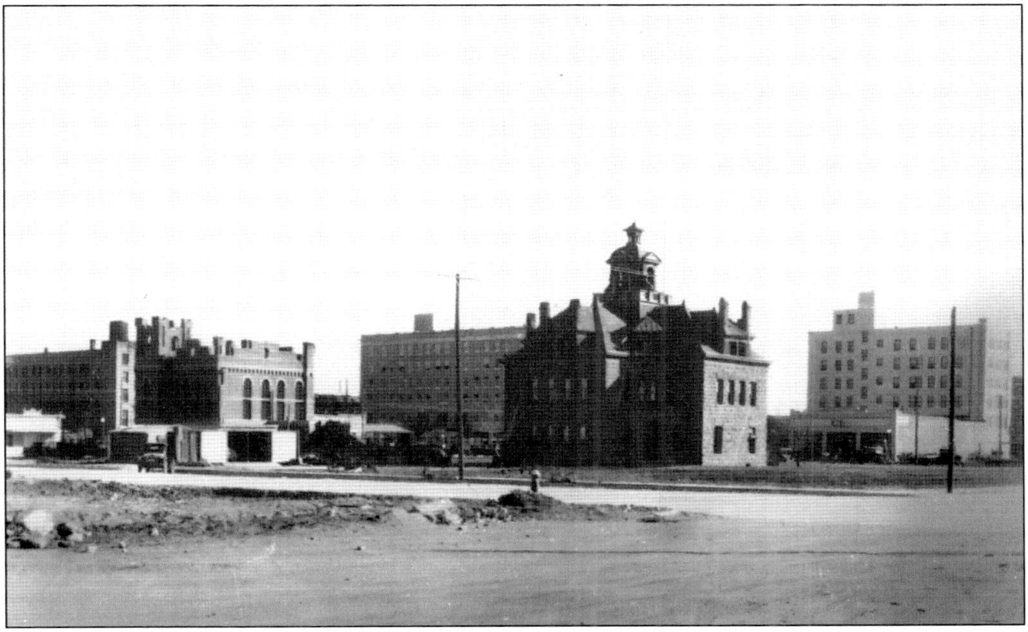

Midland was well into a new growth phase. On a single day in April 1928, a Lions Club formally organized, a Rotary Club received a new charter, and the Midland Chamber of Commerce held a meeting to elect new officers and directors. The new Scharbauer and Thomas Buildings dwarfed the courthouse, seen here from the north. The aerial view (see page 2) was even more dramatic, yet the biggest project was yet to come.

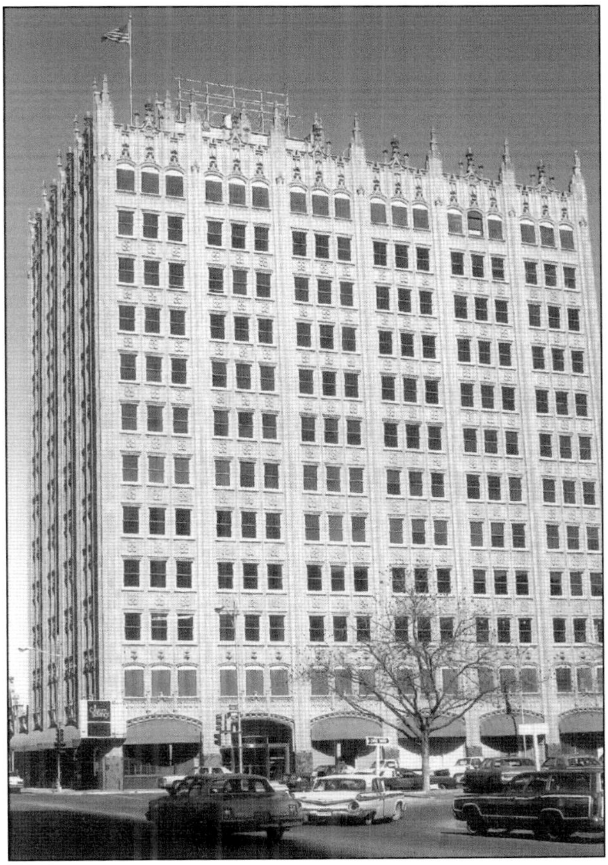

On Christmas Day 1927, T. S. Hogan, an oil operator and former Montana senator, announced plans to erect a 12-story office building. Quickly dubbed "Hogan's Folly," the Petroleum Building opened for business on July 5, 1929. Prominent Fort Worth architect Wyatt C. Hedrick designed the building with crenulated spires and decorative stonework. Though it would remain nearly empty in the early 1930s with hay stored on the lower floors, Hogan's vision would triumph. Seen at right in the 1960s, it remains a Midland landmark today.

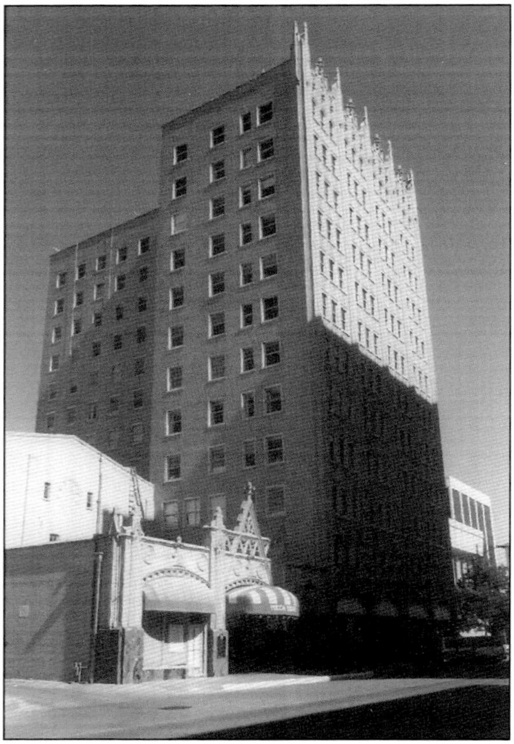

Hogan's creation became the tallest building between Fort Worth and El Paso. When it opened in 1929, it was grander and more ornate than anything in Midland and easily accommodated the 54 oil companies that had representatives in town. The building also achieved another distinction when the cut-sandstone and black marble Yucca Theater (shown here as it appears today) was added to the north side of the Petroleum Building.

H. B. Layman of New York designed the Yucca's interior. It required two years to complete. The style was Assyrian architecture. The interior had gilded lions, reliefs of winged bulls, ornate columns, and elaborate light fixtures. In 1928, Hogan told the *Midland Reporter*, "It is not enough to offer prospective citizens brick and stone. The spirit too must be fed. It must be surrounded by beauty."

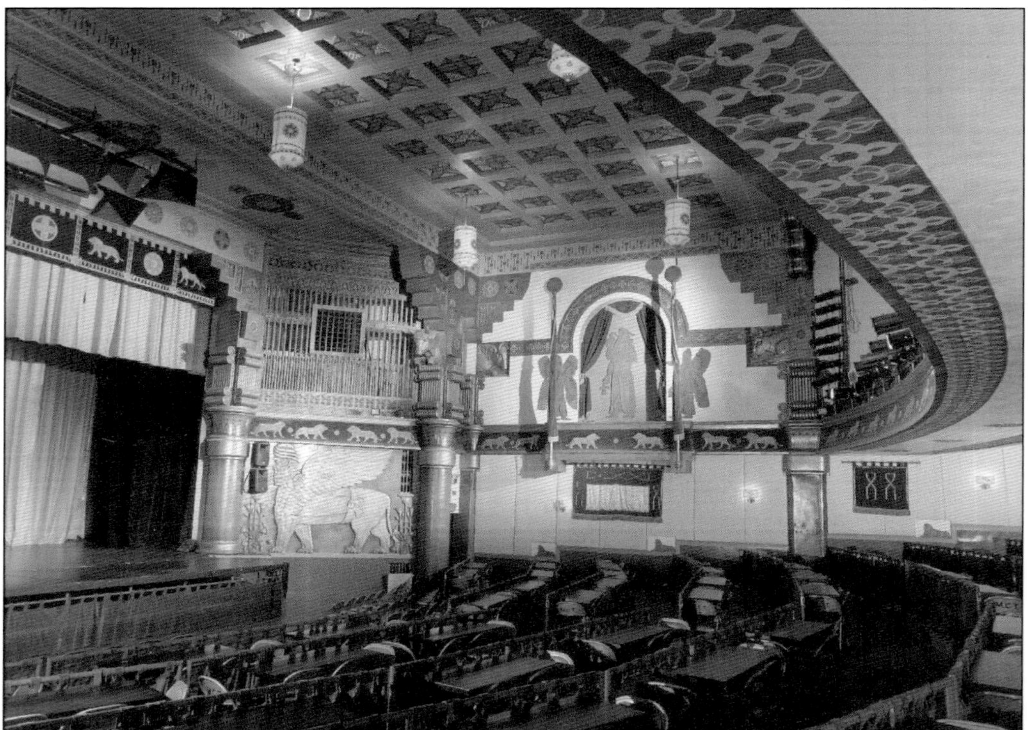

The Yucca began as a vaudeville and musical theater house. The opening night program on December 5, 1929, included a "deluxe stage presentation" with 10 acts and a "rambling stage band." The feature film was *Rio Rita*, an "all talking, all singing, musical spectacle." The next night was a midnight premiere of Mack Sennett's first talking feature. The Yucca remained open during the Depression years, even when the Hogan Building held only cotton and hay.

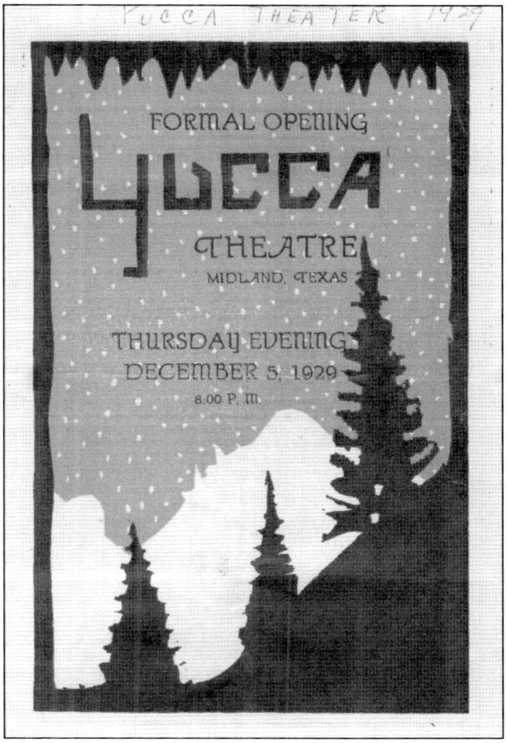

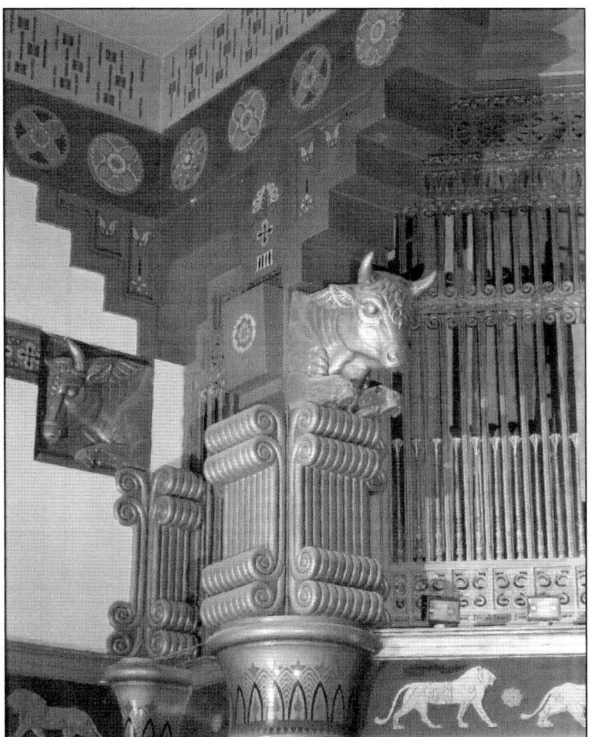

Advertisements declared the Yucca to be "the pride of the Southwest and the largest all purpose theater between Fort Worth and El Paso. All programs presented in this theater will be synchronized sound, music and talking, reproduced over RCA Photophone major reproducing and projection equipment." The Yucca Theatre was closed as a movie theater in 1974. It was restored in 1981 and is now used for live performances, operated by the Summer Mummers.

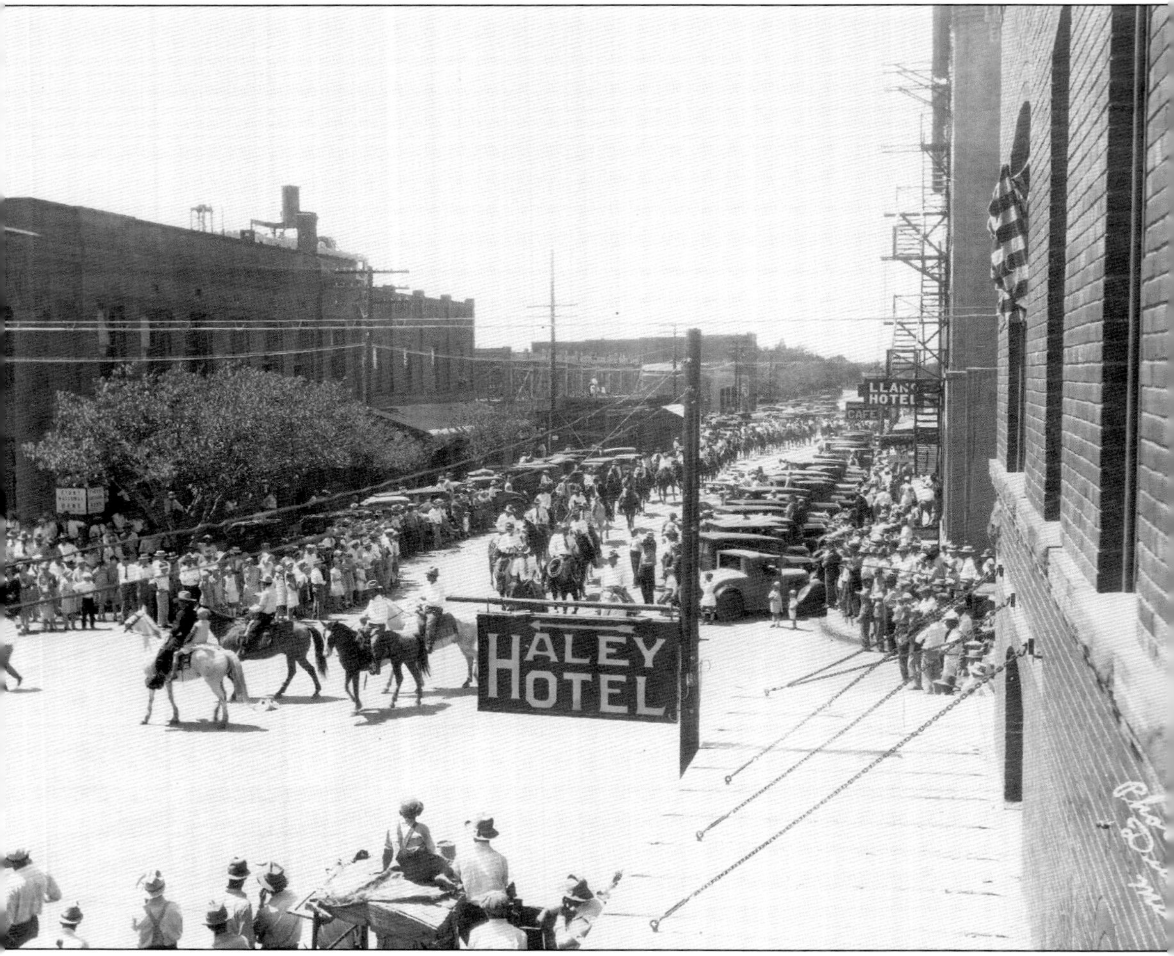

This c. 1927 parade photograph captures the spirit of 1920s Midland, still linked to western roots but at the beginning of the petroleum industry that will redefine it forever. A line of horsemen winds from the west, and somewhere behind them is the deserted campus of Midland College. They turn south onto Main Street, a sign pointing toward the Haley Hotel. To their left on Wall Street, the Scharbauer Hotel rises. The top of the Thomas Building can be seen behind it.

Four

Tough Times in Depression and War

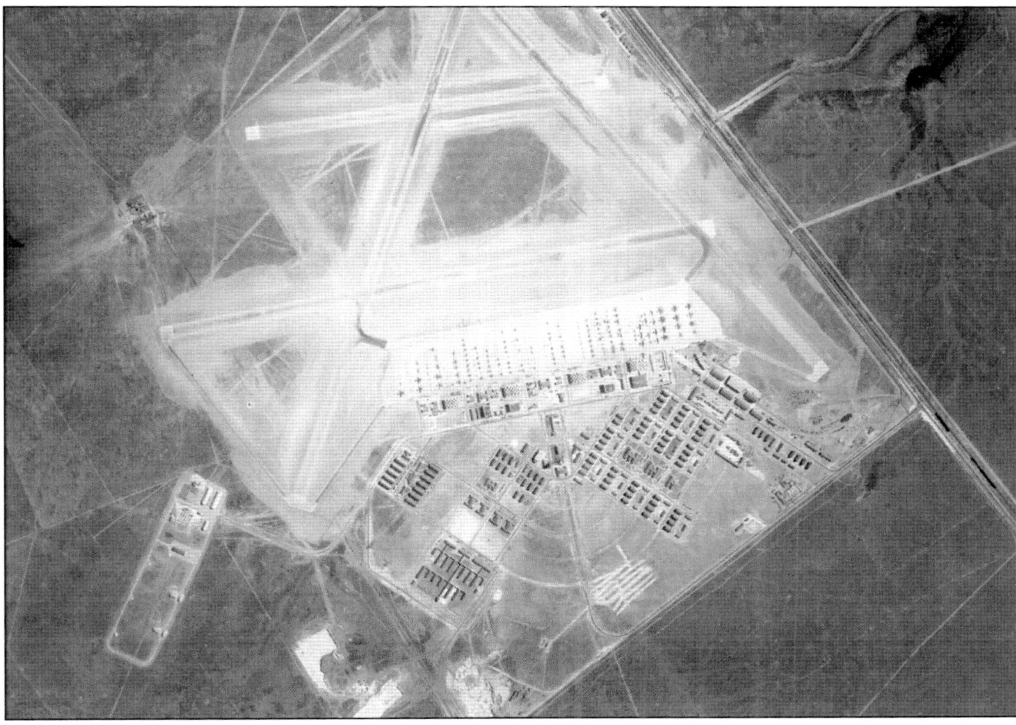

Midland was not immune to the struggles the United States faced in the 1930s and 1940s, but its location again provided the town with unique opportunities. Demand for petroleum continued to rise, especially as war loomed. In addition, Midland's remoteness, the open terrain, and a good airport presented a special wartime prospect as revealed in this 1942 classified photograph of the Midland Army Air Field. (Courtesy of the Permian Historical Society Archives.)

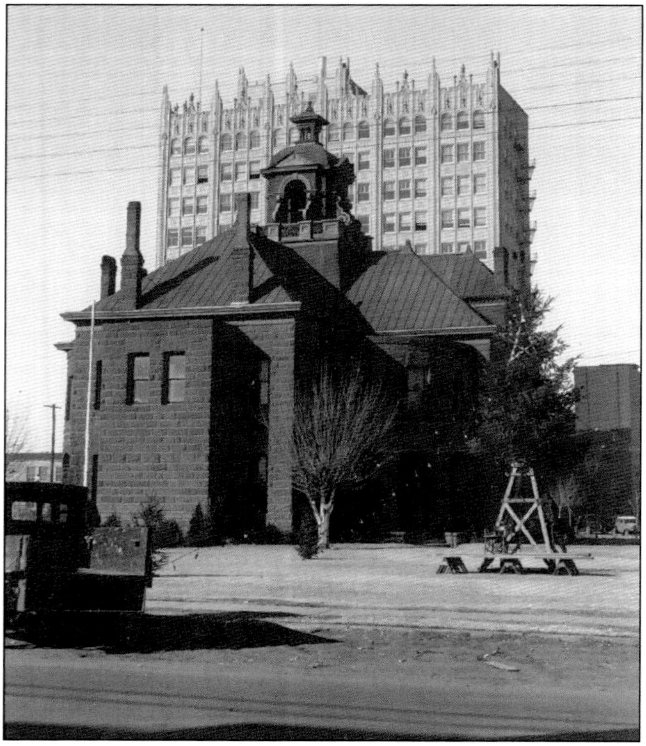

By 1930, Midland had grown to over 5,000 people. The city had a new country club, a new library, and a new theater group—the Midland Players. In the still flush times of the late 1920s, the old courthouse appeared small in the shadow of the new Hogan Building. People were ready for something grander. Bonds for a new courthouse passed almost two to one in September 1929.

In December 1929, county commissioners sold the red sandstone courthouse building for $1—a fact that made *Ripley's Believe It Or Not*. Dr. John Thomas built his home on Colorado Street (seen below) from the courthouse stones.

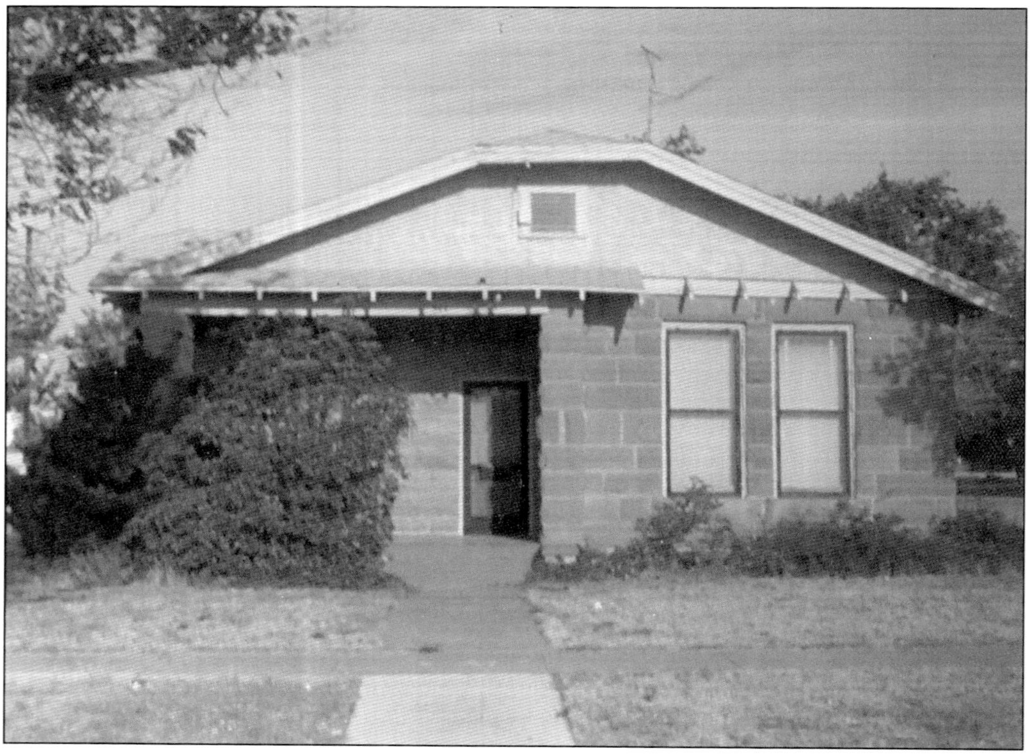

By the date of this photograph, December 14, 1930, a new impressive art deco courthouse stood on Wall Street. Hard times followed, as the Great Depression deepened and East Texas oil flooded the market, dropping the price of West Texas crude to 10¢ a barrel. T. S. Hogan eventually lost his building. Midlanders pulled together to help one another as much as possible before seeking federal aid.

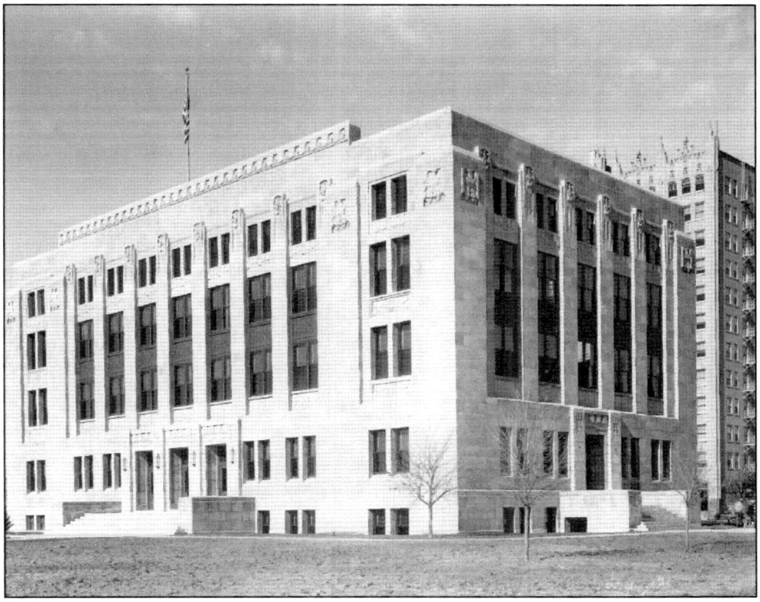

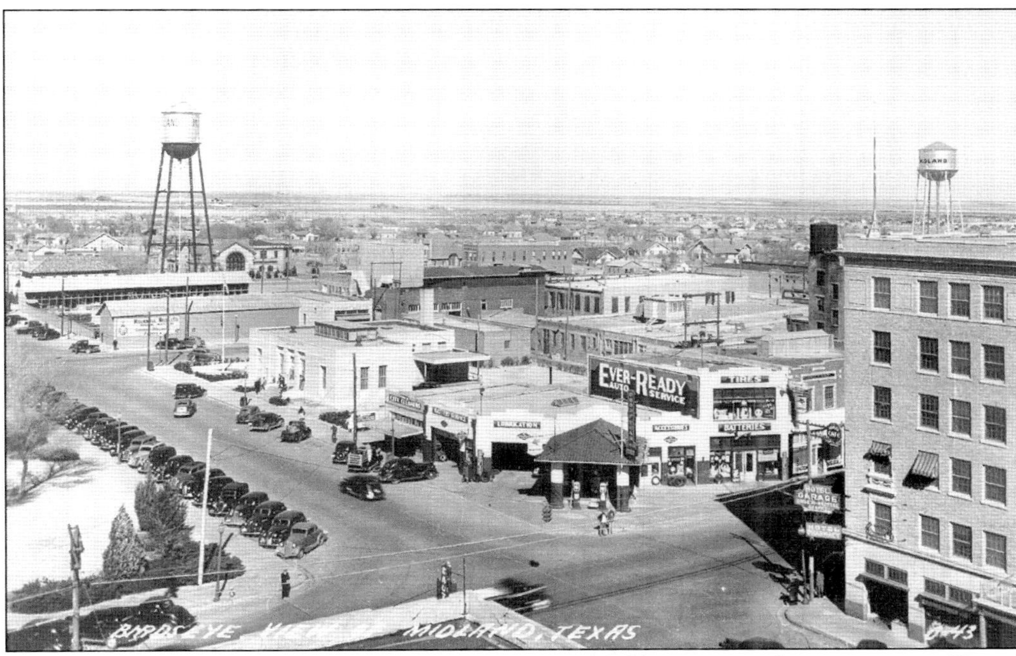

The Midland economy revived by the mid-1930s. New oil fields in surrounding counties reaffirmed the Permian Basin's status as a major oil-producing region. In 1935, local leaders persuaded Humble Oil Company to relocate area operations to the Petroleum Building's 10th floor. Humble loaded over 70 employee houses on trucks and moved them from the McCamey Camp to Midland. This image from the late 1930s or early 1940s captures the busy nature of downtown in these years.

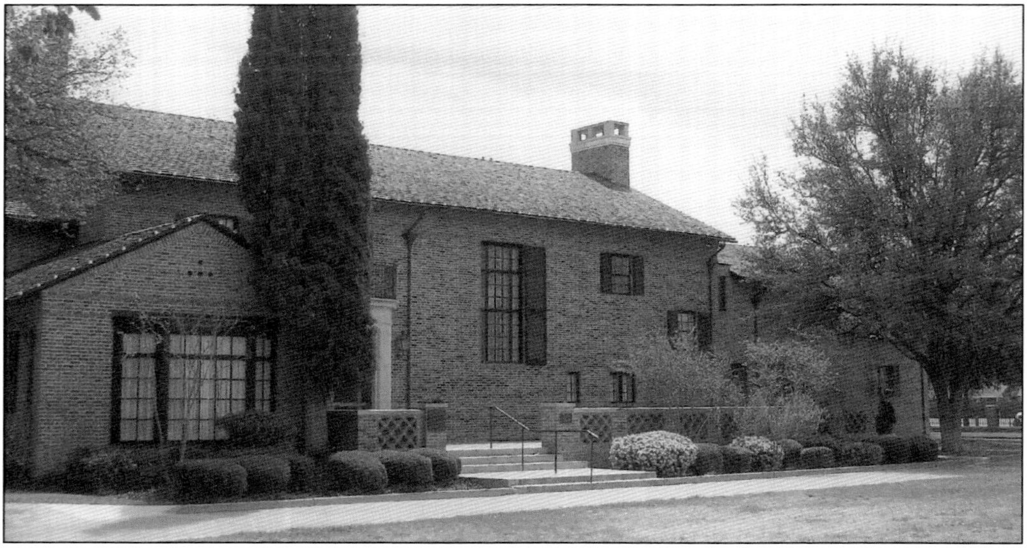

In 1937, Fred Turner completed a home in Midland's new West End addition. Turner, an oil scout turned independent operator, won drilling rights in the Yates Oil Field in a court case that reached the Texas Supreme Court in 1933. In May 1934, "The Fred Turner Jr. No. 1" oil well was completed with an estimated potential of 152,000 barrels a day. Turner and his family moved from a small two-bedroom home to this two-story brick mansion built by Dallas architect Anton Korn. The Eclectic Movement–style home reflects elements of Colonial Revival, Tudor, and Mediterranean styles. (Photograph by author.)

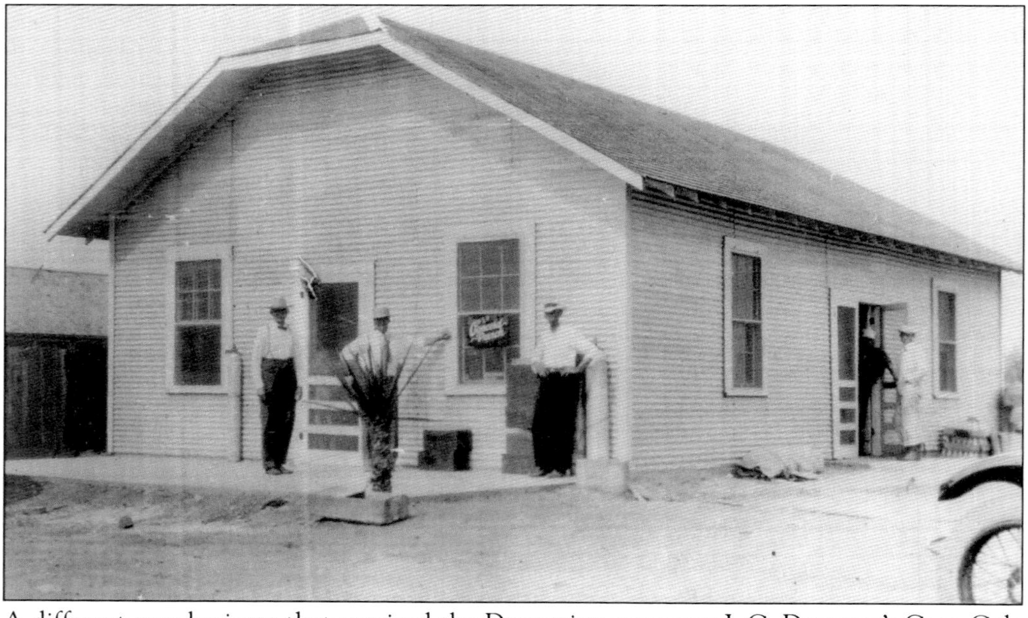

A different area business that survived the Depression years was J. C. Dunagan's Coca-Cola Bottling Company. In 1926, Dunagan established the Midland Bottling Company. The following year, he built a plant in Monahans and, in 1929, added a third in McCamey. Pictured in front of the Midland office are C. B. Dunagan (left), father of John Dunagan, and John C. Dunagan (right). (Courtesy of the Permian Historical Society Archives.)

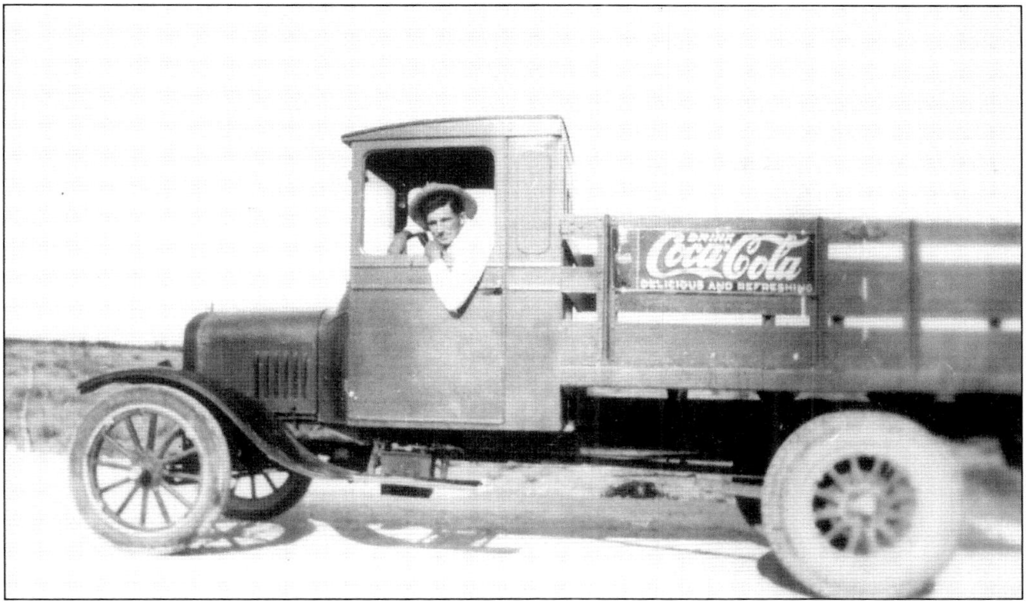

Dunagan's Coca-Cola trucks became a familiar site around the area. This postcard depicts an unidentified driver in an older truck on a dusty West Texas road sometime around 1932. The Midland Bottling Company supplied the city as well. At its opening of *Gone With the Wind*, the Yucca Theater advertised that, for the first time, patrons could buy Coca-Cola with crushed ice in the lobby. (Courtesy of the Permian Historical Society Archives.)

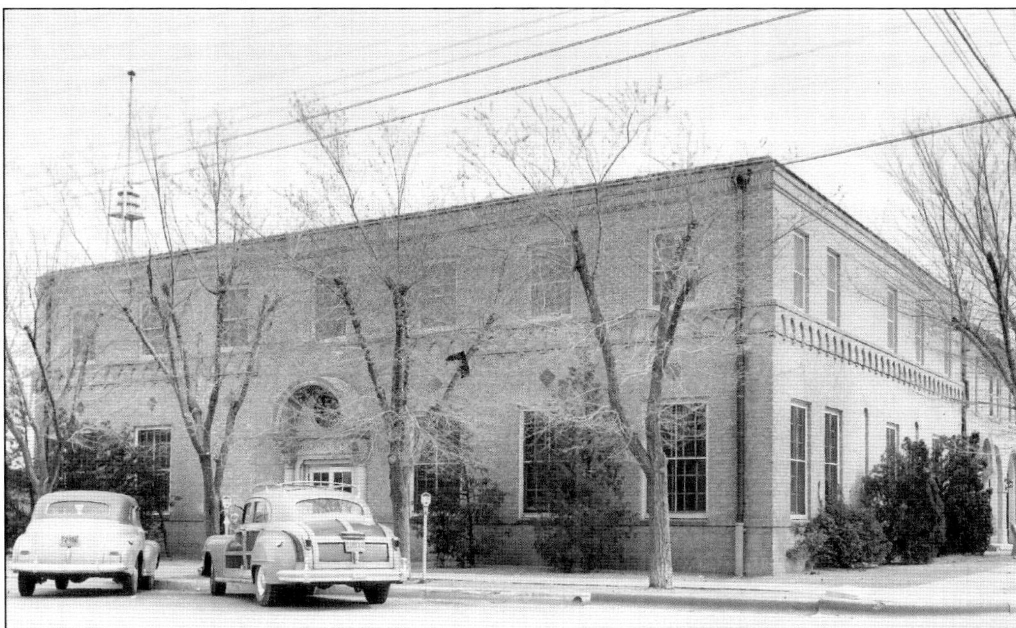

The City of Midland also constructed new offices in these years. On November 12, 1929, the cornerstone was laid for a new city hall building at the corner of Illinois and Lorraine Streets. This building (pictured in the 1940s) served as city hall for 35 years.

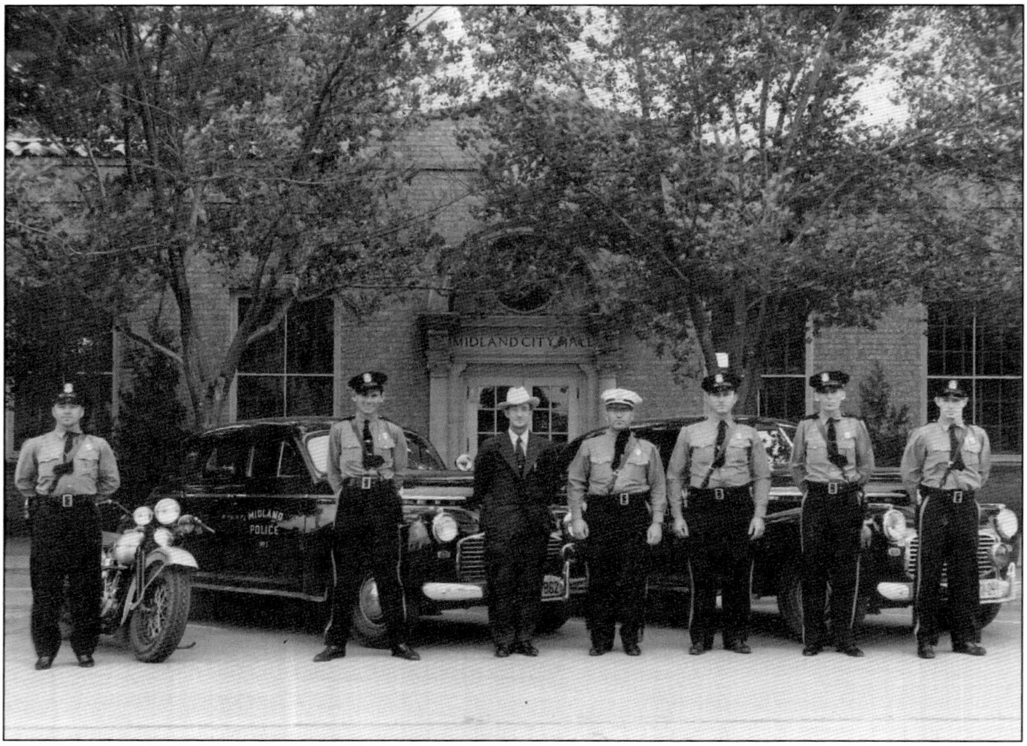

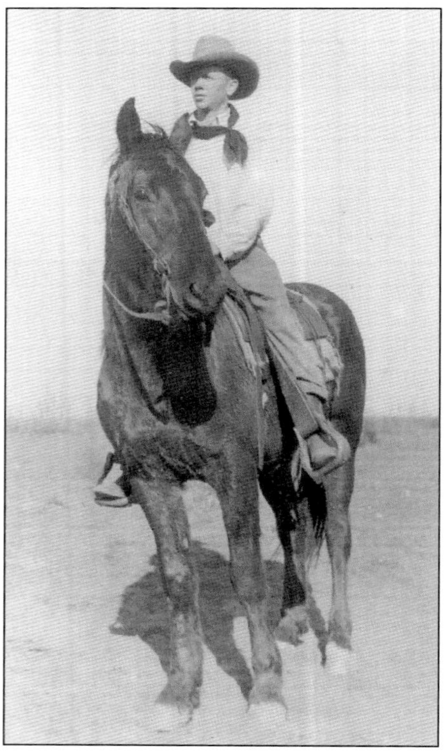

The police force grew along with the expanding city. Police officers on April 1, 1941, included, from left to right, Frank Manning, W. C. Durham, Bill Moreland, Mac McCaslin, Glen Hudson, Jake Merritt, and Charlie Adkins.

Ranching remained important in the local economy but also saw tough years. One young cattleman, J. Evetts Haley (shown here around 1923), became a chronicler of ranching on the plains. After Midland College, Haley attended West Texas State in Canyon. Graduating in 1925, he worked for the Panhandle Plains Historical Museum collecting artifacts and reminiscences. In 1929, *The XIT Ranch of Texas* launched his historical career, followed by *Charles Goodnight: Cowman and Plainsman* in 1936. Throughout his life, Haley remained a working cattleman. (Courtesy of the Nita Stewart Haley Memorial Library, Midland, Texas.)

In 1933, Evelyn Scarborough married Tom Lineberry, a young man who operated the elevator in the Petroleum Building, in a wedding at the "Big House" in Midland. The daughter of early-day rancher W. F. Scarborough, Evelyn received her bachelor's degree from the first graduating class of Texas Tech in Lubbock. When her father died unexpectedly in 1939, the young couple inherited the 45,000-acre Frying Pan Ranch with a large debt. They worked "shoulder to shoulder" until they retired that debt in 1950.

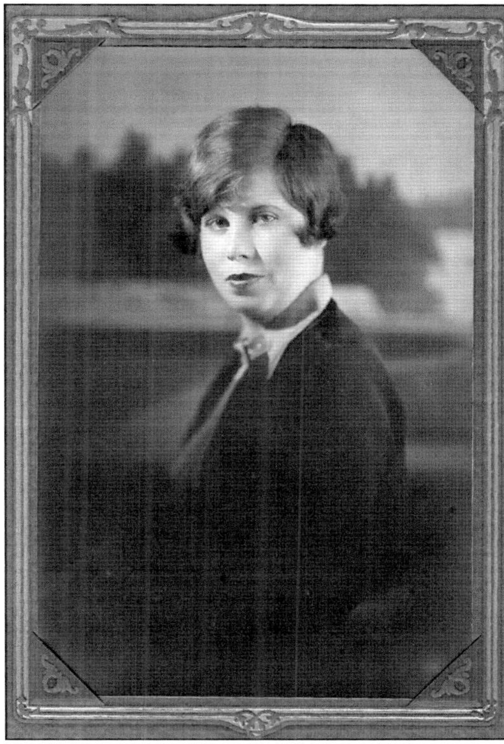

Even in hard times, business went on, and in the West, a good pair of boots helped define the measure of a man. Friday's Boot Shop (shown here around 1937) operated on west Wall Street, across from the Scharbauer Hotel. From left to right are George Friday, Horace Friday, unidentified, Bob Lee, Durward Friday, Earl Kinsey, Fred Jones, Dick Jones, and Clint Jefferson.

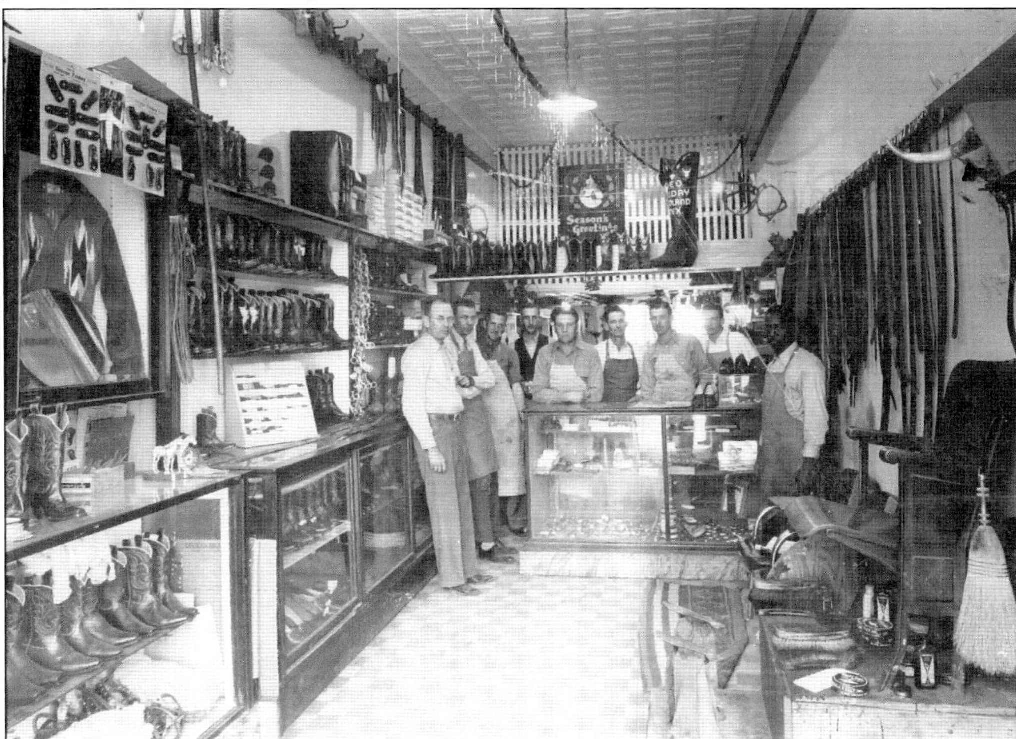

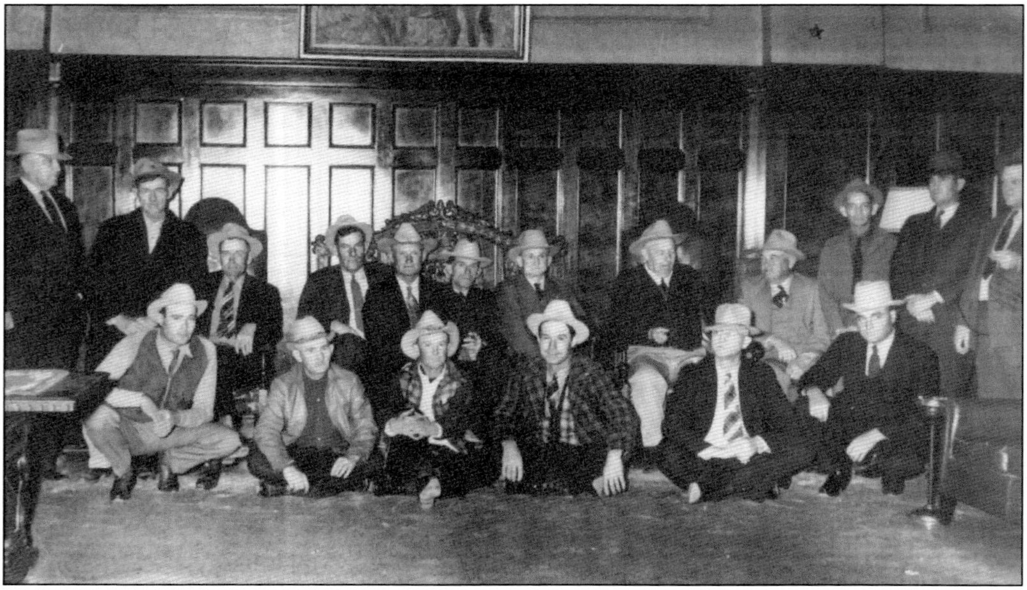

Rodeos continued as big annual events in Midland. In this 1939 photograph, titled "Rodeo Time," several prominent Midland figures pose in the lobby of the Scharbauer Hotel. Pictured are, from left to right, (first row) Clay Floyd, Claude Cowden, Gene Harwell, L. E. Cook, Ed Dozier, and H. H. Castleberry; (second row) Sam Preston, Will Wesson, Lewis Beyer, A. B. Stickney, J. H. Underwood, Young Lee, Charles Allen, Ollie King, Spencer Jowell, C. A. McClintic, R. B. Cowden, and Clyde Cowden.

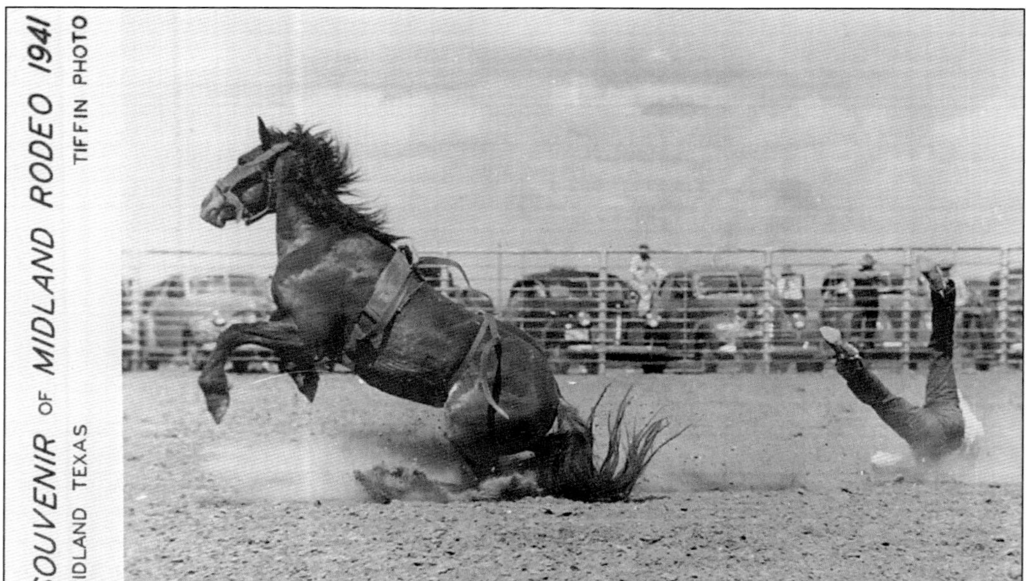

This souvenir postcard for the 1941 rodeo was an award-winning picture. Photographer L. H. Tiffin took this action shot during the 1940 rodeo. It was named as one of the Associated Press's best pictures of the year.

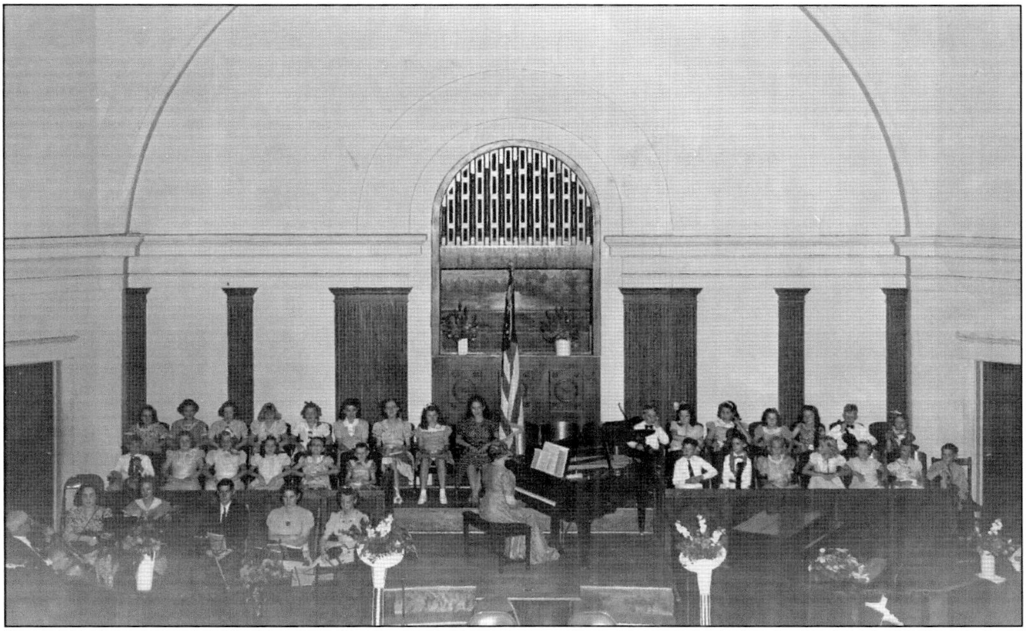

Even as America edged closer to war, other social and cultural events continued. The Watson School of Music held a recital at the First Baptist Church on June 6, 1941. Three years later, June 6 would earn lasting distinction as D-Day. A year earlier, Midland had already joined the nation's preparedness effort as it became increasingly clear the United States could not avoid entering World War II.

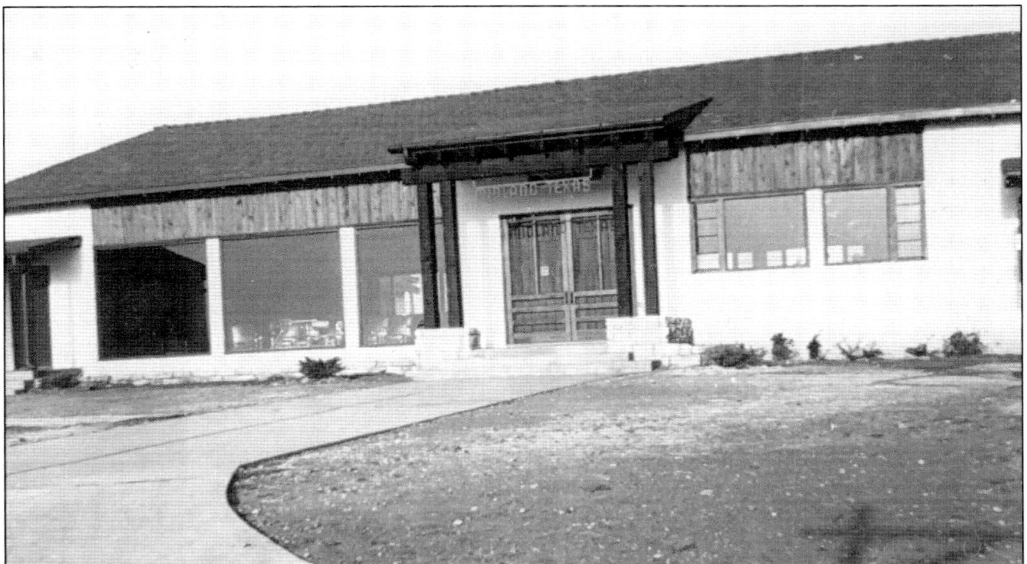

In 1927, oilman Samuel Addison Sloan created a small airport midway between Midland and Odessa on 220 acres leased from Clarence Scharbauer. After Samuel died in a plane crash, his brother, William, continued to operate Sloan Field. The city of Midland purchased the airfield on July 1, 1939, for $14,500. By that time, the Army Air Corps Flying Cadets used the field as a routine stop on cross-country training flights. This undated photograph shows the old terminal building.

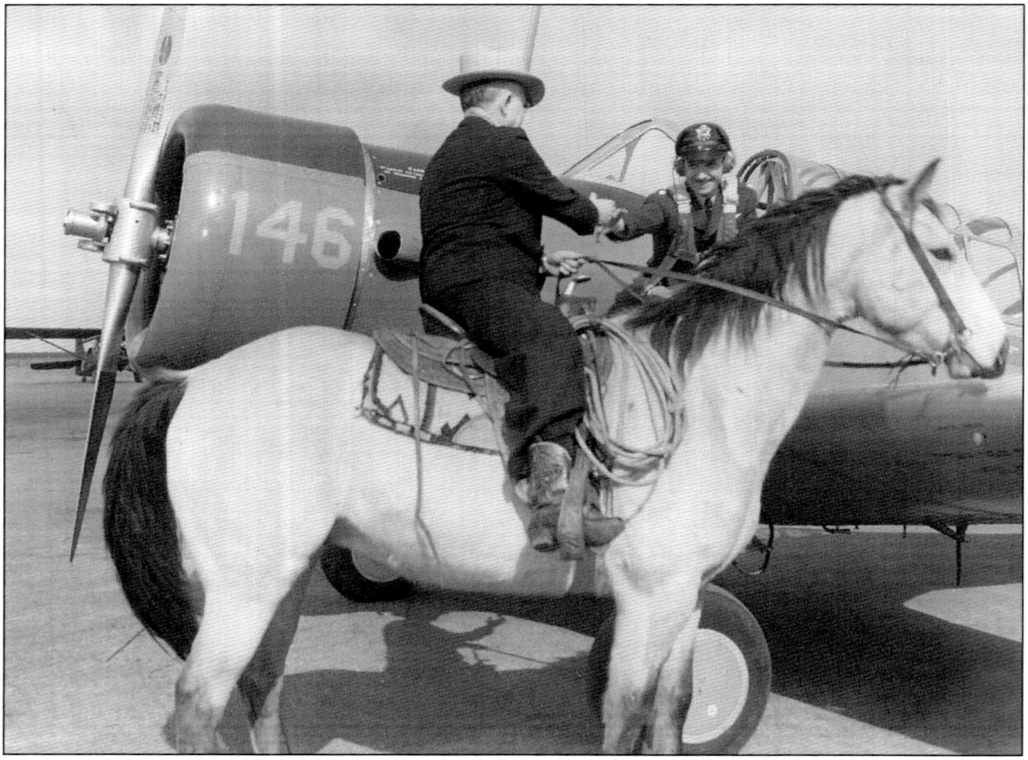

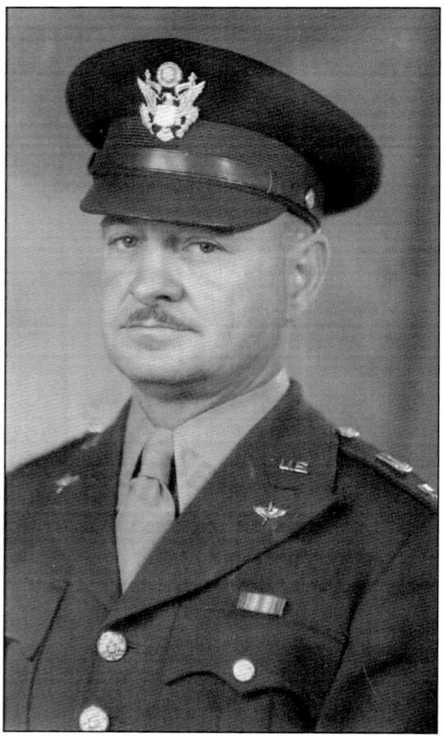

Several prominent Midlanders, including Marvin C. Ulmer, mayor and president of First National Bank, and Bill Collyns, Midland Chamber of Commerce manager, initiated a campaign to establish a military base at the airport. An additional 450 acres acquired from Clarence Scharbauer and over $150,000 in improvements created an attractive package. In June 1941, the federal government leased the airport for a $1 a year. Pictured above, Mayor Ulmer, mounted on one of Clarence Scharbauer's horses, greets Col. Isaiah Davies, first commanding officer of Midland Army Air Field, upon his arrival in November 1942.

Following his World War I service, George McCormick returned to Midland, where he worked as purchasing agent and city manager. With the outbreak of World War II, McCormick returned to active duty and served as an officer at the Midland base. He was a captain there at the time this photograph was taken in November 1942. He later served in England as a major with the 8th Air Force Reconnaissance Group.

The flat terrain and frequently clear skies provided optimum conditions for a bombardier training school. Soldiers would receive instruction and practice in accurately aiming and releasing bombs during large-scale aerial attacks on the Axis powers. As the use of bombardiers was a new military strategy, the Midland Army Field played a significant role in its development. A field manual (cover shown here) was issued each year of the base's operation (1941–1946). The photograph shows the primary training plane, the Cessna Advanced Trainer (AT) 11, on the flight line. (Courtesy of the Permian Historical Society Archives.)

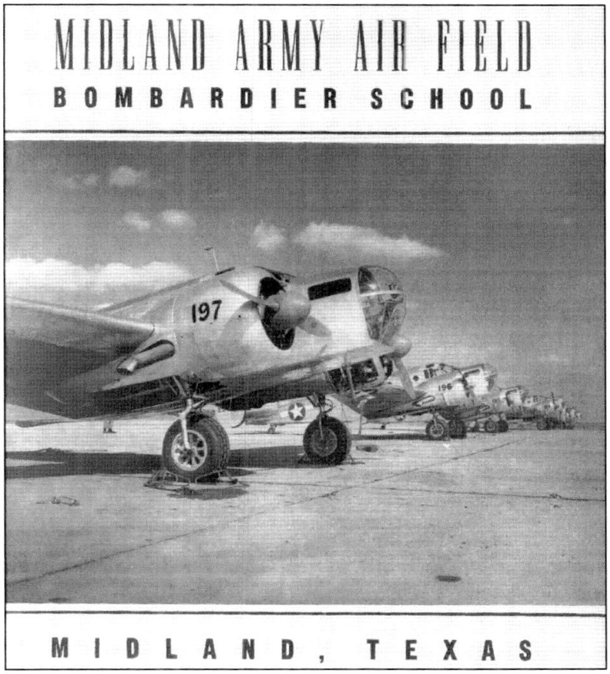

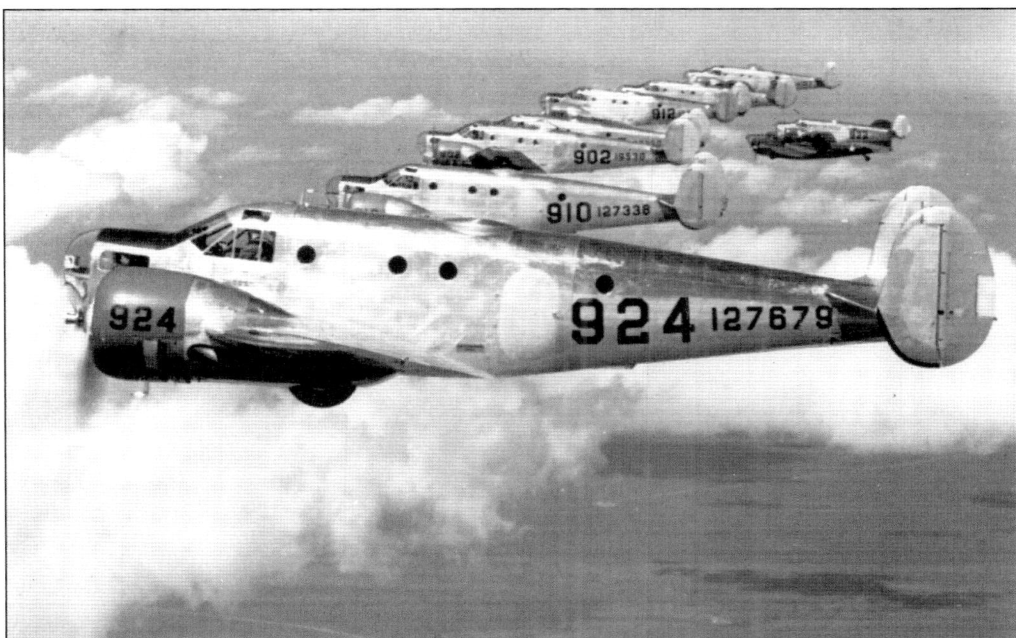

Construction began in July 1941 and proceeded quickly, accelerated by the attack on Pearl Harbor. The first class of flying cadets, designated "42-6," arrived on February 6, 1942. The cadets received 12 weeks of ground and flight training, rigorous physical activity, and military discipline in a 16-hour day. Here a group of cadets train in flight. The base grew into a significant facility with a monthly payroll in excess of $1 million at its height. (Courtesy of the Permian Historical Society Archives.)

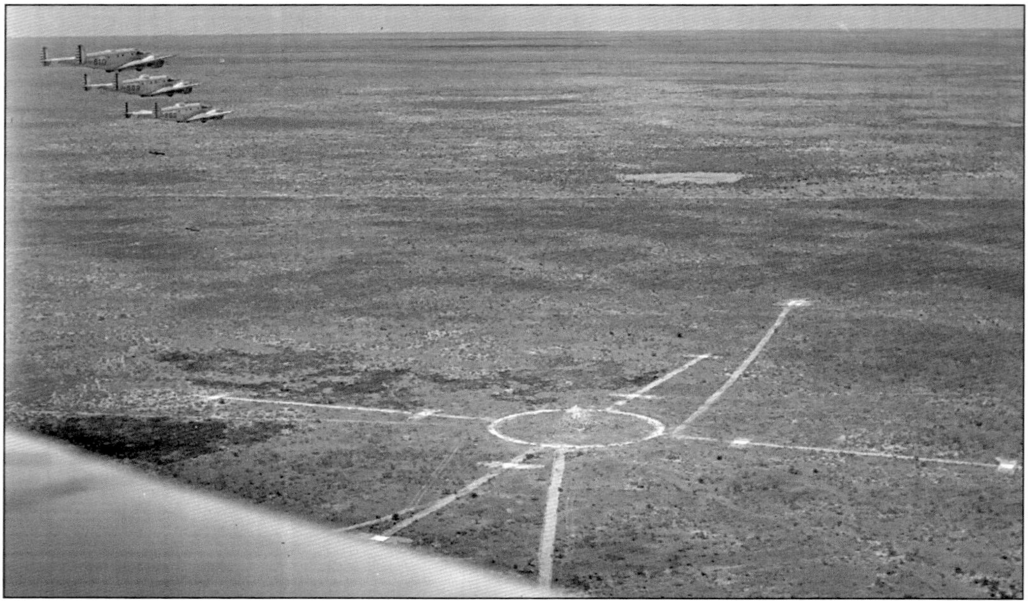

The army leased 23 different ranges on ranches around the area, including the C Ranch, with range crews assigned to maintain the white caliche targets and fight any fires started by the bombs. Cadets were soon dropping up to 1,000 bombs a day, six days a week, earning the nickname "Heaven from Hell Men." In this image, planes approach a target area.

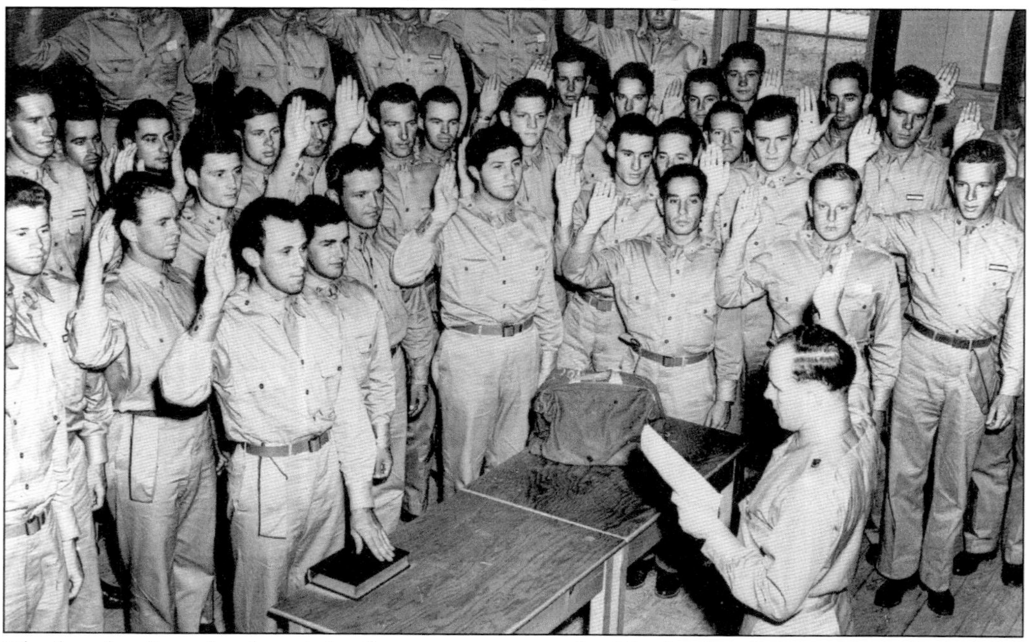

The bombardiers developed deadly accuracy using the Norden bombsight, a closely guarded secret at the time. Before being allowed to see the bombsight, cadets (as shown here) swore an oath that originated at Midland Army Air Field to protect its secrecy "if need be, with life itself." The Norden bombsight is in the canvas bag on the table. (Courtesy of the Permian Historical Society Archives.)

Midland Army Air Field pioneered several new techniques and inventions. Midland civilian Bruce Goode invented a bomb-loading machine. The steel practice bombs held a three-pound black powder spotting charge and weighed 100 pounds, 85 of which were sand. Hand-loading the bombs was exhausting, slow work, and the bombs varied slightly in weight and moisture content, affecting bombing accuracy. Goode's machine (shown here) filled five bombs at a time with gas-dried and accurately measured sand. (Courtesy of the Permian Historical Society Archives.)

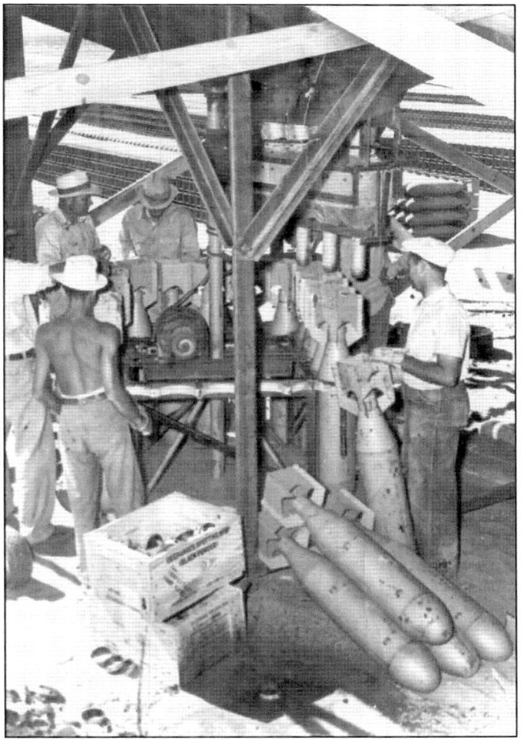

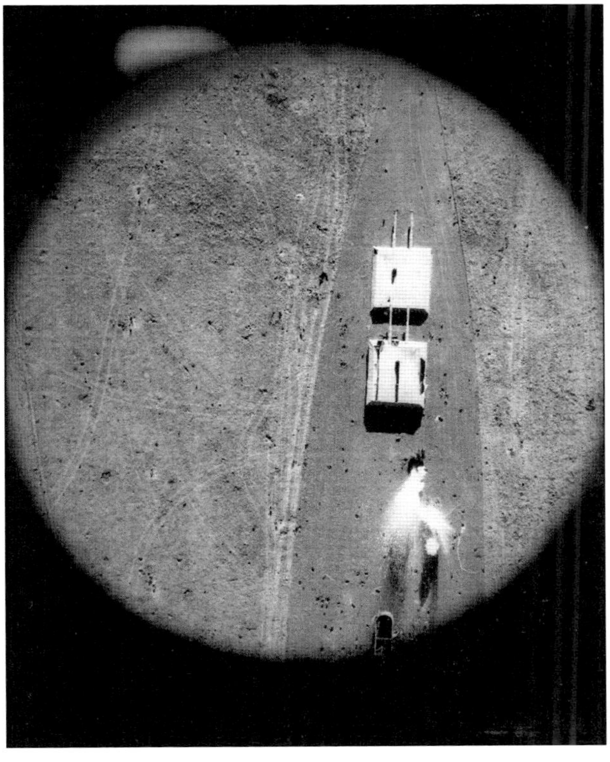

Another innovation begun at the Midland field was the photographic scoring of all practice bombs dropped. Cadets flew practice runs in pairs, one cadet manning the bombsight and the other serving as photographer, then trading assignments. Up to 95 percent of all bombs dropped were photographically scored. This photograph records a bombardier's hit. (Courtesy of the Permian Historical Society Archives.)

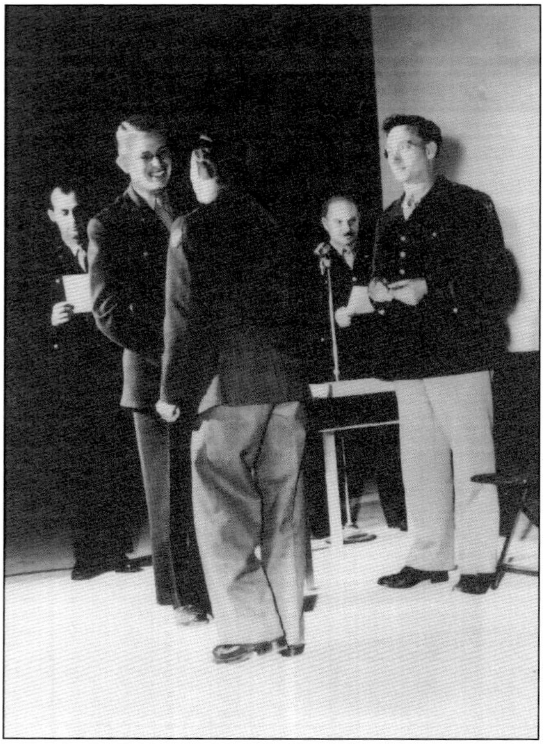

The first class of cadets graduated in April 1942. Maj. Gen. Hubert R. Harmon, commander of the Gulf Coast Air Forces Training Center, flew in for the event. Each cadet received newly designed silver wings with a bomb falling across a circular target. Over the next three years, classes arrived at three-week intervals and graduated in 12 weeks. Classes averaged 150 cadets. In 1943, over 2,700 cadets received wings. In this graduation ceremony from 1942, Captain McCormick is the second from the right.

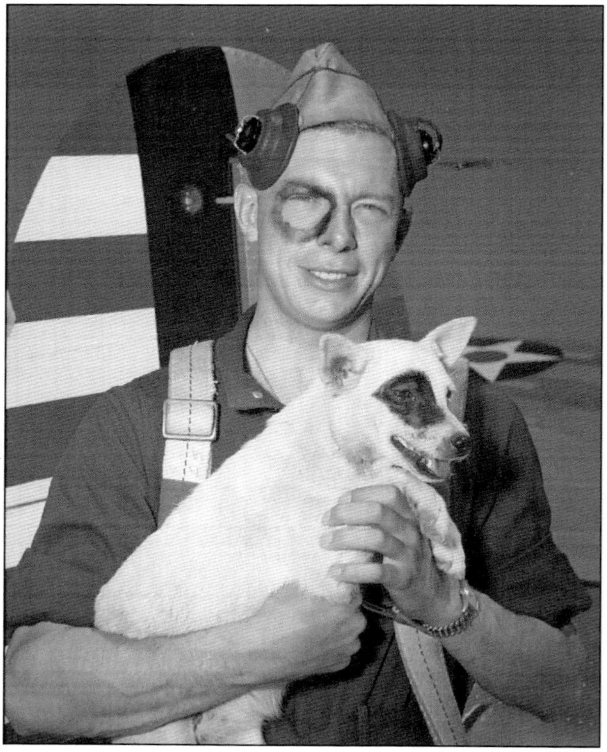

Base commander Gen. Isaiah Davies believed strongly in the value of strategic bombing. He supported a campaign to convince the military and the public of the value of bombardiers to the war effort. The May 18, 1942, issue of *Life* magazine featured a cover story on the base. The six-page photograph essay drove home the point that "the bombardier is the key to victory." The young cadets with their black right eyes (caused by peering through the rubber eyepiece of the bombsight) made great copy.

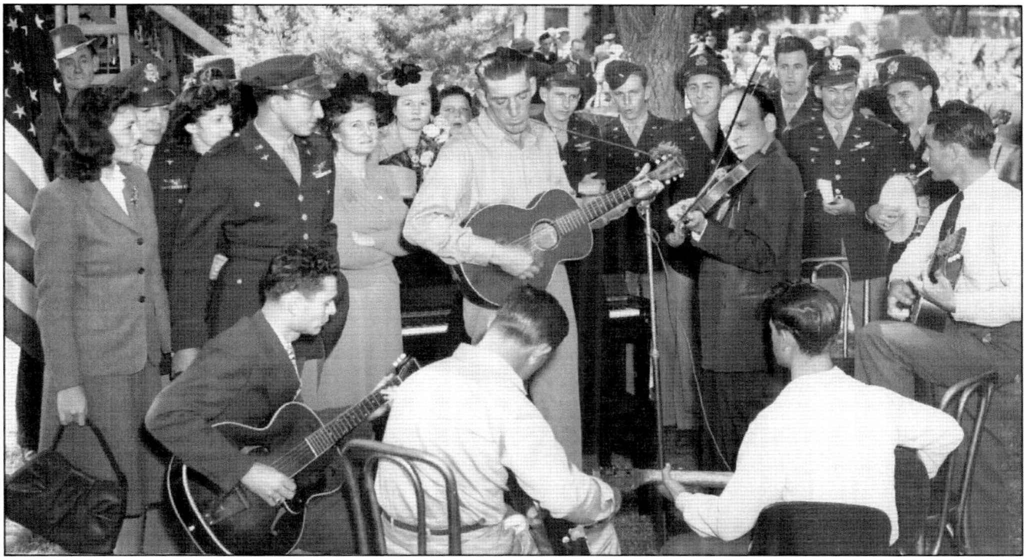

The young men also proved popular in Midland. The caption for this official photograph from the Army Air Field Training Command reads, "Personnel from Midland Army Air Field enjoy festivities at a barbecue in the backyard of the J. E. 'Bob' Hill residence." This was one of numerous functions given by the Hills for the airmen. Several cadets met their future brides in Midland. A number chose to return after the war and make Midland their home.

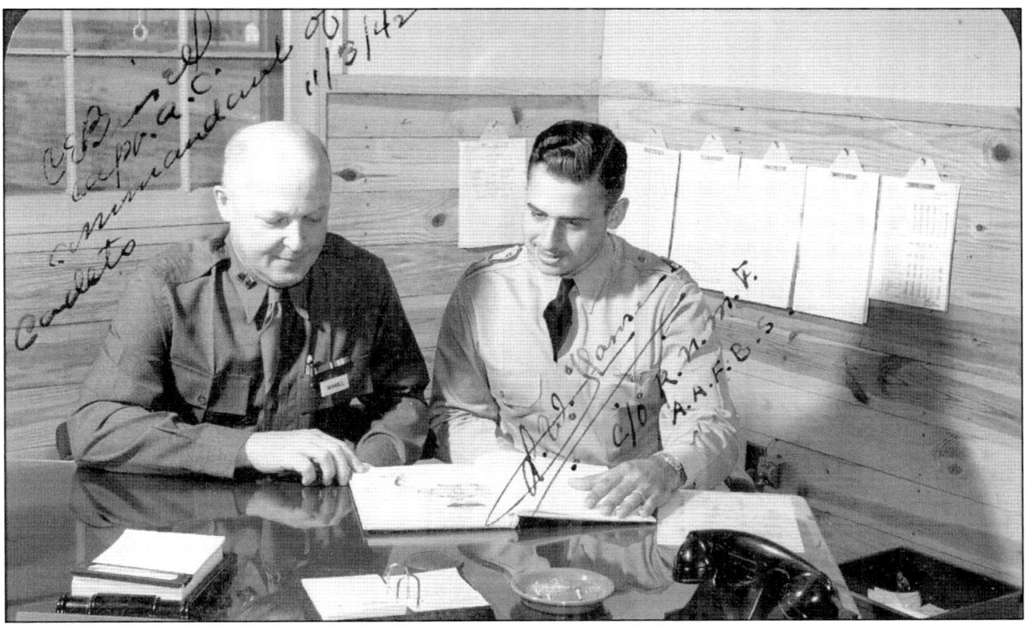

Clarence E. Bissell (left) arrived at the base early in the war as a reserve captain and became a lifetime Midland resident. He served for a time as commandant of cadets (as he signed here in 1942). Bissell and his wife returned to Midland after the war where he began an insurance business. He became an expert on local Native American artifacts and amassed an extensive collection, which he donated to Midland's Museum of the Southwest. The man on the right is identified as L. W. Hansen. (Courtesy of the Permian Historical Society Archives.)

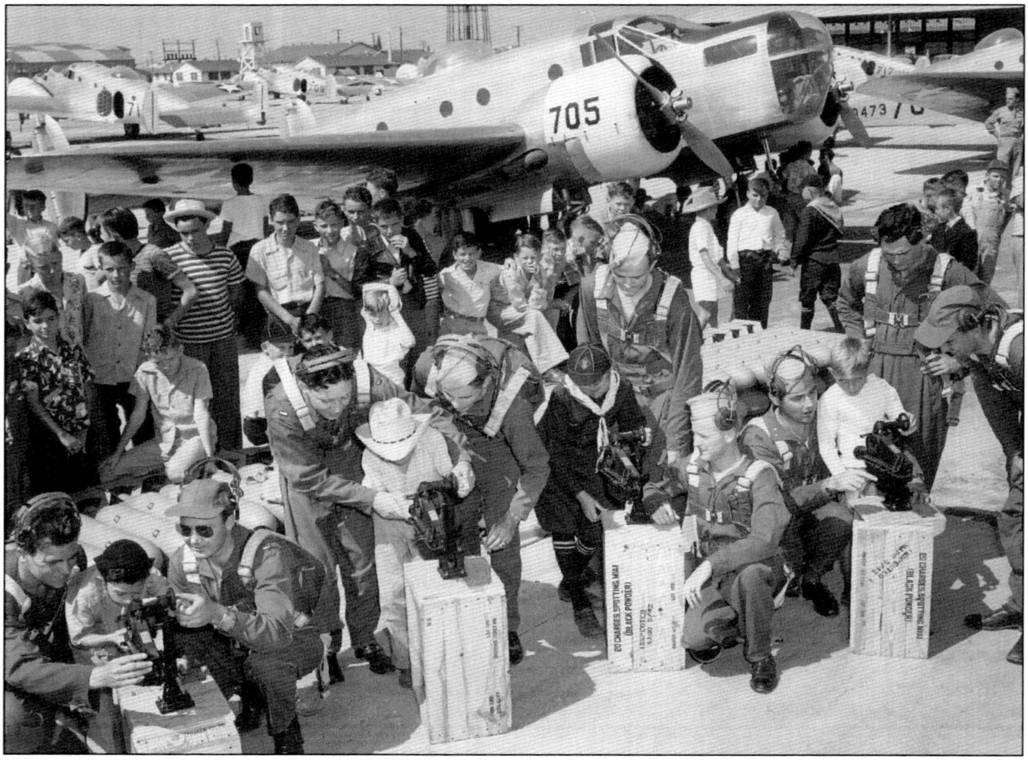

Local support also came through the Future Bombardiers of America (FBA) program. Boys from ages 8 to 16 joined and received tours of the base with special opportunities, as in this photograph of FBA members peering through the famous bombsights after swearing their own oath, modeled on that of the bombardiers. Rapid technology changes altered the nature of bombing, and the school eventually closed in 1946. The airfield returned to the city as a public airport. During its short career, the Midland Army Air Field played a pivotal role in the development of the bombardier program, and many still consider it to have been the world's greatest bombardier college.

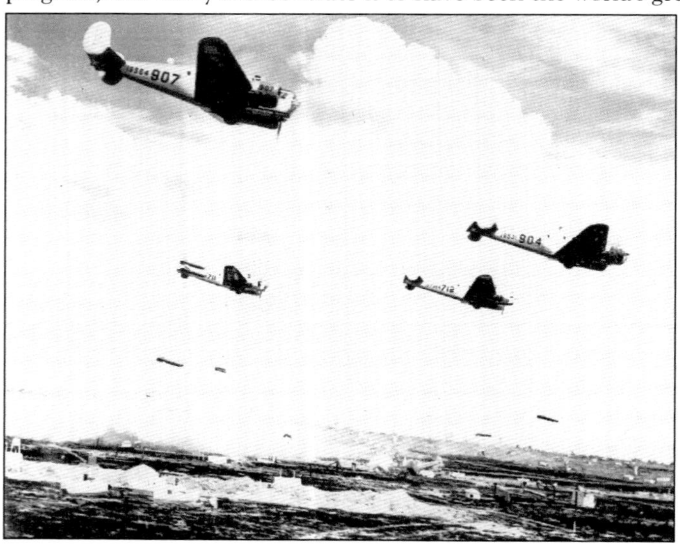

The height of publicity came with the July 4, 1942, bombing of "little Tokyo," a target 12 miles south of the base. Reporters, feature writers, and even the Hollywood film crew for the movie *Bombardier* came for the event. Three thousand vehicles, carrying some 20,000 spectators, created a dusty traffic jam stretching for miles. The spectacular show included more than 70 AT-11s, 450 men, and 1,500 bombs. (Courtesy of the Permian Historical Society Archives.)

Five

Boom and Bust and Boom in the Tall City

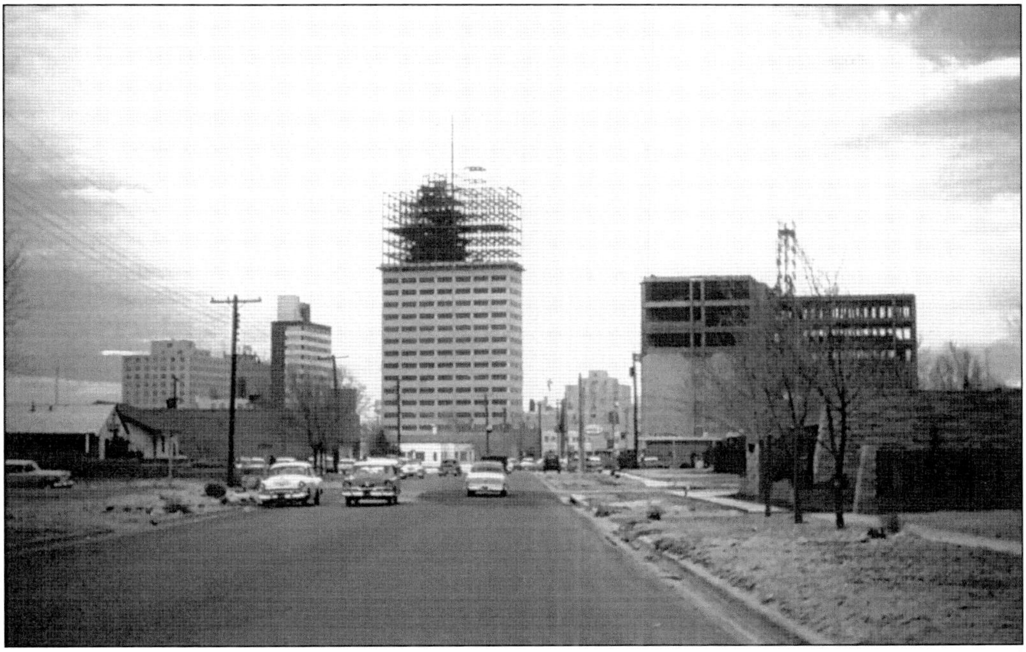

In the summer of 1956, Jeff George, a young geologist with a new college degree, came to Midland to work for Humble Oil. George also had a new camera. Seeking photography subjects, he chose the changing face of downtown Midland. George's photographs (here of the Humble Building addition and the new Wilco Building) reflect the boom spirit that characterized Midland through much of the second half of the century. Yet more than the skyline would change during those years. (Photograph by Jeff George.)

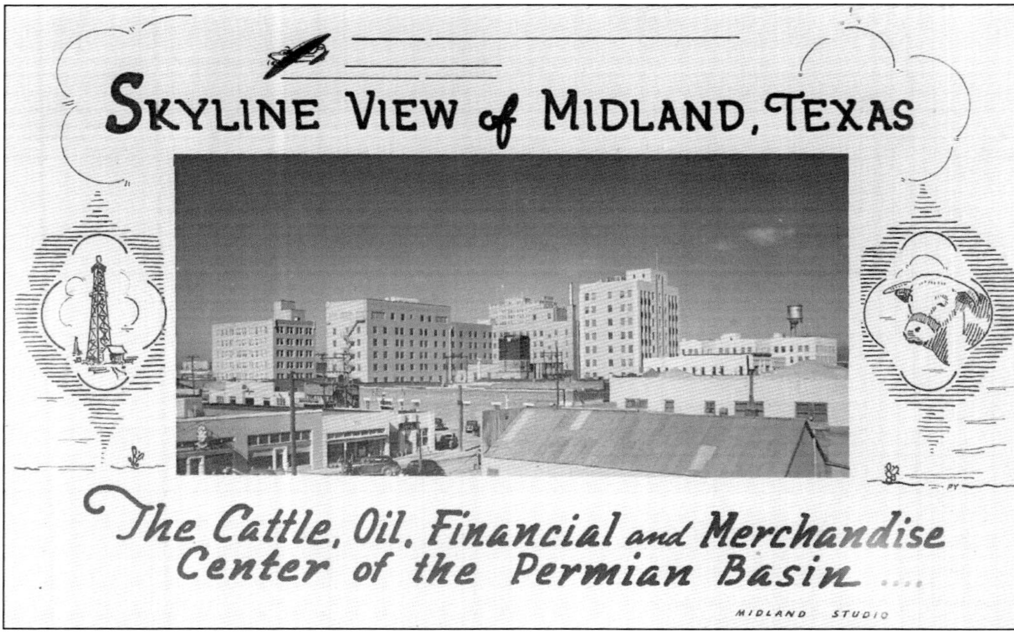

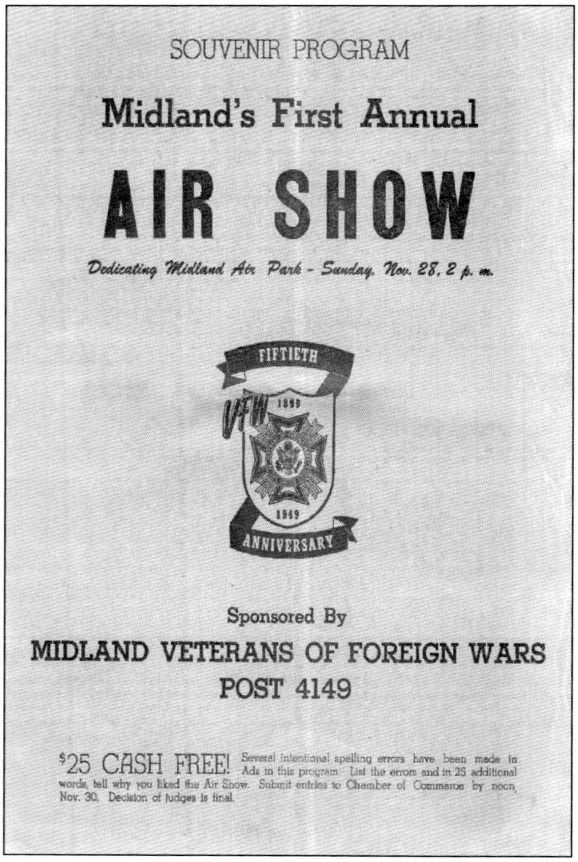

The postwar Midland skyline looked much as it had at the end of the booming 1920s. One major change was the remodeling of the First National Bank in 1936 (the tall building right of center). Clarence Scharbauer Sr., bank president for many years, died in 1942, and Marvin Ulmer became president. The Scharbauer Hotel dominates the center of the photograph, with the Petroleum Building rising in the background. The Llano Hotel (below the water tower) had been renamed the Crawford in 1939.

The Veterans of Foreign Wars organized the first air show in Midland in 1948 at the Midland Air Park, the airfield north of town that served the public during the war. On December 14, 1946, Midland received word that Midland Army Air Field would return to the city; there would be no permanent military base at Midland. Midland Air Park remained a small airfield. The Commemorative Air Force moved its headquarters to Midland in 1991 and produces an annual air show.

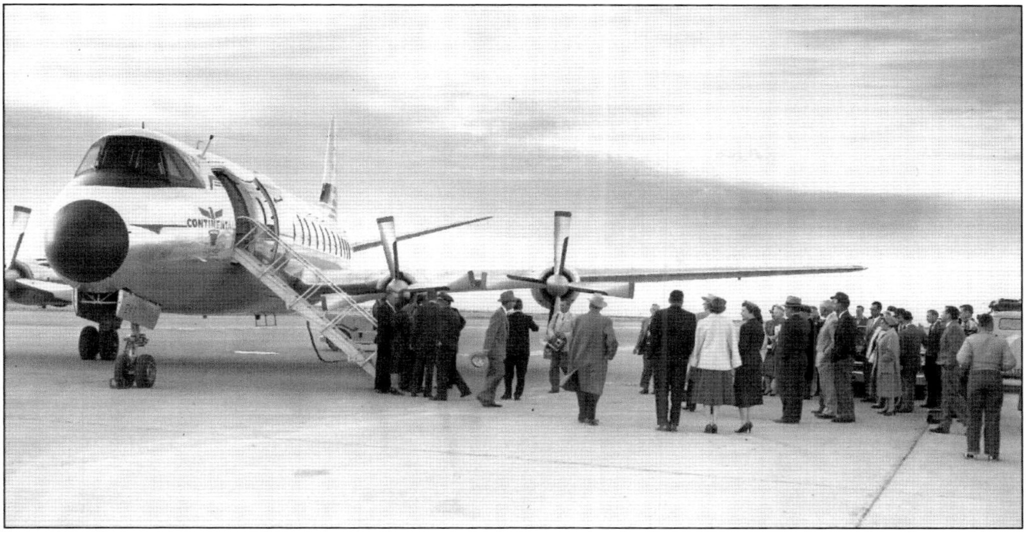

Remodeling of the terminal for civilian use was underway by August 1947. By November, three airlines—American, Continental (one of its planes shown here), and Pioneer—all operated flights out of Midland. In December, the Department of Commerce established a weather station at the airport. Midland Municipal Airport occupied a strategic position along east-west routes with many planes stopping to refuel. The airport was considered one of the better ones in West Texas.

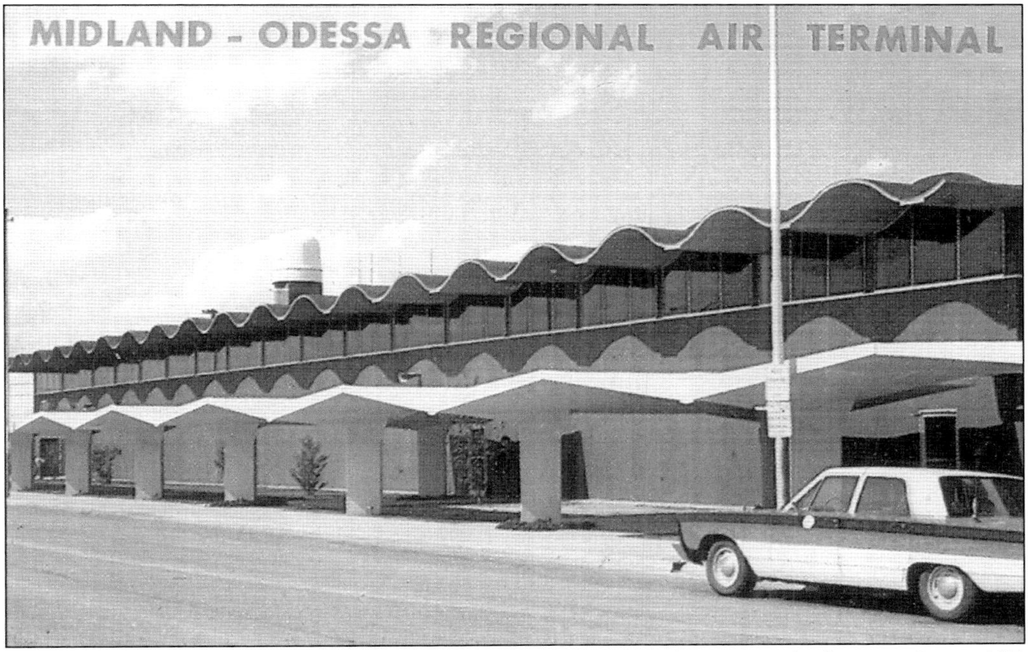

As air travel boomed in the 1950s, Midland sought to enlarge the airport facilities. In June 1957, the city council considered plans for a new, two-story terminal designed by architect J. J. Black. The $1.4 million price tag was too steep without federal money, which the city preferred not to accept. Plans were revised and the new terminal (shown here on a postcard) officially opened on January 6, 1960. The airport improved the runway system over the next two decades to accommodate larger jets and maintain its role as a regional airport.

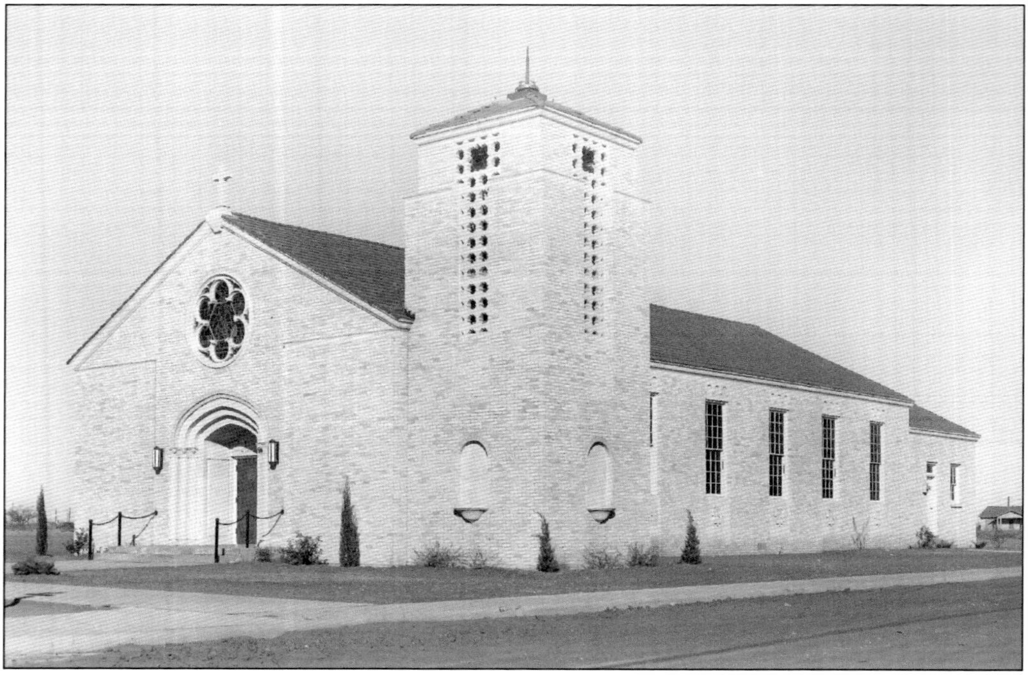

Bombardier school facilities soon served other purposes. St. Ann's Catholic parish was established in 1933 with a small sandstone church on Texas Street. By 1947, the growing congregation needed more room. The former Midland Army Air Field Chapel was acquired and relocated to the corner of Texas and M Street, where it was dedicated as St. Ann's in October 1948. This photograph is from that time period. In 1951, a school and convent were added to the site.

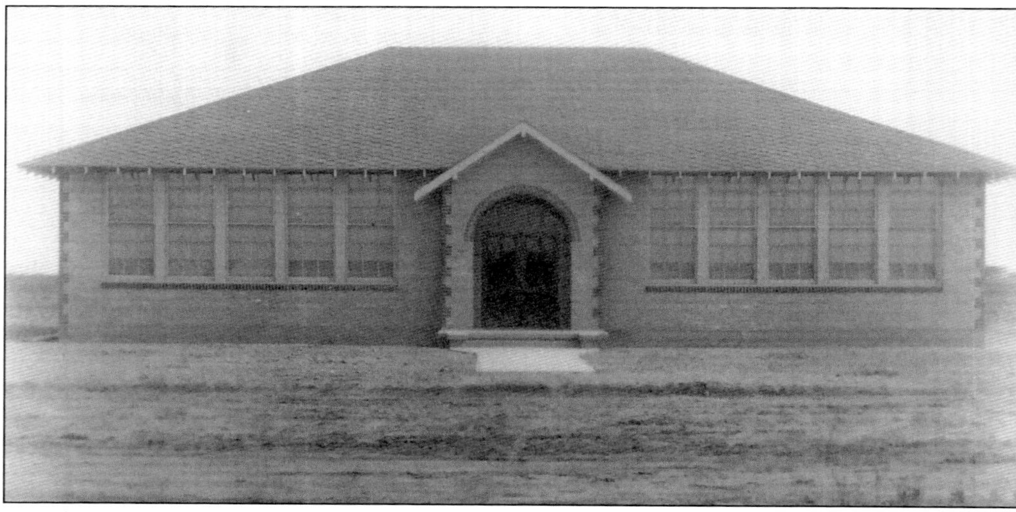

Another airport building became the new Carver School building. A significant number of blacks migrated to Midland in the 1920s, seeking work in agriculture and as domestic help. In 1932, $6,000 was allocated to establish a "colored school." In 1943, the facility became Carver School in honor of George Washington Carver. After the close of the war, a bombardier barracks was converted into this brick structure as the new home for Carver School, as Midland schools remained segregated.

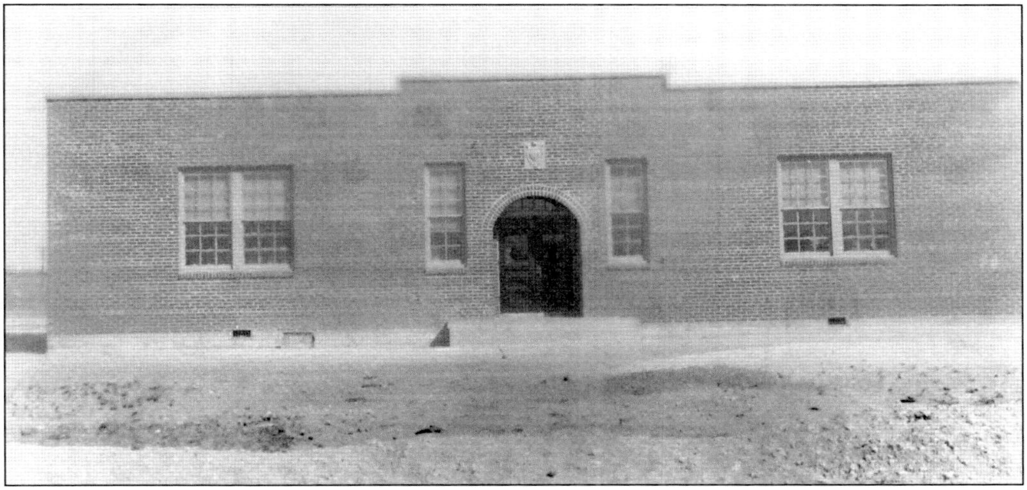

Midland established the "Mexican School" for Hispanic children in 1928, with instruction through grade eight. Hispanics had been a part of the Midland community from the early years. Several railroad workers relocated to Midland, working on ranches and farms. A small Hispanic community had grown up on the east side of Midland by 1915. Hispanics began acquiring jobs with the city in the mid-1940s. The first Hispanic students attended Midland High in 1948. The Mexican School later became De Zavala Elementary.

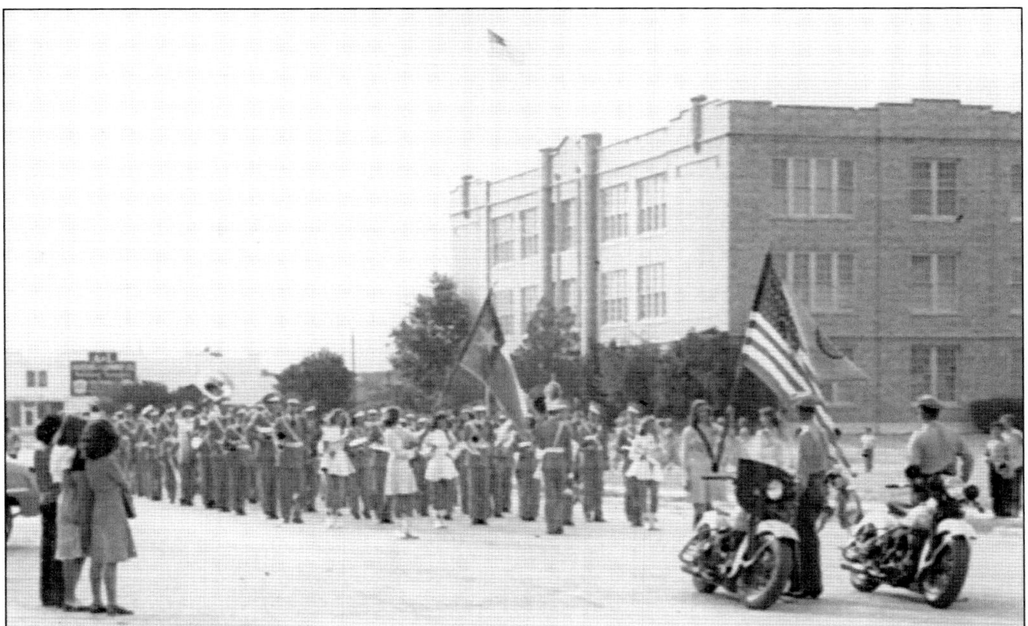

Midland's schools grew significantly from the North School days. Midland High School (in background) was erected in 1928 for a price of $150,000 and considered one of the finest in the state. Two years later, Cowden Junior High was built for $100,000. Francis Williams, Midland County librarian in the 1970s, took this photograph on October 24, 1947. The Midland High School band lines up for the parade before the football game between the Midland Bulldogs and the Abilene Eagles. (Photograph by Francis Williams; courtesy of Burr Williams.)

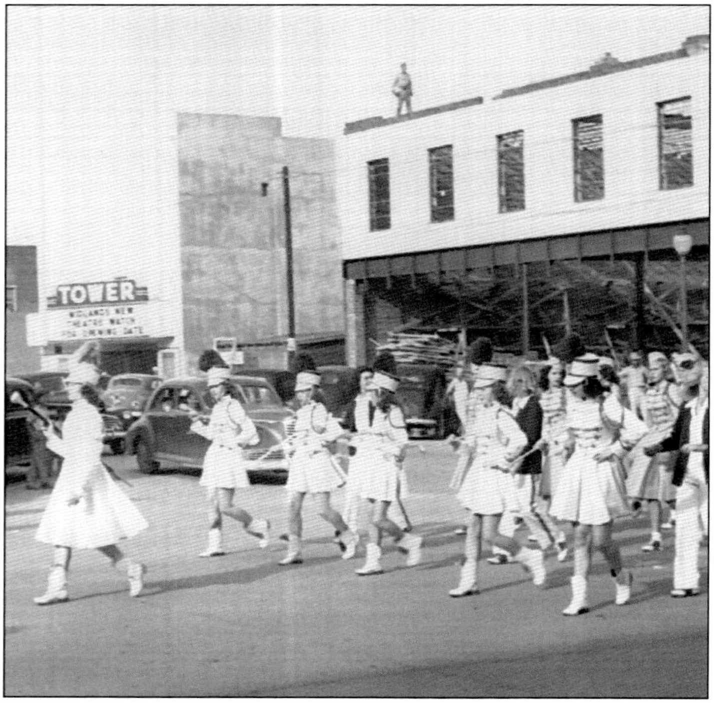

As the band marches through downtown, traces of the postwar changes are visible. The new Tower Theater announced its grand opening as Midland's fourth movie house, joining the Yucca, Ritz, and Rex. On October 28, 1947, *It's A Wonderful Life* became the opening feature for a price of 35¢. A workman standing atop the new construction next door paused to watch the parade. The Midland High Bulldogs lost the game 20-0. (Photograph by Francis Williams; courtesy of Burr Williams.)

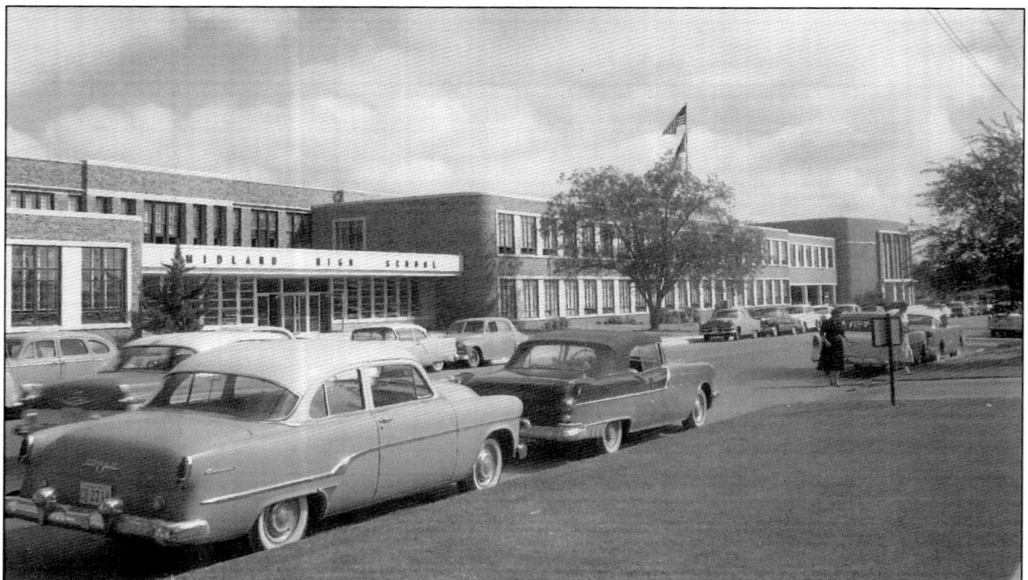

Construction on a new Midland High School facility began in 1948; the class of 1950 was the first to graduate from the new facility. The new Midland High School auditorium (on the far right in this 1950s photograph) was part of a feature article in the October 26, 1952, *Los Angeles Examiner* on "Fabulous Midland." Giles Wright, special staff writer, remarked on the rising skyscrapers in this city of 30,000 residents: "Last year, more than $1 million a month was spent in new building." The Midland High School student yearbook's name expressed it well. The *Catoico* derived its name from the combination of cattle, oil, and cotton.

Big changes lay ahead for the parade students. By 1962, Midland's population grew to 62,000, with student enrollment above 15,000. Ten new elementary schools, two junior highs, a second high school (Robert E. Lee in 1963), and more schools in the black community reflected the growth. These years also marked the beginnings of desegregation in Midland. In 1956, the first black students attended white schools. A process began in 1967 to dismantle all dual schools by 1969. Carver High School closed in 1968. Geneva Harris, bused to Lee High School her senior year, recalled it many years later as "the end of an era." Midland schools would not become fully integrated until 1976. (Photograph by Francis Williams; courtesy of Burr Williams.)

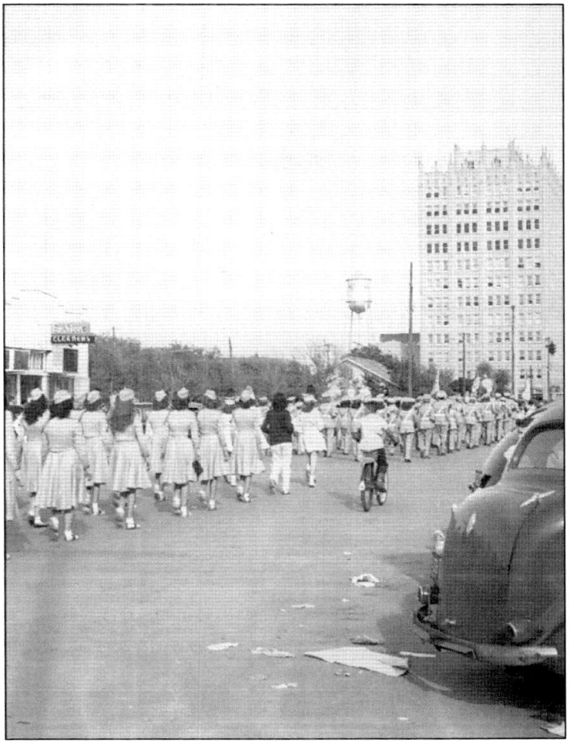

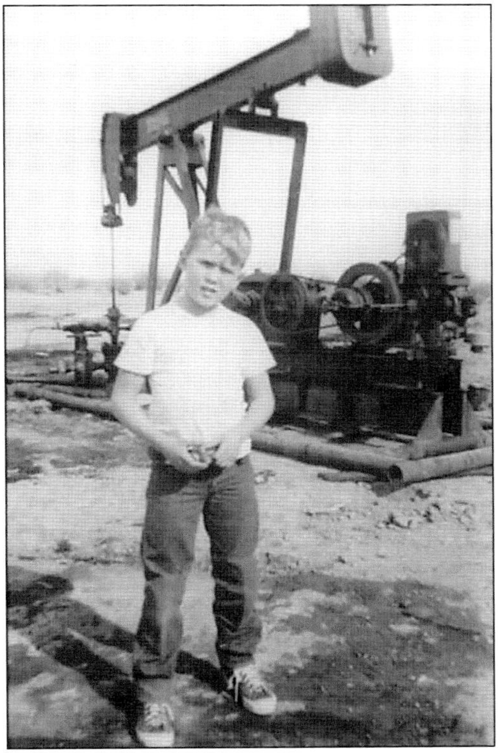

Future president George W. Bush (seen here as a young boy) was among the students attending a Midland school in the late 1940s. Also future president George H. W. Bush moved his family to Midland, where he worked in the oil business. They lived in a modest home on Ohio Street. Young George attended Sam Houston Elementary and San Jacinto Junior High School. In 1959, the Bush family moved to Houston. (Courtesy of the George H. W. Bush Presidential Library and the George W. Bush Childhood Home.)

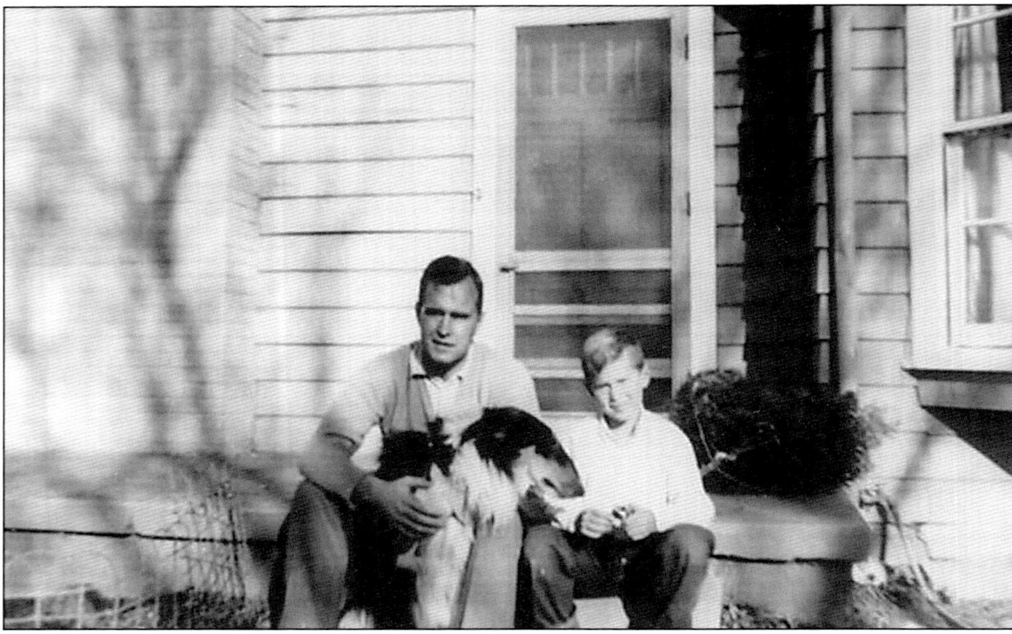

Two future U.S. presidents relax in front of their Midland home in this 1950s photograph. George H. W. Bush cofounded the Zapata Petroleum Corporation in Midland in 1953, became president of the Zapata Offshore Company in 1954, and moved the company to Houston in 1958. George W. Bush met Laura Welch, a librarian and also a former Midland resident, in 1977. That same year, they were married in Midland's First United Methodist Church on Main Street. (Courtesy of the George H. W. Bush Presidential Library and the George W. Bush Childhood Home.)

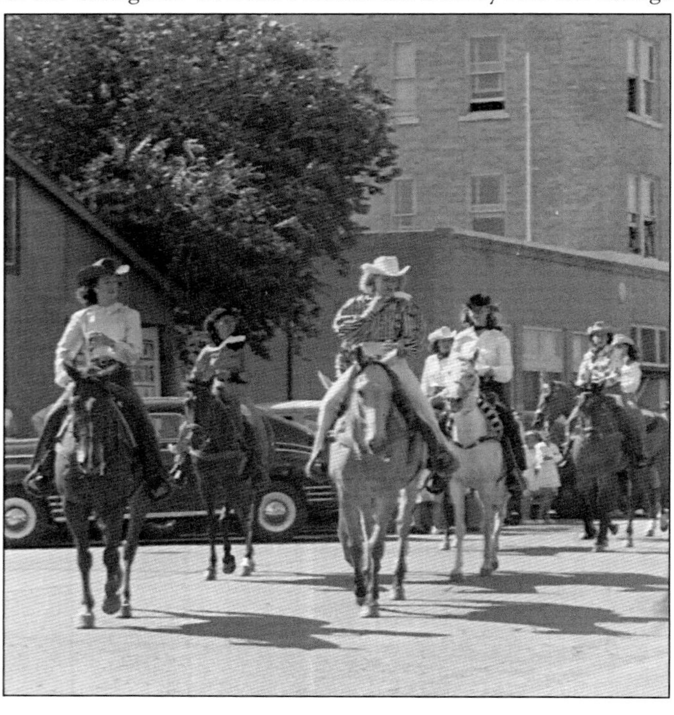

Rodeo remained a Midland tradition for another decade. In 1935, the Midland World Championship Rodeo was inaugurated. Beginning in 1944, early June became the annual rodeo time. As this photograph from the 1947 parade demonstrates, the contestants and the city had changed considerably from earlier years (compare to page 74). The last Midland Rodeo was held in June 1959. (Photograph by Francis Williams; courtesy of Burr Williams.)

Over the years, several special guests attended the rodeo. In 1950, Texas governor Allen Shivers (center) became the guest of honor. Robert L. Wood (left) and J. Ed Warren (right) prepare to join Governor Shivers in sampling the barbecue at the Midland Baseball Park. Shivers served as governor of Texas from 1949 to 1957.

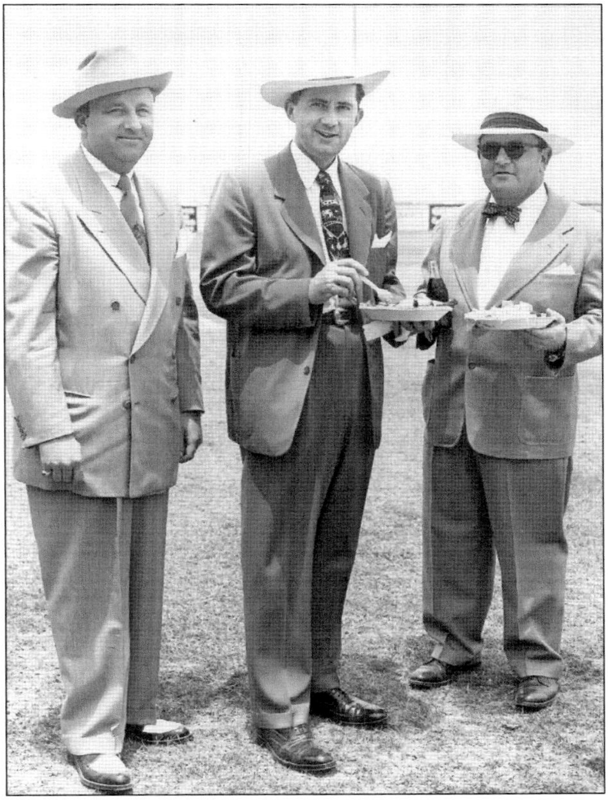

In 1948, Strom Thurmond, governor of South Carolina, led a group out of the Democratic National Convention over Harry Truman's civil rights platform. They formed the States' Rights Democratic Party (also called Dixiecrats) and chose Thurmond as their presidential candidate. On his Texas campaign, Thurmond (right) visited the Scharbauer Hotel. In the first row at left are Midlanders F. W. Barnett and Jim Allison, publisher of the *Midland Reporter Telegram*; Jim Armstrong and Richard Brooks stand behind them in the second row on the left. Truman carried Midland County in the election.

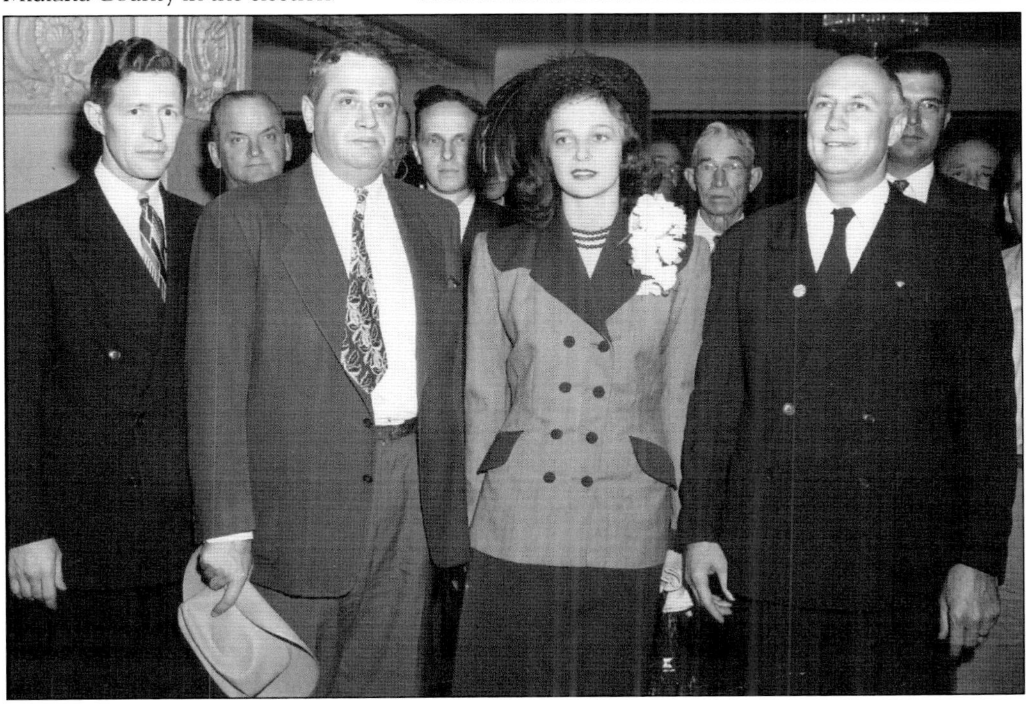

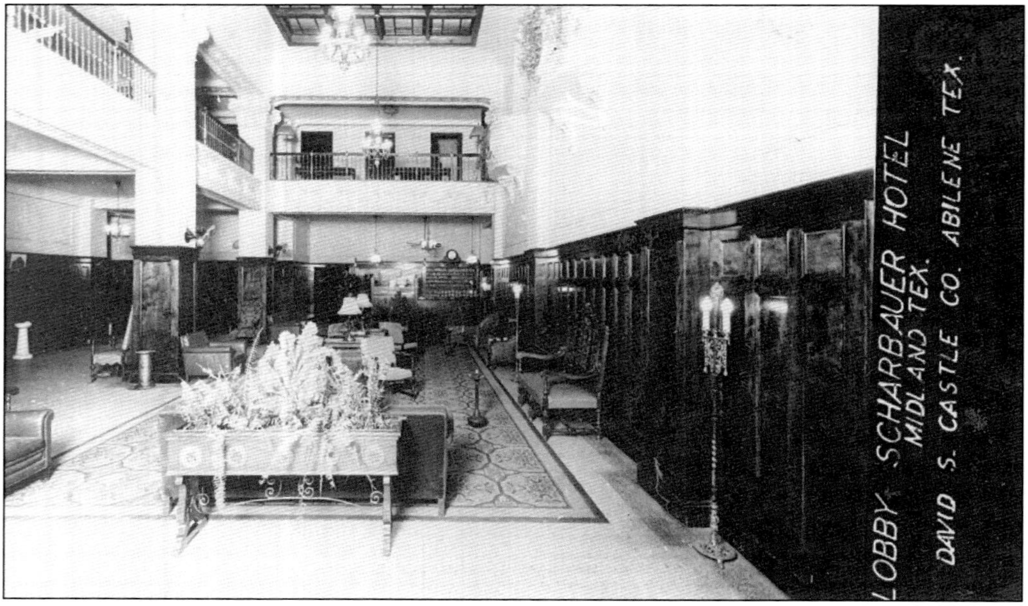

By 1949, the Scharbauer Hotel was the "Showplace of the Southwest." In that year, *Life* magazine featured a photograph of the ornate lobby filled with small groups of cattlemen and oil entrepreneurs. The caption stated that over $50 million in cattle and oil deals were transacted there each year—more than anywhere else in the country. At its peak, the hotel (with the lobby pictured above) had 350 guest rooms and a penthouse on the seventh floor. The Scharbauer was imploded in 1973, and a 14-story Hilton hotel was erected on the site.

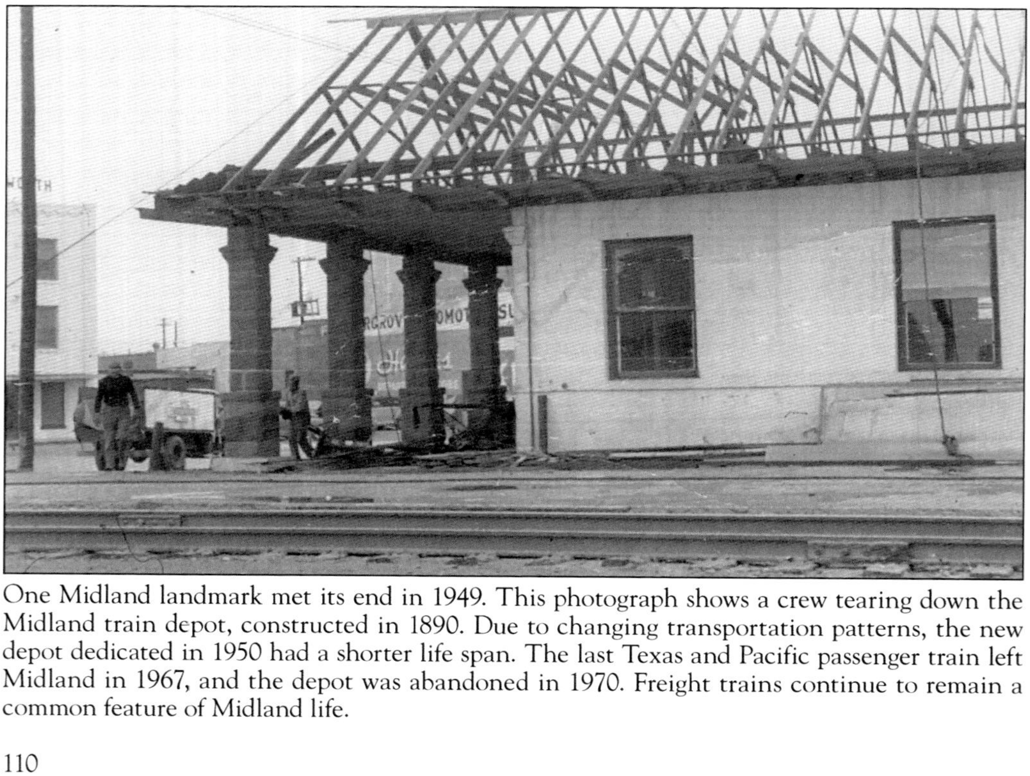

One Midland landmark met its end in 1949. This photograph shows a crew tearing down the Midland train depot, constructed in 1890. Due to changing transportation patterns, the new depot dedicated in 1950 had a shorter life span. The last Texas and Pacific passenger train left Midland in 1967, and the depot was abandoned in 1970. Freight trains continue to remain a common feature of Midland life.

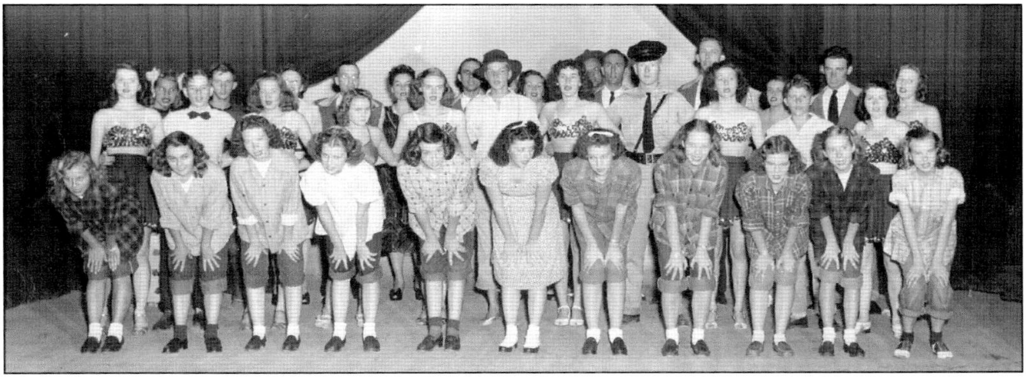

Art Cole, a former Midland army airfield staff sergeant, founded the Midland Community Theater (MCT) in 1946 and served as its director for over 30 years. Productions were first held downtown in the City-County Auditorium, a tin Quonset-type building. In 1978, the newly constructed Cole Theatre became MCT's home. This photograph is of an August 1946 variety show. Dorothy Harrison (first row, second from right) was a member of the Harrison family, who performed in many theater productions over the years. Robert Short (second row, second from the left) later became author of the 1965 best seller the *Gospel According to Peanuts*, which pioneered the study of religion through popular culture. (Courtesy of Shirley Ireland.)

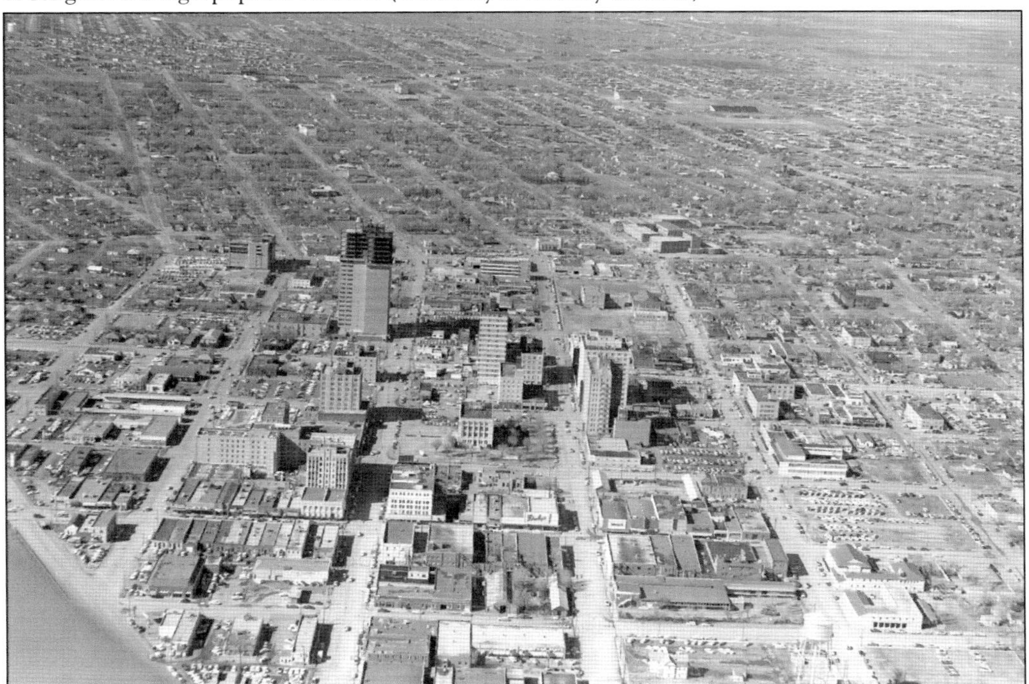

The under-construction Wilco Building (left of center) dominates this 1957 scene. The courthouse (lower center) is dwarfed by the surrounding buildings. The Petroleum Building (right of courthouse) now shares the skyline with several competitors. The city sprawls westward beyond the old Midland Christian College site. The new Midland High School is right of center. The First Baptist Church has moved to its new home near the stadium (upper right). The new Midland Memorial Hospital (upper center) opened in 1950. Main Street has a thriving business district and Midland National and the Crawford Hotel (formerly the Llano) still stand on Wall Street (lower left of center).

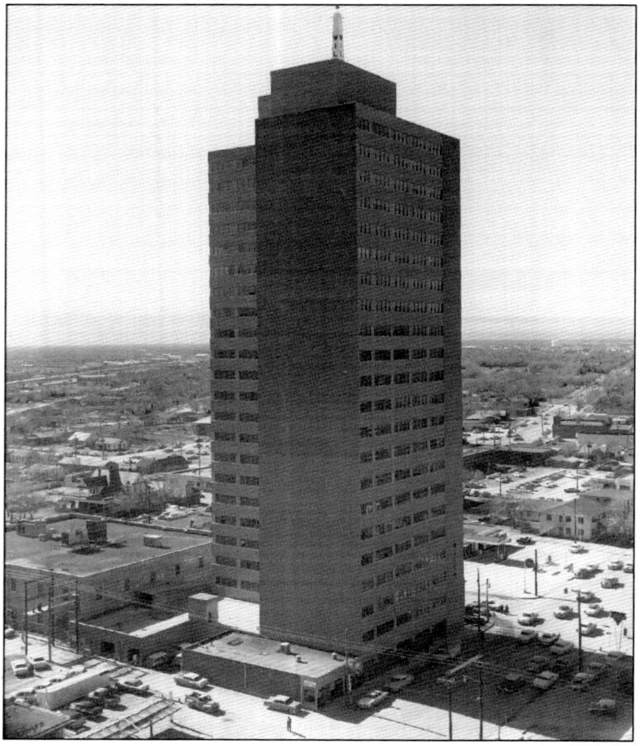

The Wilco Building, completed in 1958, (the date of this photograph) stands 22 stories tall. It became the tallest building between Fort Worth and Phoenix, Arizona, greatly adding to Midland's ability to operate as an oil administrative center. By the end of the decade, office space in Midland grew from 360,000 square feet to over 2 million. In 1958, over 120 independent consulting geologists and other petroleum-related professionals worked with some 150 oil companies and related organizations. The plentiful office space and favorable climate for investment create an environment encouraging easy intercommunication.

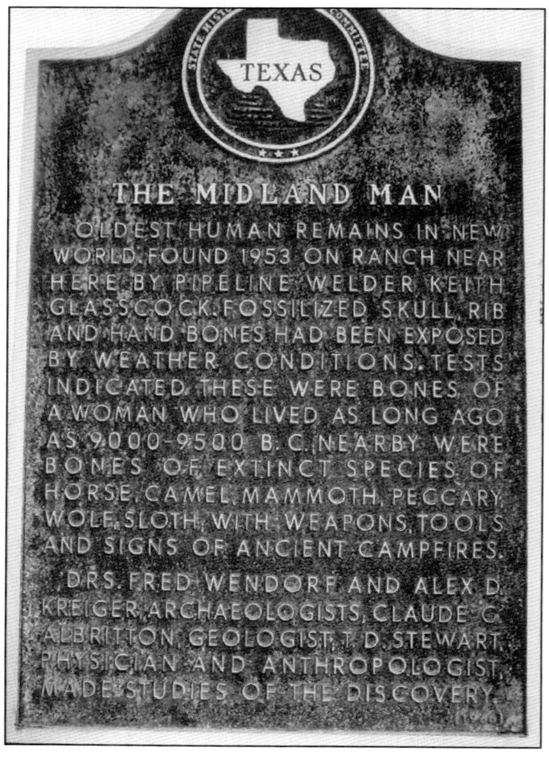

Midland became a center of prehistoric study in 1953. Pipeline welder Keith Glasscock found a skull and other bone fragments in a "blowout"—a depression created in wind-blown sand. Tests by archeologists indicated they were the bones of a woman (dubbed "Midland Minnie") who lived in the area over 10,000 years ago, making them among the oldest human remains discovered in the new world. Professional arguments continue over her age, perhaps as much as 37,000 years old. (Photograph by the author.)

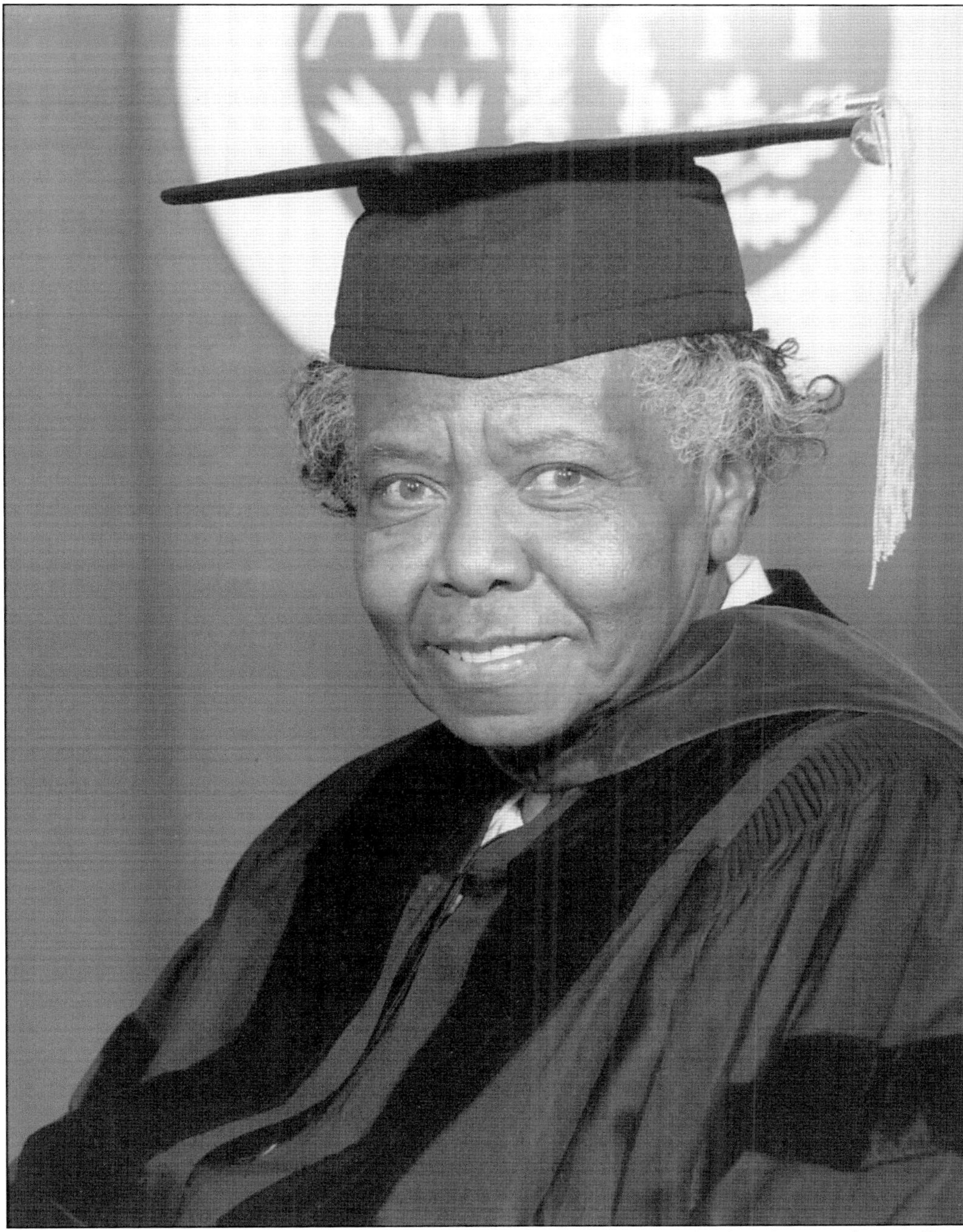

In 1951, on their way to California by train, Dr. Viola Coleman and her husband stopped in Midland and found a welcoming environment. She began a medical practice at the new Midland Memorial Hospital. Dr. Coleman began quiet desegregation efforts in the hospital. She desegregated her waiting room and then ended it in the lunchroom simply by eating there one day. Dr. Coleman helped launch an EMT program and played an instrumental role in the desegregation of Midland Schools. Dr. Coleman died in 2005 after over 50 years of community service. (Courtesy of the Permian Historical Society Archives.)

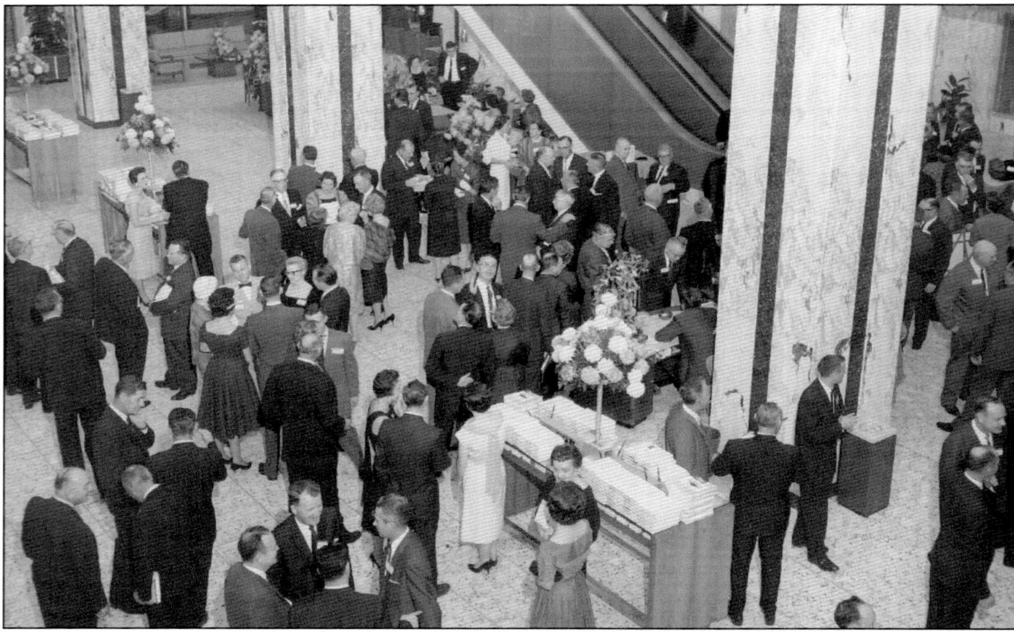

In 1959, Midland First National moved from its longtime home on Main Street. This photograph records the grand opening of the new eight-story building at West Wall and Colorado Streets. That same year, the bank published *Land of the High Sky*, a history of Midland written by John Howard Griffin, who later became more well known for his 1961 best seller *Black Like Me*.

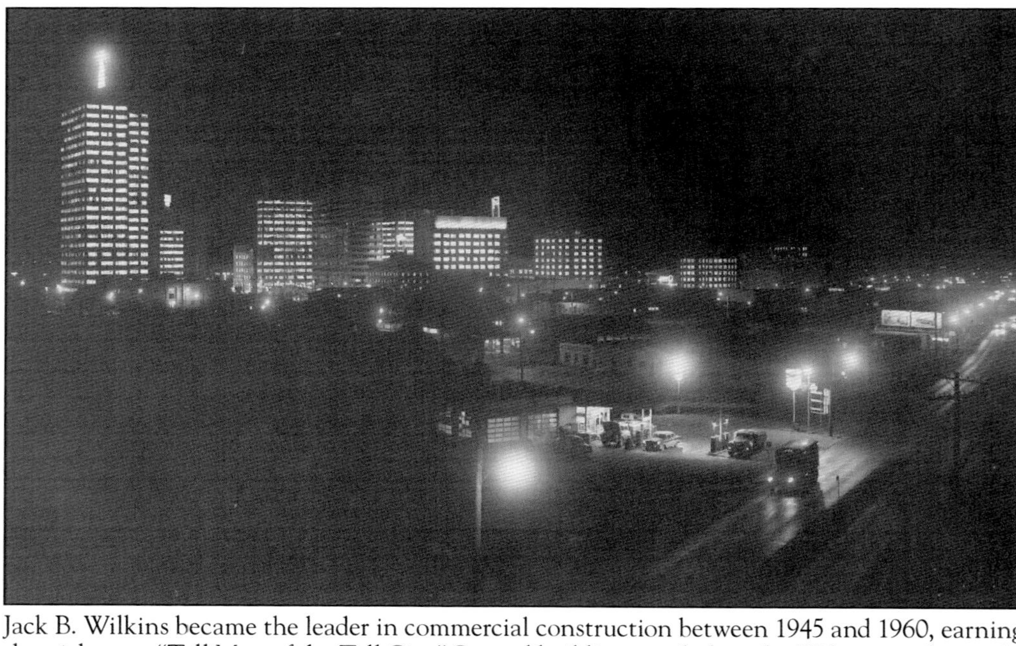

Jack B. Wilkins became the leader in commercial construction between 1945 and 1960, earning the nickname "Tall Man of the Tall City." Several buildings, including the Wilco, were his work. This photograph from the late 1950s bears the caption, "Midland at night all lighted up." The tower atop the Wilco Building (left) glows like a giant candle. This skyline was visible for miles to travelers along U.S. Highway 80 (later Interstate 20).

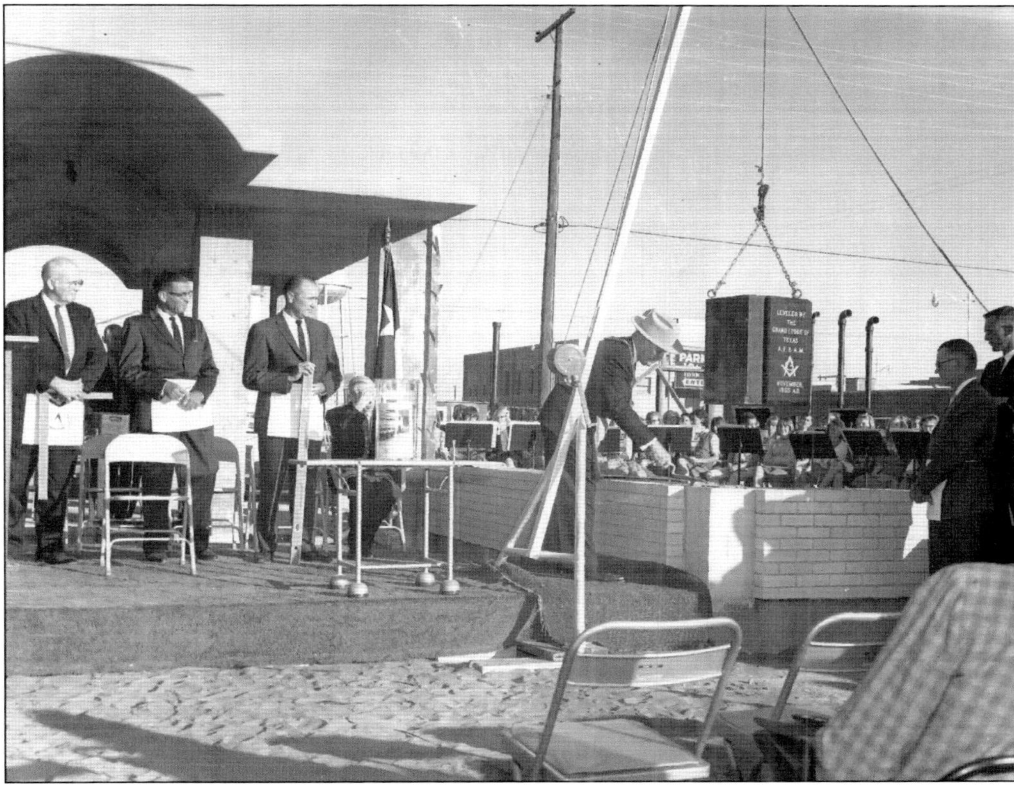

On November 12, 1965, the new city hall was dedicated, 36 years after the first city hall. In this photograph of the event, J. Carroll Hinsley, Grand Mason of the Grand Lodge of Austin, along with members of Midland Lodge No. 623, levels the granite cornerstone of the building. Leveling cornerstones for public buildings and other structures is Masonic tradition.

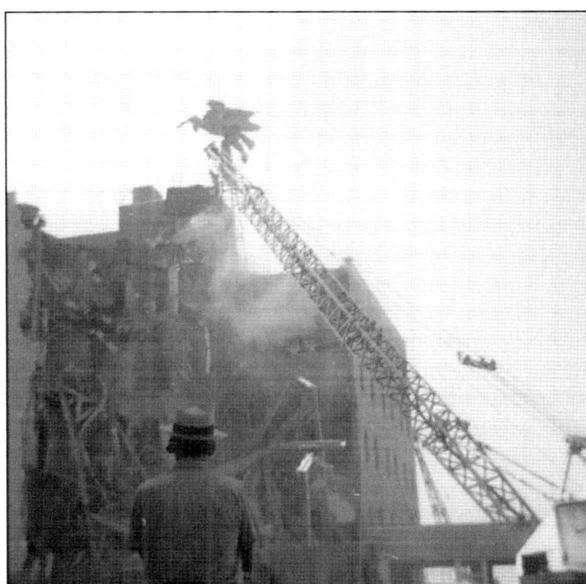

The rise of cheap foreign oil in the early 1960s brought tougher times for the domestic industry. Midland suffered a population loss through most of the 1960s, as several major oil companies closed their doors and others cut staff. Many homes and offices stood vacant, and confidence was low. In 1968, a wrecking ball destroyed the Mobil Oil Building. In this photograph, its iconic red pegasus "Peggy" trademark remains precariously atop the wreckage. Local tradition claims the horse still resides somewhere in Midland.

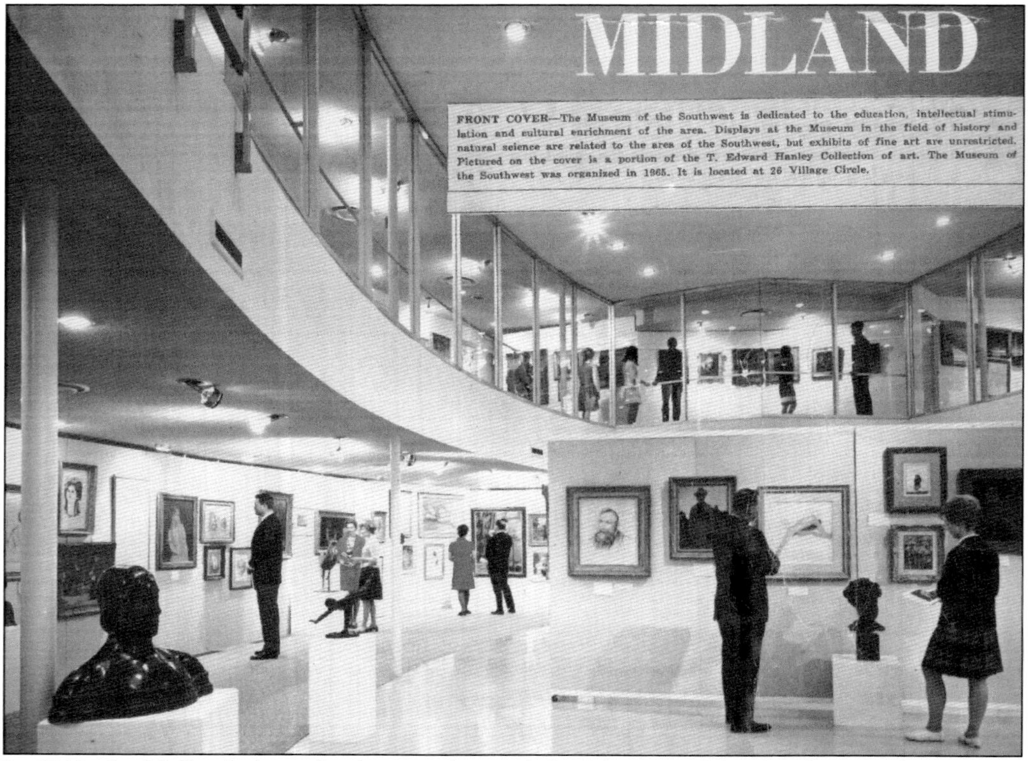

In 1968, the Midland phone book cover featured the Museum of the Southwest. The museum incorporated in 1965 when the Junior League of Midland voted to establish a regional museum devoted to art, history, and science. The museum opened in a facility on West Wall, with Gov. John Connolly cutting the ribbon. In 1966, the museum relocated to 26 Village Circle (the facility shown here). In July 1968, the museum found a permanent home in the Turner Mansion (page 88).

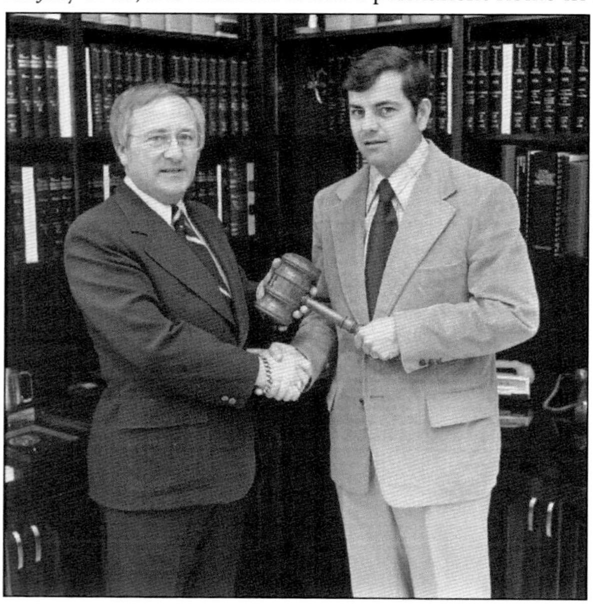

Tom Craddick (right) won election to the Texas House of Representatives as a Republican in 1968, one of three in a southern state still heavily Democratic. By 1976, Craddick had won his fifth term, and the number of Republicans had grown to 17. The caption for this undated photograph reads, "Speaker Billy Clayton and Rep. Tom Craddick engage in a bit of gavel swapping." Clayton first won the speaker's office in 1975 and presided until 1983. In 1975, Clayton named Craddick as chairman of the House Natural Resources Committee, making him the first Republican to chair a Texas legislative committee in over a century. In 2003, Craddick became the first Republican speaker in Texas since Reconstruction.

In 1970, the courthouse was renovated. A fifth floor, supported by pillars, was added. The courthouse quickly acquired the nickname "the Greek Temple." In 1976, the city purchased the Crawford Hotel and adjacent property to construct a convention center and park plaza. The area became Bicentennial Plaza. The Crawford was demolished the following year. In 1985, Midland celebrated the county's centennial in a remodeled plaza area.

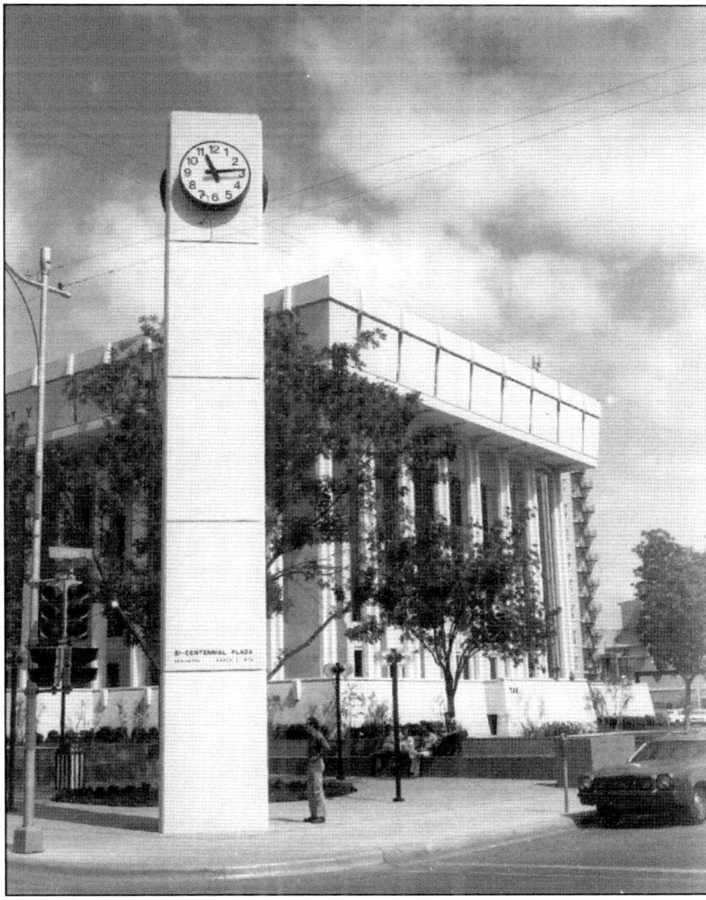

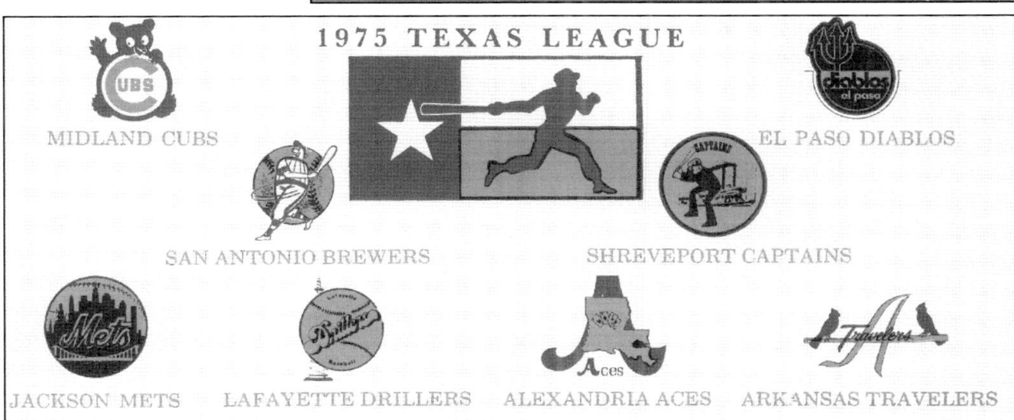

Midland had baseball teams from the early years. From 1927 to 1940, Los Patrillos, a Hispanic team, played in Midland. A black semipro team, the Indians, played during the 1940s. The Double-A Texas League came to Midland in 1972, and the Midland Cubs played in this league until 1984. Midland then became the Angels until 1998. The Midland Rockhounds, an affiliate of the Oakland A's, have played in the Scharbauer Sports Complex since 2002. This 1975 Cubs program lists the league members. (Courtesy of the Permian Historical Society Archives.)

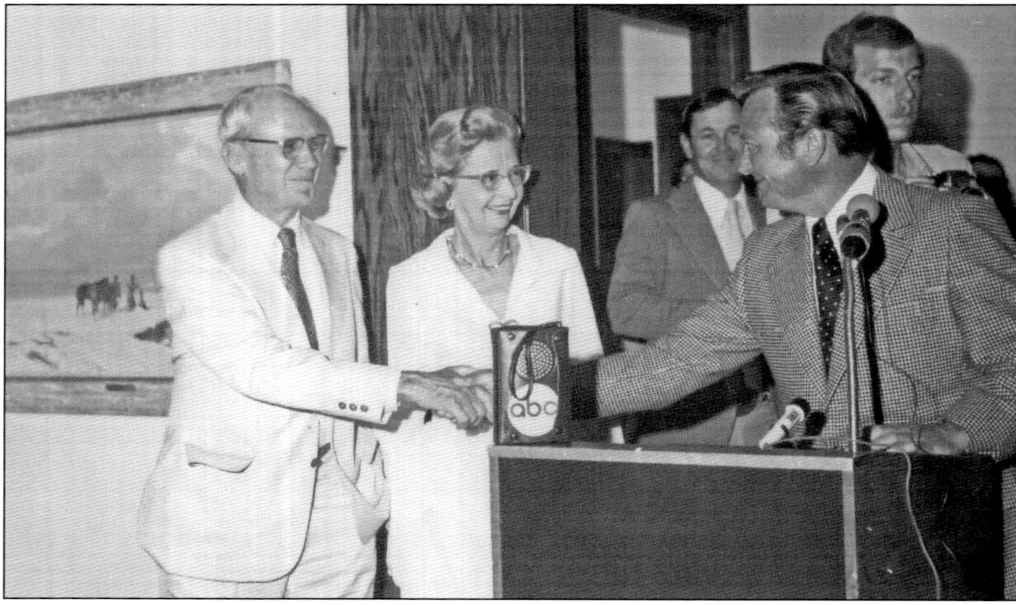

J. Evetts Haley returned to Midland in 1976 for the dedication of a library and history center. The event took place on July 5, Haley's 75th birthday. Haley started a trust in 1961 in memory of his wife, Nita Steward Haley, who died in 1958. Library trustee J. C. Barnes greets Haley and his second wife, Rosalind, during the dedication program. The library, located at 1805 West Indiana Avenue, contains one of the largest collections of Western literature, history, and artifacts (including the original bell from the Alamo). The Special Collections Room includes the photographs of J. Irwin Smith, noted frontier photographer, as well as Haley's books and research materials. (Courtesy of the Nita Stewart Haley Memorial Library, Midland, Texas.)

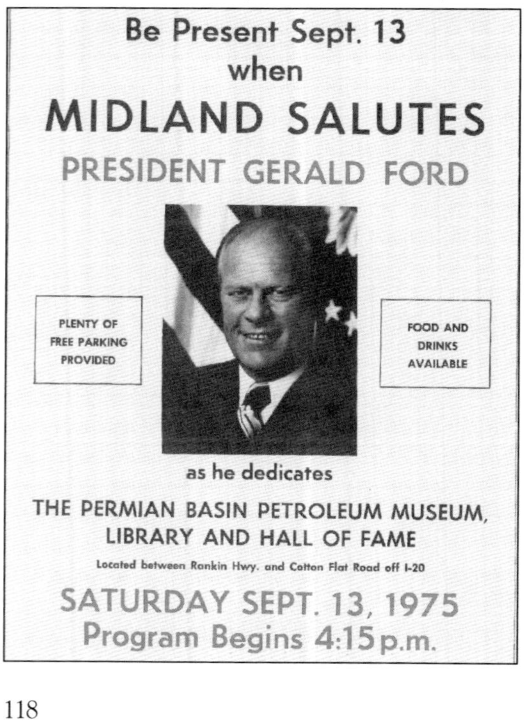

The Permian Basin Petroleum Museum opened in 1975. This flyer announcing the event featured Pres. Gerald Ford as the primary speaker. At the opening, visitors toured a West Texas boomtown and a marine diorama of the way the region may have looked 230 million years earlier. An archives and library collected documents and photographs of the oil industry. A hall of fame honored those who made outstanding contributions to the petroleum industry. In 1999, the 100th member was inducted into the hall.

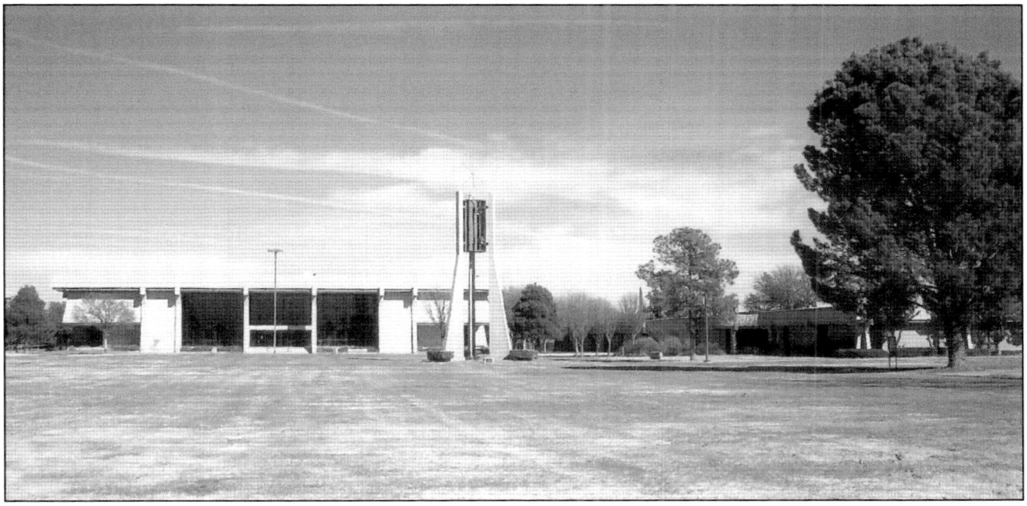

Midland received a new college in 1975. In 1969, voters in the Midland School District agreed to join the Odessa Junior College district, and the college began with a small building on the Andrews Highway and four instructors. In 1972, Midlanders decided to create their own college district. A 115-acre site near Midland Air Park was purchased. By January 1975, three buildings were ready, and spring classes began on the new campus. Since that time, Midland College has continued growing to become a prestigious regional college. (Photograph by author.)

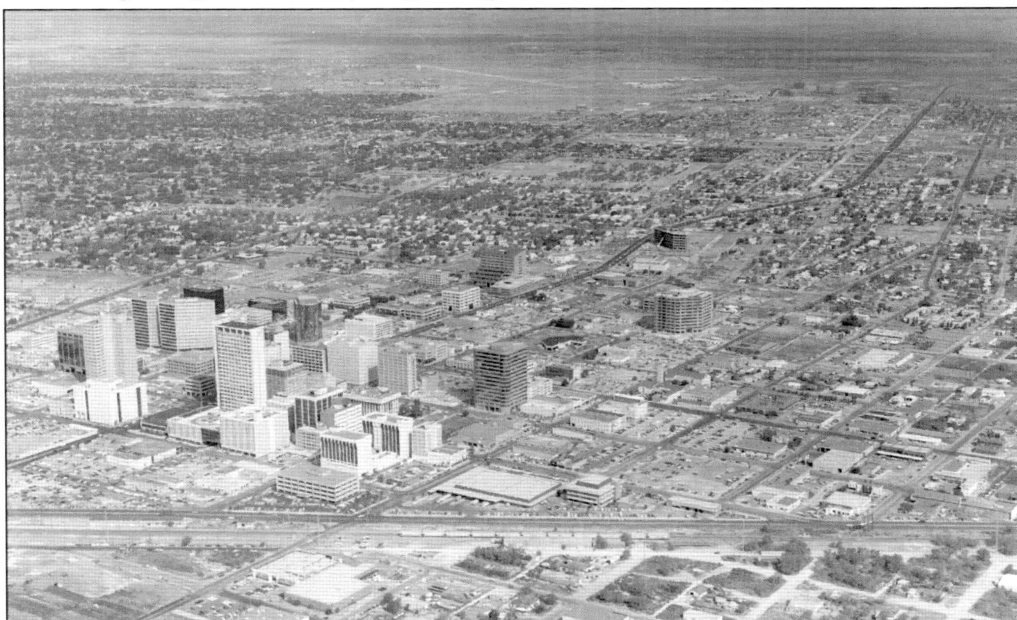

By 1970, the oil industry had rebounded and Midland again boomed. Between 1974 and 1983, eighteen new office buildings were constructed. This 1982 aerial photograph records Midland from the southeast. Highway 80 runs along the bottom of the picture, and downtown occupies the center. There are several new buildings with more modern architecture, including the Bank of America at 24 stories. (Courtesy of the Permian Historical Society Archives, the Bill Shoopman Collection.)

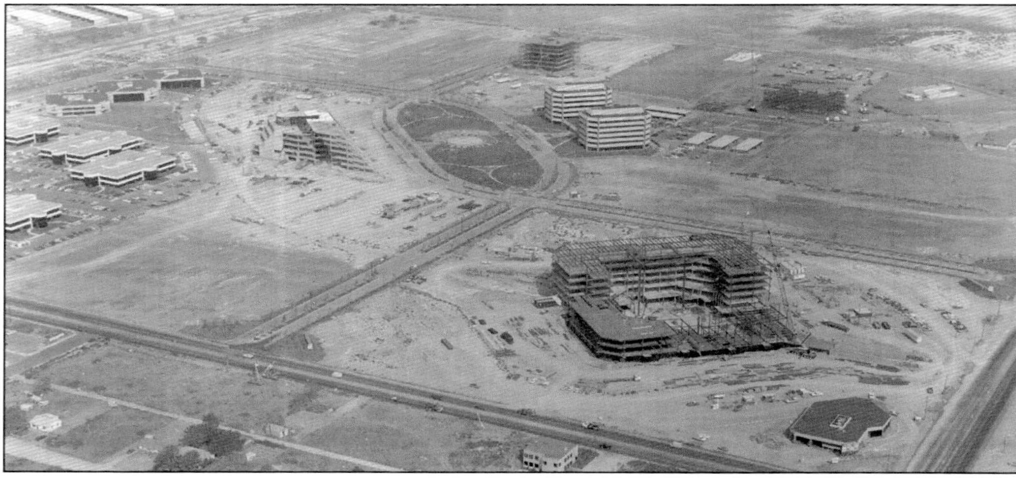

A second Tall City business district arose in 1982. Clayton "Claytie" Williams Jr., West Texas rancher and independent oilman, in early 1981, formed Claydesta Corporation, a Midland-based commercial real estate development firm; the name was derived from Claytie and wife Modesta's names. A 183-acre office complex (shown here under construction in 1982) on the north side of Midland near the airpark formed the centerpiece of the venture. In 1990, Williams ran for governor of Texas, losing to Democrat Ann Richards in a controversial election. (Courtesy of the Permian Historical Society Archives, the Bill Shoopman Collection.)

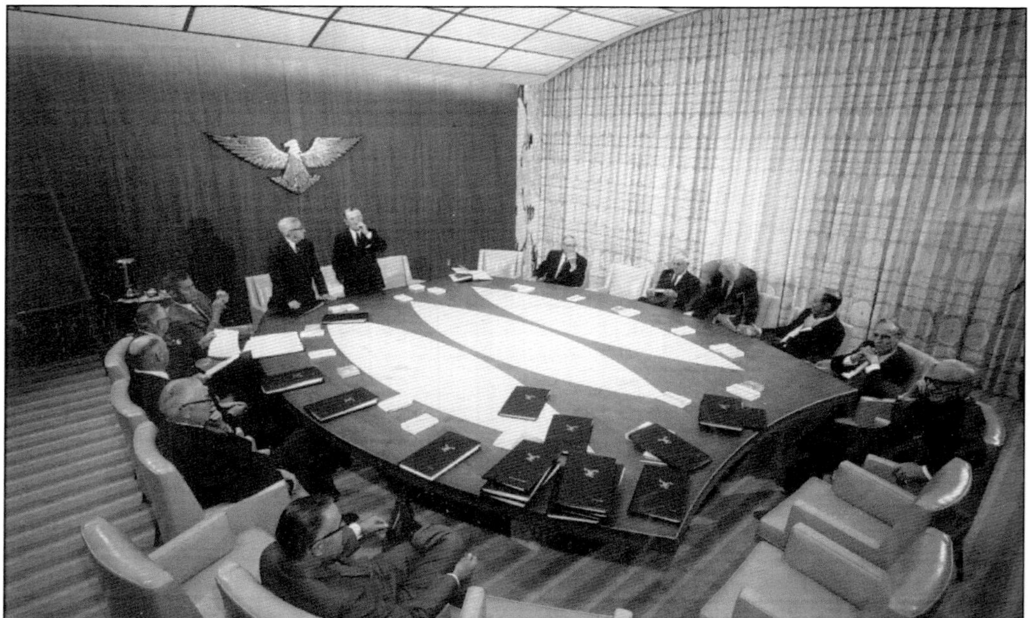

At the boom's height in 1981, First National Bank was Texas's largest bank, with assets of over $1.4 billion. Two years later, it failed. In October 1983, it reopened as Republic Bank First National Midland. Midland National Bank was already gone, having been purchased by First City Bancorporation in the mid-1970s. After several failures and buyouts, it became a Wells Fargo bank location. This late-1960s image shows the First National Bank boardroom in more successful times. Bank president John P. Butler stands on the right at the head of the table.

After the Yucca Theater closed in 1981, a group undertook its restoration as the home of the Summer Mummers, a live show performed each summer since 1949. The show includes a locally written melodrama with a formulaic plot. After the melodrama, a "moviola" begins, which is a silent slapstick film featuring the play's characters (and others) who continue the story in different areas of Midland in a series of "acts" best compared to vaudeville routines. Acts vary each year, though some have become annual favorites. Here Olio perennials and local actresses Shirley Ireland (left) and Mary Lou Cassidy (right) survive a barrage of oatmeal for a 2003 moviola scene. (Courtesy of Shirley Ireland.)

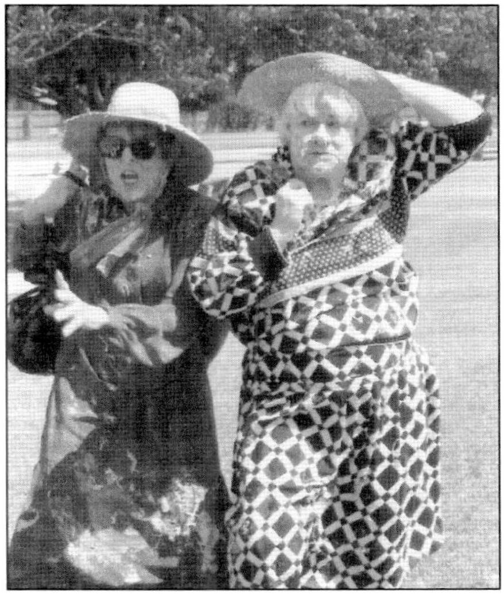

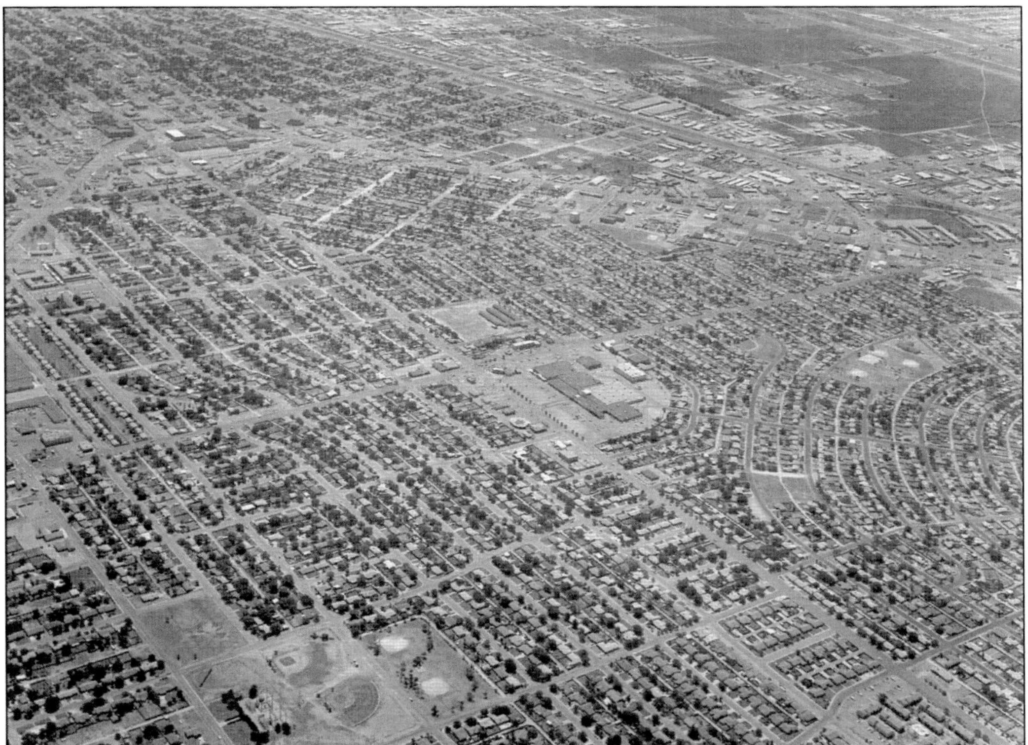

In 1950, Midland leaders produced the first comprehensive city plan. Included were provisions for new schools, parks, and subdivisions. A vision of newer neighborhoods that stressed "charm and individuality" rather than a gridiron system of uniform blocks and right angle streets became the pattern as Midland grew. This 1986 aerial view to the southeast of a newer section of west Midland demonstrates how that plan guided the city's growth. Andrew Highway runs diagonally from the left edge of the photograph to intersect Illinois Street at Midland Memorial Hospital. (Courtesy of the Permian Historical Society Archives, the Bill Shoopman Collection.)

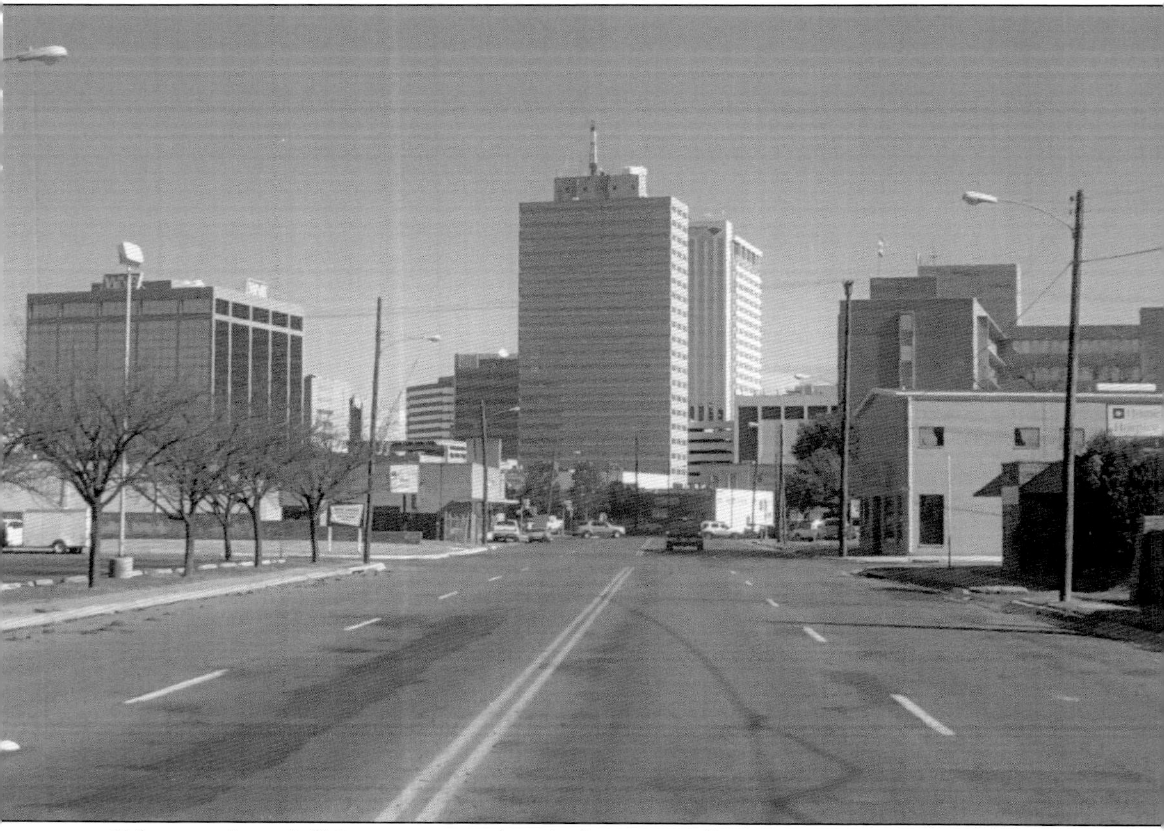

Fifty years later, Jeff George returned to the locations of his 1956 photographs to take new shots. This 2007 view down Missouri Street records a skyline considerably different from that on page 101. The Wilco Building remained, but had lost it preeminence to the Bank of America Building (behind the Wilco Building). In many respects, Midland grew into a modern, more complex city during these years. Yet it remained a city squarely built upon its earlier foundations. The Petroleum Building remained (almost hidden on the left behind the light pole), and the Midland High School yearbook was still the *Catoico*. (Photograph by Jeff George.)

Six

On the World Stage in the 21st Century

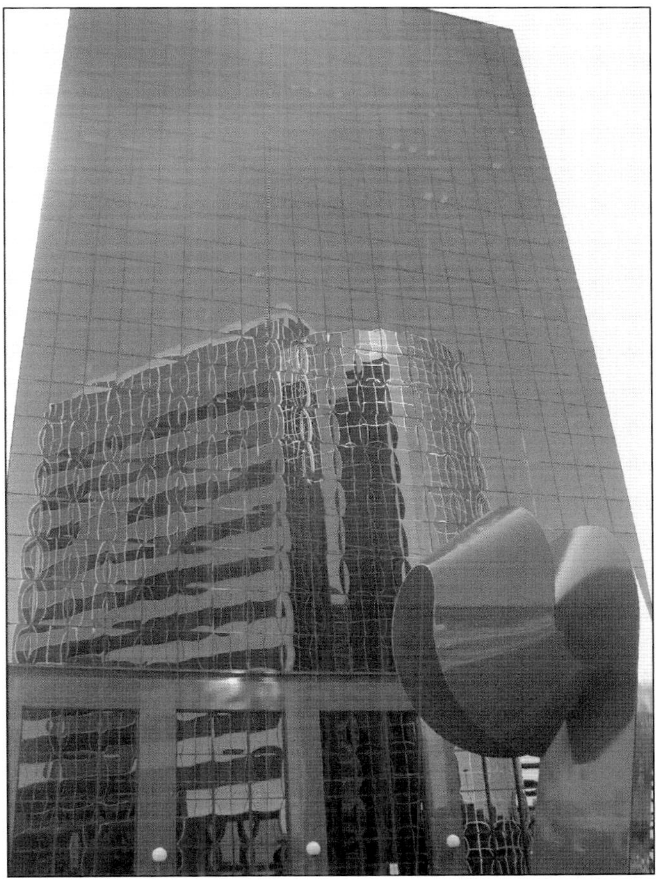

At the dawn of the 21st century, Midland was a city of over 100,000 that sprawled for miles across the Llano, its skyline dominated by tall office buildings of glass and steel. It had already gained national attention in 1987, with the dramatic rescue of "Baby Jessica," an 18-month-old child who fell into a narrow well. A team of rescuers worked for over 58 hours to free her, using both paramedic training and oil-field technology. Former Midland resident George W. Bush served as Texas governor from 1995 to 2000 before winning the presidency. Rep. Tom Craddick became Speaker of the Texas House in 2003 and presided until 2009. During the next decade, with Bush in the White House, the city received international attention. The town that began as a dusty little railroad stop had gained a place on the world stage. (Photograph by author.)

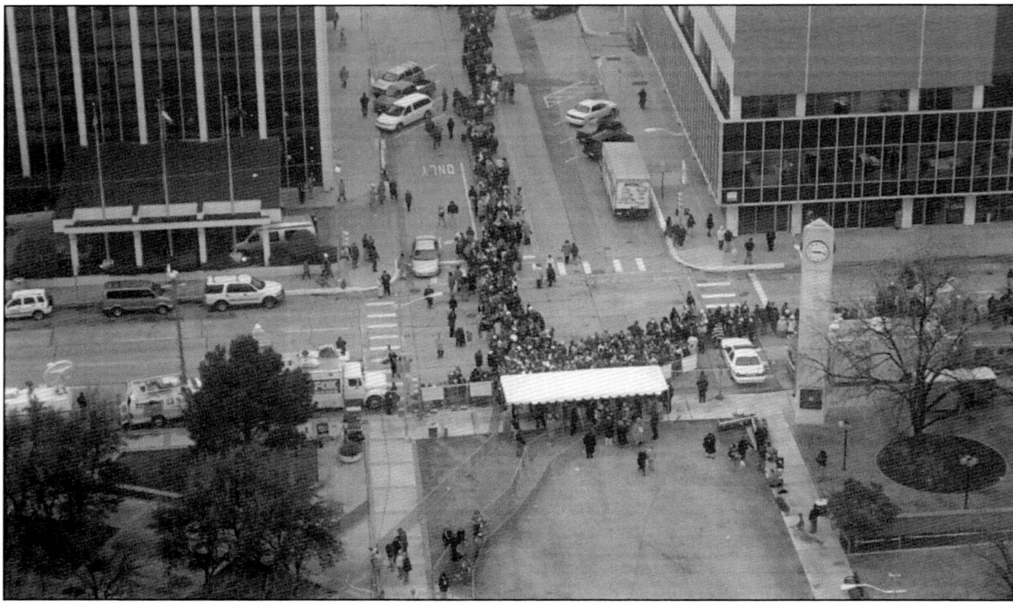

Early on January 17, 2001, lines began forming outside Centennial Plaza next to the courthouse. Though the temperature was 31 degrees, no one left. They had come to see president-elect George W. Bush, stopping in town on his way to be sworn in as President of the United States. Over 20,000 people crowded into the plaza; others watched on JumboTron screens for the arrival of the former Midlander.

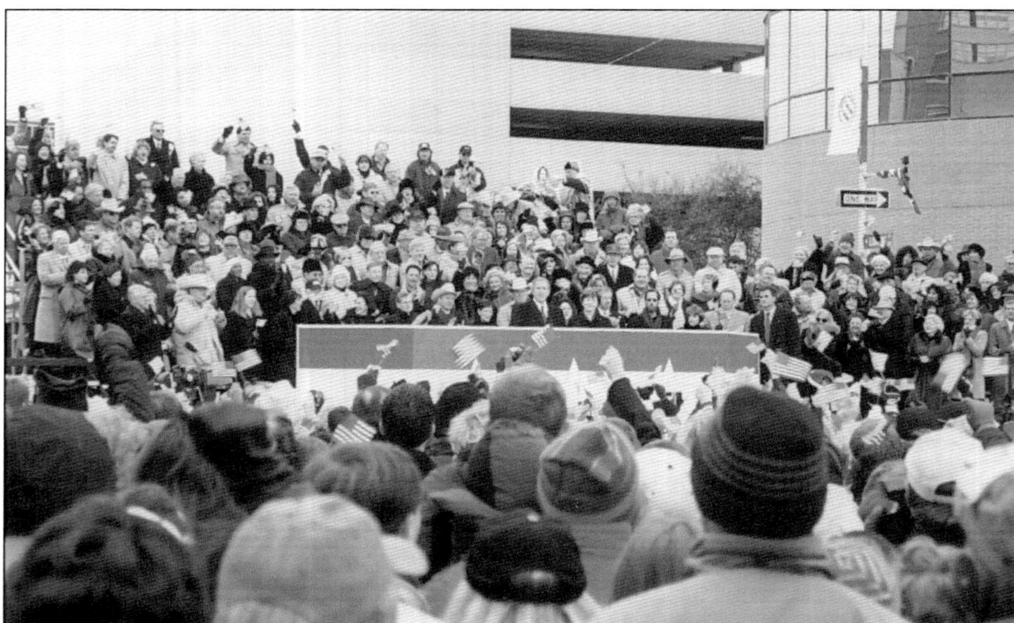

With his wife, Laura, beside him and several dignitaries joining him on the stage (including Texas House member Tom Craddick), Bush told the crowd, "This place has shaped the values that will shape our service to the nation." Brandishing a white cowboy hat, he promised them, "I'm leaving Texas, but not forever. This is my home."

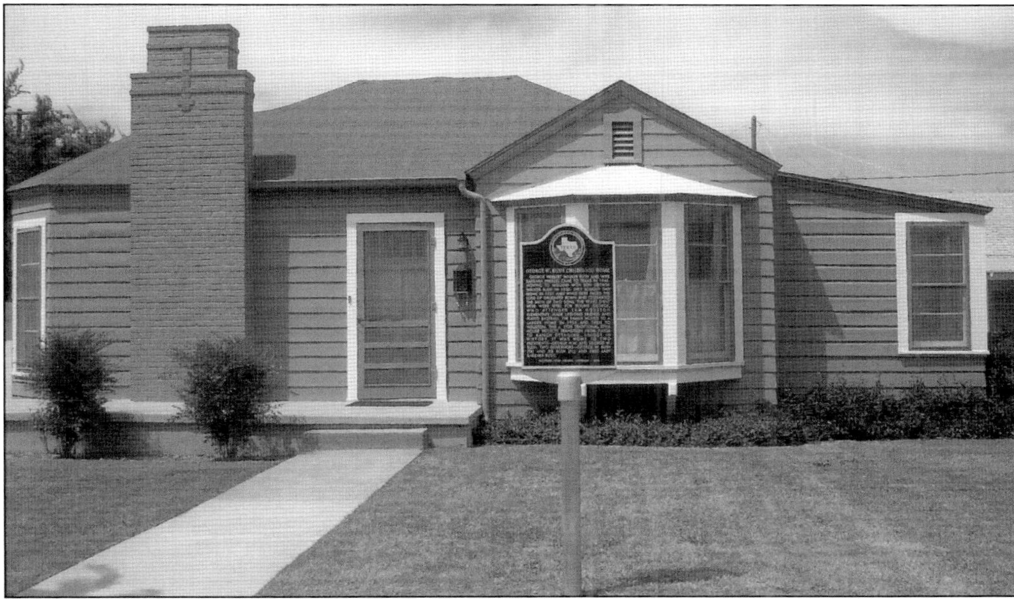

The George W. Bush Childhood Home at 1412 West Ohio Avenue is unique in American history as home to two presidents (George H. W. Bush and George W. Bush), two governors (George W. Bush of Texas and Jeb Bush of Florida), and a first lady (Barbara Bush). The Bush Childhood Home became a museum in 2001 and was restored to the look and furnishings of the years when the Bush family occupied it. (Photograph by the author.)

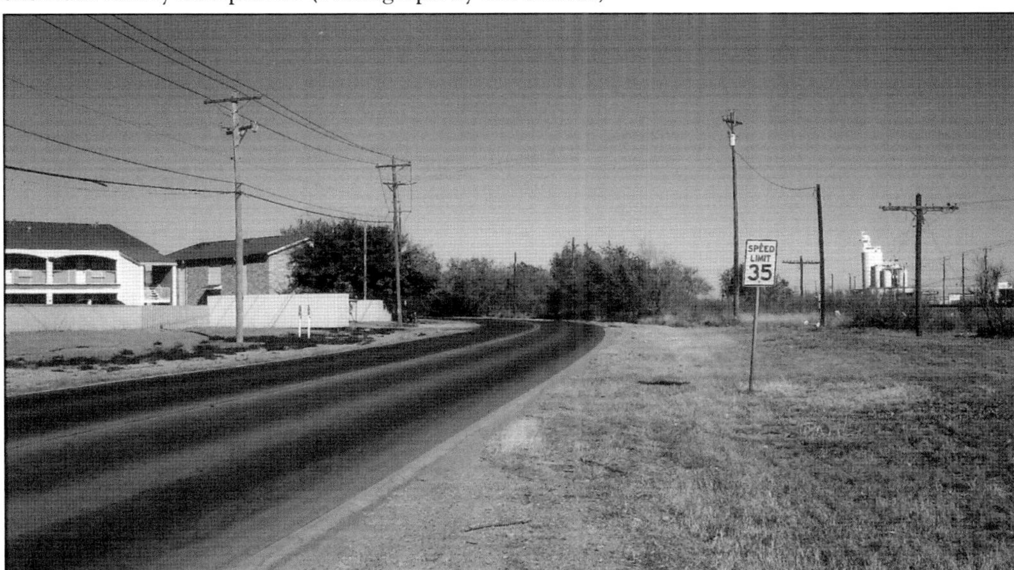

Other traces of the past remain. The Bankhead Highway (shown here) still runs for a few blocks beside the Texas and Pacific Railroad Line. The Sibley Nature Center preserves a few acres of land as it was before the Llano was settled. The Petroleum Museum continues to recognize the region's petroleum industry, both past and present. The museum added a new wing showcasing the innovative Chaparral racing cars designed by Formula One driver Jim Hall of Midland. (Photograph by the author.)

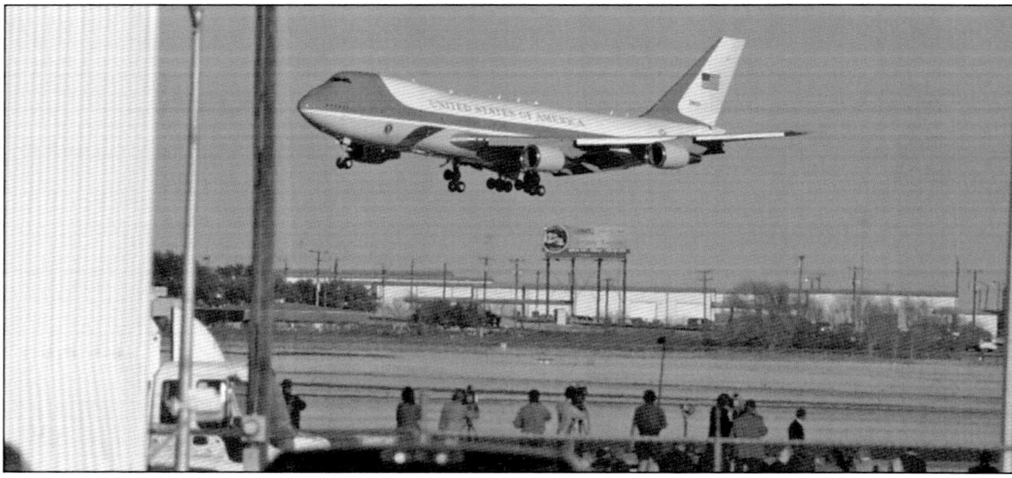

On January 20, 2009, only hours after passing the presidency to Barack Obama, former president George W. Bush returned to Midland for his first public appearance after leaving office. His plane (designated Special Air Mission 28000), landing here at Midland International Airport, flew low over downtown Midland where a crowd of over 30,000 in Centennial Plaza awaited Bush's arrival. Many had come hours earlier to stake out a good spot. (Photograph by Ron Hodges.)

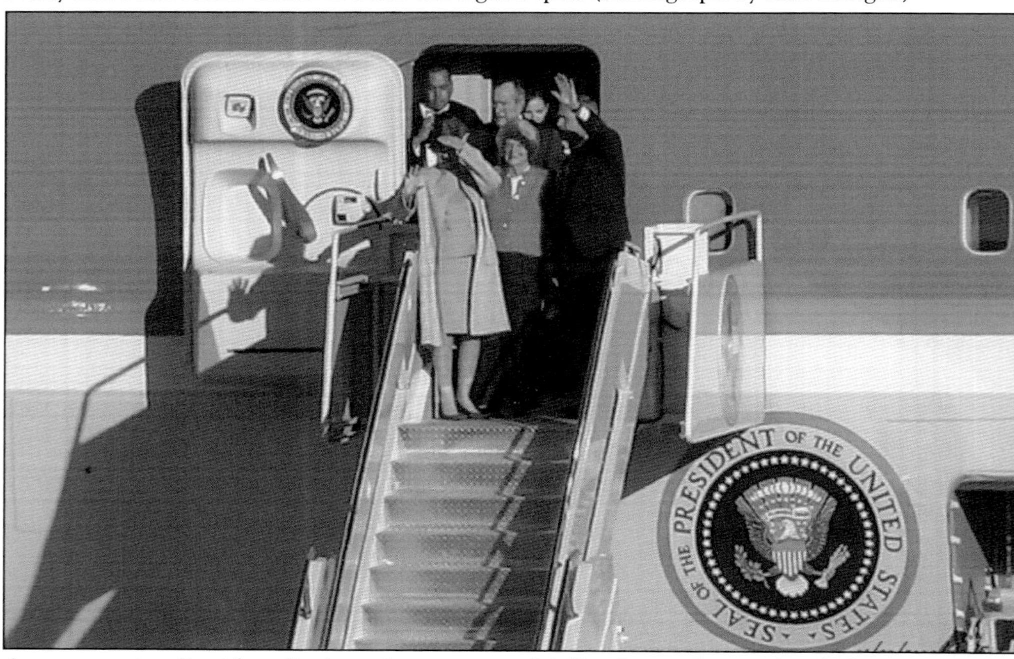

Accompanying President Bush on his return to Midland were former first lady Laura, former president George H. W. Bush, and former first lady Barbara Bush. George W. waves to the crowd as he and Laura disembark from the plane. His parents wait just behind. Dignitaries joining the group downtown included former speaker of the Texas House of Representatives Tom Craddick, Texas governor Rick Perry, and U.S. Congressman Mike Conaway. Commenting on the challenges of his presidency, Bush told the sympathetic crowd, "Sometimes what I did was unpopular, but that's OK. I always did what I thought was right." He wryly added, "Popularity is as fleeting as the West Texas wind." (Photograph by Ron Hodges.)

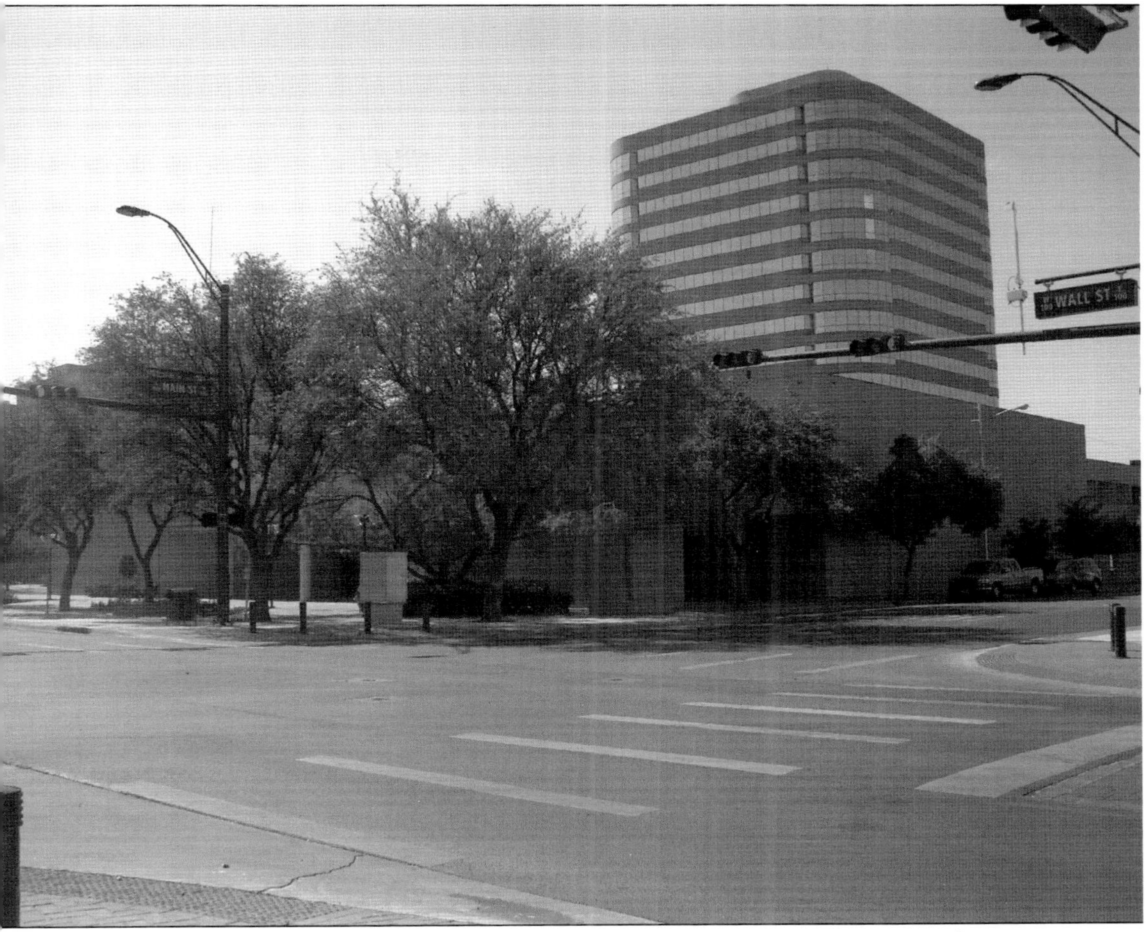

The Midland Center and Centennial Plaza now occupy the corner of Wall Street and Main Street, the same corner where the Midland National Bank stood (cover) and where cowboys lined up in front of the Llano Hotel on Christmas Day 1895. Over the years, this spot has been the meeting place for cattle barons and cotton farmers, railroaders, financiers, travelers, engineers, and presidents. Historic downtown continues to play a central role in the life of 21st-century Midland. (Photograph by the author.)

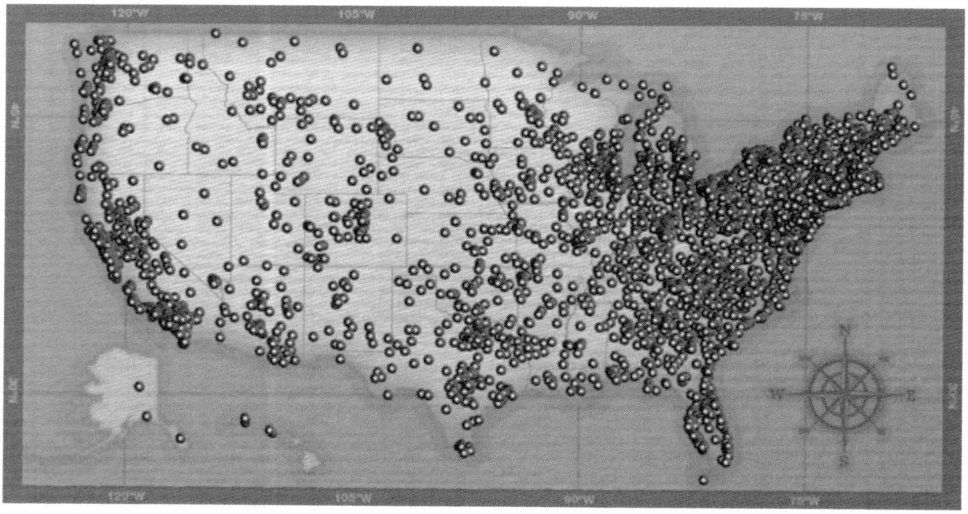